50 Great Myths

50
GREAT
MYTHS
ABOUT
RELIGIONS

JOHN MORREALL AND TAMARA SONN

WILEY Blackwell

This edition first published 2014
© 2014 John Wiley & Sons, Ltd

Registered Office
John Wiley & Sons, Ltd, The Atrium, Southern Gate, Chichester, West Sussex, PO19 8SQ, UK

Editorial Offices
350 Main Street, Malden, MA 02148–5020, USA
9600 Garsington Road, Oxford, OX4 2DQ, UK
The Atrium, Southern Gate, Chichester, West Sussex, PO19 8SQ, UK

For details of our global editorial offices, for customer services, and for information about how to apply for permission to reuse the copyright material in this book please see our website at www.wiley.com/wiley-blackwell.

The right of John Morreall and Tamara Sonn to be identified as the authors of this work has been asserted in accordance with the UK Copyright, Designs and Patents Act 1988.

Library of Congress Cataloging-in-Publication data applied for

Hardback ISBN: 978-0-470-67351-5
Paperback ISBN: 978-0-470-67350-8

A catalogue record for this book is available from the British Library.

Cover image: Dramatic sky © omersukrugoksu/iStockphoto

Set in 10.5/13pt Minion by SPi Publisher Services, Pondicherry, India
Printed in Malaysia by Ho Printing (M) Sdn Bhd

1   2014

Contents

1   Introduction: Myths and Misbelieving   1

2   Myths About Religions in General   9
    Introduction   9
    1.   All Societies Have Religions   12
    2.   Religion Is about the Spiritual   18
    3.   Religion Is about the Supernatural   21
    4.   Religion Is about Faith or Belief   23
    5.   Worship Is an Essential Part of Religion   28
    6.   Religion Is a Personal Matter   31
    7.   Science Will Eventually Replace Religion   34
    8.   Religion Causes Violence   39

3   Myths About Judaism, Jews, and Jewish Scripture   45
    Introduction   45
    1.   The Ancient Israelites Believed in One God   46
    2.   Moses Wrote the First Five Books of the Bible   50
    3.   The Book of Genesis Is Incompatible with the Theory
         of Evolution   53
    4.   Jews Believe They Were Chosen by God to Receive
         Special Privileges   60
    5.   The Jews Killed Jesus   63
    6.   Blood Libel: Jews Use Christian Blood in Their Rituals   68
    7.   Benjamin Franklin Advised the US Government
         to Expel Jews   70
    8.   *The Protocols of the Learned Elders of Zion*: Jewish
         Leaders Plot Global Takeover   73
    9.   Hanukkah Is for Jews What Christmas Is for Christians   77

4   Myths About Christianity, Christians, and Christian Scripture   80
    Introduction   80
    1.   The Four Gospels Are Eyewitnesses' Accounts
         of the Life of Jesus   81
    2.   The Bible Says that When We Die, Our Souls Go
         to Heaven or Hell   86
    3.   Jesus Was Born on December 25 in a Stable in Bethlehem   89
    4.   Jesus Was a Christian   93
    5.   Jesus Preached Family Values   97
    6.   The Image of the Crucified Jesus Has Always Been Sacred
         to Christians   101
    7.   The Church Suppressed Science in the Middle Ages   105
    8.   Catholics Are Not Christians   110
    9.   The United States Was Founded as a Christian Country   115

5   Myths About Islam, Muslims, and the Qur'an   123
    Introduction   123
    1.   Most Muslims Are Arabs and All Arabs Are Muslim   124
    2.   Muslims Worship a Different God   126
    3.   The Qur'an Condemns Judaism and Christianity   129
    4.   "Jihad" Means Holy War   135
    5.   The Qur'an Encourages Violence   138
    6.   The Qur'an Condones Mistreatment of Women   142
    7.   The Qur'an Promises Suicide Bombers 72 Heavenly Virgins   147
    8.   Muslims Reject Democracy   150
    9.   Muslims Fail to Speak Out against Terrorism   153
    10. American Muslims Want to Impose Islamic Law
         on the United States   158

6   Myths About Other Western Traditions   163
    Introduction   163
    1.   Zoroastrians Worship Fire   163
    2.   Voodoo Is Black Magic   166
    3.   Witches Worship Satan   169
    4.   Rastafarians Are Marijuana Abusers   175
    5.   Unitarian Universalists May Believe Whatever They Want   178

7   Myths About Eastern Traditions   181
    Introduction   181
    1.   Hinduism Is a Single Religious Tradition   181
    2.   Hinduism Promotes the Caste System   185

    3. Hindus Worship Idols   187
    4. Buddha Is a God for Buddhists   190
    5. The Laughing Buddha (Budai, Ho-Ti) Is Buddha   193

8   Myths About Nonbelievers   196
   Introduction   196
    1. Nonbelievers Are Ignorant about Religion   196
    2. Nonbelievers Have no Basis for Morality   198
    3. Without Religious Belief, Life Has No Purpose   202
    4. Atheism Is Just as Much a Matter of Faith as Religion Is 207

Bonus Myths   210
    1. The Bible says, "Cleanliness is next to Godliness,"
       "The Lord works in mysterious ways," "Hate the sin,
       love the sinner," "God helps those who help themselves,"
       "Money is the root of all evil," "Spare the rod and spoil
       the child," "To thine own self be true," "This too shall pass,"
       "To err is human, to forgive divine," and "Idle hands are
       the Devil's workshop."   211
    2. The Bible Forbids Eating Pork Because It Causes Illness 216
    3. The Apocalypse Is the End of the World Foretold in Scripture 220
    4. Satan and His Devils Torture Humans in Hell   224
    5. Cherubs Are Cute, Childlike Angels   226
    6. Christians Were Systematically Persecuted by the Romans 229
    7. There Was a Female Pope Named Joan   233
    8. Saint Patrick Drove the Snakes out of Ireland   238

Index   242

1

Introduction: Myths and Misbelieving

Might I suggest that [people doubting religious narratives] use the tactic used by many modern Jews dealing with biblical narratives that defy credulity, from a six-day story of creation to Jonah living inside a large fish. We distinguish between left-brain narratives (meant to convey factual truth) and right-brain narratives (meant to make a point through a story; the message will be true even if the story isn't factually defensible). (Rabbi Harold Kushner (2013))

Two Meanings of "Myth"

This book was inspired by another Wiley Blackwell book, *50 Great Myths of Popular Psychology* by Scott Lilienfeld *et al.* (2010), in which "myth" means a widespread belief that is not well supported by evidence. Some of our myths are like that, such as the beliefs that Moses wrote the first five books of the Bible, and that Jesus was born in a stable in Bethlehem on December 25. But we also count as myths common beliefs that are questionable for other reasons, such as that they conflict with the teachings of the religions of the believers. Some Muslims (and countless non-Muslims), for example, believe that the Qur'an promises suicide bombers 72 heavenly virgins. In the Qur'an, however, both suicide and terrorism are condemned as grave sins. Many Christians believe that Satan and his devils torture humans in hell, but that actually conflicts with basic Christian teachings. When we call something a "myth," then, our meaning is close to the dictionary

50 Great Myths About Religions, First Edition. John Morreall and Tamara Sonn.
© 2014 John Wiley & Sons, Ltd. Published 2014 by John Wiley & Sons, Ltd.

definition for "misbelief": a myth is a wrong, false, or unorthodox belief or opinion, especially in religion.

There is a second meaning of "myth" that we should mention, because it is important in the academic field of Religious Studies. When scholars of religion talk about "myths," they generally mean traditional stories that explain important aspects of life, such as where we came from, why we're here, who our heroes are and what makes them special, and how we should live. A good example is the story in Genesis about Adam and Eve disobeying God by eating of the tree of the knowledge of good and evil, and then being cast out of the Garden by God. This description of the origin of evil, and stories like it, are often characterized by extraordinary and even supernatural events, and some people believe they are literally true – true in the same way that a traffic report or a medical diagnosis is true. They believe the stories are accurate representations of things that really happened. But many scholars believe that such myths are not to be judged on the basis of historic or scientific accuracy. In fact, these stories generally developed before modern criteria of historical and scientific accuracy. They are often about things in the deep recesses of prehistory, and sometimes about things in the far distant future. As such, they are beyond the realms of history and science. But we cherish them anyway because they help us understand who we are and answer some of the most pressing questions in life, including why bad things happen, who can be trusted, and what might happen next.

As we listen to stories like Adam and Eve in the Garden, we sometimes get a sense that we are in touch with higher reality. We are in the realm of the transcendent, a realm beyond the frailties and limitations that characterize everyday reality. Myths of this kind are commonly transmitted in religions, so much so that many scholars include myths as essential components of religions. Another example of this kind of myth is the Creation Story in the Bible and the Qur'an. According to that story, a single almighty personal God created the earth and everything upon it in just a few days, and provided all that was needed for his most cherished creatures, human beings. Stories like this provide a measure of assurance that things are basically as they should be and there is a reason for us to carry on, even in the most difficult circumstances.

When viewed from this perspective, myths in religion – in their own unique way – can be considered true. They provide context, continuity, and comfort for the communities who share them. They are thus true for the people who believe them. The fourth-century Roman historian Sallustius spoke from this perspective when he said, "Myths are things that never happened but always are" (Sallustius, 1996). Joseph Campbell, among the twentieth century's best known mythologists, called myths "the womb of mankind's initiation into life and death" (1969: 12). The University of Chicago's Wendy Doniger (1998) presents myths as imaginative expressions of universal human experiences, which allow us to communicate across cultures. British scholar Karen Armstrong (2005: 4) stresses the sacred aspect of myth, saying that myths speak "of another plane that exists alongside our own world, and that in some sense supports it. Belief in this invisible but more powerful reality, sometimes called the world of the gods, is a basic theme of mythology." For scholars such as these, myths are very much like what Pablo Picasso said about art: "a lie which makes us realize truth" (Borofsy, 1923).

Other scholars caution against such a romantic view of myth. The University of Chicago's Bruce Lincoln (2000: 147) describes myths as "*ideology* in narrative form." As such, like any other ideology, myths establish identity and distinguish "us" from "them." They also establish and legitimatize a group's internal order. Lincoln is primarily concerned with myths that have condoned and even encouraged exclusivist identities of the type that devalue other groups, such as those promoting Europe's anti-Semitism. Far from the comfort of sacred planes, the myths discussed by Lincoln have profound – and sometimes disastrous – practical implications.

Writers such as Christopher Hitchens, Sam Harris, and Richard Dawkins also advocate a critical approach to religious myths. They are concerned that too many people can't tell the difference between the "special" or "sacred" kind of truth conveyed in the imaginative stories of mythology, and ordinary truth like that found in newspapers. Too many people can't distinguish between transcendent myth and literal truth. They fail to recognize the importance of verifying truth claims instead of blindly accepting them on the basis of unaccountable authority. Again, that can lead to serious problems in real life. Take the example of the creation story. It is one thing to find in it assurance that life has a purpose and a goal, but quite another to insist that this story is literally true and that any science that demonstrates otherwise, such as the theory of evolution, must therefore be dismissed as an attack on a higher, unquestionable authority. Yet that seems to be what is happening. A 2012 Gallup Poll indicates that 46% of Americans believe that the description of creation in Genesis is literally true. This figure represents an increase of 2% from 1982, no doubt reflecting a tendency to teach "creationism" instead of – or as a suitable alternative to – science. In 2013, *The New York Times* reported that a survey of more than 900 biology teachers in the United States revealed that nearly 13% teach various forms of the creation story as "valid scientific alternatives to Darwinian evolutionary theory" (Rich, 2013) – this despite a US Supreme Court ruling prohibiting the teaching of "creation myths" as science (*Edwards v. Aguillard*, 482 US 578, [1987]). Similarly, the spread of creationism in Europe prompted the Parliament of the Council of Europe to pass a resolution in 2007 entitled "The Dangers of Creationism in Education." The resolution warns that denying the science behind the theory of evolution in favor of unquestioning belief in a particular group's creation myth could undermine the research necessary to deal with the major challenges facing humanity today, such as epidemic disease and environmental disasters.

We recognize and respect the scholarly notion of myths as stories conveying transcendent truths – truths immune from the rigors of scientific method. But for the purposes of this book, we use the skeptical view of myths: widely believed claims that are not well supported by historic or scientific evidence. Our emphasis will be on the major traditions of the West – Judaism, Christianity, and Islam. But we will include some stories about smaller Western traditions, as well as some Western myths about Eastern traditions. We will also discuss some common misbeliefs about people who lack religious beliefs – atheists and agnostics.

References

Armstrong, K. (2005) *A Short History of Myth*, Canongate, Edinburgh.

Borofsky, S. (1923) Picasso Speaks, The Arts, May 1923, in *Picasso: Fifty Years of His Art* by A.H. Barr Jr., published for The Museum of Modern Art by Arno Press, New York, 1980, www.gallerywalk.org/PM_Picasso.html (accessed January 10, 2014).

Campbell, J. (1969) *Bios and Mythos*, Scriptor Press, Portland, OR.

Council of Europe (2007) Resolution 1580: The Dangers of Creationism in Education. http://assembly.coe.int/main.asp?link=/documents/adoptedtext/ta07/eres1580.htm (accessed January 6, 2014).

Doniger, W. (1998) *The Implied Spider: Politics and Theology in Myth*, Columbia University Press, New York.

Gallup (2012) In U.S., 3 in 10 Say They Take the Bible Literally, July 8, www.gallup.com/poll/148427/say-bible-literally.aspx (accessed January 10, 2014).

Kushner, H. (2013) Letter. *New York Times* (Jul 29).

Lilienfeld, S.O., Lynn, S.J., Ruscio, J. and Beyerstein, B. (2010) *50 Great Myths of Popular Psychology: Shattering Widespread Misconceptions about Human Behavior*, John Wiley & Sons, Ltd, Chichester.

Lincoln, B. (2000) *Theorizing Myth: Narrative, Ideology, and Scholarship*, University of Chicago Press, Chicago.

Rich, M. (2013) Creationists on Texas panel for biology textbooks. *The New York Times* (Sep 28), www.nytimes.com/2013/09/29/education/creationists-on-texas-panel-for-biology-textbooks.html?_r=0 (accessed January 6, 2014).

Sallustius (1996) Concerning the Gods and the Universe, Ars Pub.

Where Do Myths Come From?

There are several things about human beings that predispose them to create and circulate myths like the ones in this book. We'll suggest eight. The first, and most flattering to our human self-image, is that, as the ancient philosopher Aristotle said, we are *rational* animals. We are constantly trying to understand the world around us and make sense of what we experience. We want to know why some people are allies and others enemies, how we can be successful, why we failed, and countless other things.

In trying to understand the world, we look for similarities between current experiences and past experiences. We link new things to what we already know, thus creating concepts of types of things, as when we classify a new acquaintance as "a student" or "a Muslim." In thinking this way, we naturally create generalizations about all or most members of a group, based on a certain feature that some members of that group may have. If we have had a negative encounter with someone, for example, we often form a negative stereotype of all members of whatever group that individual represents to us.

A second feature of human beings that leads us to create myths is that we are *social* animals. We are born into groups and are nurtured by them. Our family and community are the initial source of our safety and security. We must therefore be able to identify our own group and learn to live in harmony with them, and be able to distinguish between them and those who might be a threat to us. Early humans lived in tribes, as many still do. Getting along with the rest of one's tribe requires keeping track of who all of them are, how they are related to each other, whether they are cooperative or dangerous, etc. One theory of why the human brain evolved so quickly over the last three million years is that once our ancestors came down from the trees and began living in social groups on the African savannah, they needed to remember more and more information about larger and larger numbers of people. That's why a large part of the human brain today is devoted to recognizing faces and filling in background information on them. It is also why so many myths deal with identifying our own group as distinct from other groups.

We keep up with who is doing what with whom, and to whom, not only by direct observation but also by talking with people about other people who aren't present. That's a third feature of human beings that leads to mythmaking: we are *gossiping* animals.

A fourth feature that makes us mythmakers is that we are *moral* animals. In thinking and talking about people, we assess their honesty, generosity, courage, loyalty to the group, and so on – or their lack of these features. Just as the stories we create about our own group tend to stress its positive points, the stories we tell about outsiders tend to stress the reasons we should not trust them. Indeed, most myths about other groups, like most gossip, put people in a bad light. As we shall see, there are few flattering myths about other people's religions.

The fifth thing about human beings that leads to mythmaking is that we are *storytelling* animals. Around the world, for tens of thousands of years, people have created narratives – to explain events, honor heroes, teach children moral lessons, entertain each other, and for many other purposes. We store information about people mostly as stories about them, and before the invention of writing a few thousand years ago, stories were the basic form in which human beings retained most information about anything at all. That's over 98% of our history, so it's no wonder that we still love to create, tell, and listen to good stories.

And we are not just storytellers, but *imaginative* storytellers, a sixth feature that leads to mythmaking. While stories sometimes convey accurate information, accuracy is not a necessary characteristic of good stories. Humans love storytelling so much that long ago they began creating what we now call "fiction." As Walter Ong (1982) has pointed out in his studies of oral cultures, the more creative a story is, the more likely it is to be remembered. So if we are telling a story about an ancestor whose courage and strength we valorize, descriptions of extraordinary – even superhuman – courage and strength might well be the most likely to be passed on from one generation to the next. Similarly, if we feel threatened by a particular group, we may well exaggerate their negative traits.

This point about heroes to admire and villains to fear brings up a seventh feature of humans that leads to myths: we are *emotional* animals. For a story to grab our interest, be remembered, and get passed on, it helps if it elicits emotions such as admiration for heroes, fear, sexual desire, awe, pride in our group, and hatred of other groups. Some people today complain about all the sex and violence in the media, but sex and violence have always been central to storytelling, starting with the Bible and Greek literature. Think of the story in Chapter 11 of the Second Book of Samuel of how, after King David impregnated Bathsheba, he arranged to have her husband killed in battle. Think of Sophocles' tragedy *Oedipus Rex*, in which Oedipus kills his father and marries his mother. The same part of the brain that processes emotions – the limbic system – also converts short-term memories to long-term memories. Direct experience of an emotionally arousing event is usually the most powerful way to make something impress us and register in our long-term memory, but an emotionally arousing story is probably the second most powerful.

Myths make sense not only of what we experience, but also of what we do. With myths we can provide reasons for our actions. When one group of people persecutes another, for example, negative myths about the target group are often used as justification: those people poison our wells, steal our children, worship devils, perform black magic, and so on. The myths we will examine about Jews, Muslims, and nonbelievers, for example, were mostly created by their enemies. We started our list of human features by saying that we are rational animals. But with Sigmund Freud, we can add that we are also *rationalizing* animals. That's our eighth – not as flattering – feature.

In our scientific, technological culture, we may think of ourselves as having grown beyond myths, but an hour reading tabloid newspapers, surfing the web, or watching television shows reveals that these eight human traits and the myths they spawn are still alive and well. We are still gossips who think in ethnic and religious stereotypes. We still love a good story that evokes admiration for heroes, fear, sexual desire, awe, pride in our group, or hatred of other groups. We're still prone to tribalism, as in our allegiance to our country's military forces, and to sports teams. Hero worship flourishes not just in the military and in sports, but in movies and the music industry. And xenophobia – fear of people outside our group – is still rampant, as the persistence of anti-Semitism and Islamophobia shows.

Electronic media have only made the creation and circulation of myths easier and faster. Modern myths are often called "urban myths" or "urban legends," and people have created whole web sites to scrutinize them. Snopes.com, for example, describes itself as "the definitive Internet reference source for urban legends, folklore, myths, rumors, and misinformation." The American television show *MythBusters* (Discovery Channel) tests urban myths like the claims that being painted with gold or being hit by a penny dropped from the top of the Empire State Building can be deadly. Many urban legends are about religion, such as the story about geologists drilling in Siberia who accidentally punched through to hell, or the one about the "Second Coming Project" that is trying to clone Jesus from the DNA of relics, or the claim that some airlines refuse to pair a Christian pilot with a Christian co-pilot because the Rapture might snatch away both of them, leaving the plane to crash. We will leave such myths to snopes.com and *MythBusters*, and focus on a sampling of some of the world's more persistent myths. They fall into the following general categories:

- Common misbeliefs about religions in general
- Common beliefs about the origins of various religions that have been shown to be questionable in the light of historical research
- Beliefs within religious traditions that are popularly believed but are not part of official doctrine
- False allegations about certain religious communities' beliefs and practices, held by people outside those communities.

References

Ong, W. (1982) *Orality and Literacy*, Routledge, New York.
Snopes.com (accessed January 6, 2014).

2

Myths About Religions in General

1. All Societies Have Religions
2. Religion Is about the Spiritual
3. Religion Is about the Supernatural
4. Religion Is about Faith or Belief
5. Worship Is an Essential Part of Religion
6. Religion Is a Personal Matter
7. Science Will Eventually Replace Religion
8. Religion Causes Violence

Introduction

Most people think they have a pretty good idea of what religion is. Many who grow up in one religious tradition use it as a model for religions in general. As they hear about other people's religions, they look for similarities with their own and assume they have a basic understanding about other religions. In other words, they use their own religion as a stereotype for all religions. The problem is that there has been a huge range of diverse religions throughout history. According to the *World Christian Encyclopedia* (Barrett *et al.*, 2001: vi), there are now over 10 000 religions, and they differ in many ways.

For example, the Greek Orthodox Church and the Church of Jesus Christ of Latter Day Saints (Mormons) are both Christian, but they differ in their understanding of what God has revealed, who Jesus is, what happens after death, and dozens of other points. Among the Western monotheistic traditions of Judaism, Christianity, and Islam, the first rejects the idea that

50 Great Myths About Religions, First Edition. John Morreall and Tamara Sonn.
© 2014 John Wiley & Sons, Ltd. Published 2014 by John Wiley & Sons, Ltd.

Jesus was the Messiah, the second accepts it and says that Jesus is also God, and the third accepts that Jesus was the Messiah and even that he will come again, but rejects the idea that Jesus is God. Even greater differences are evident when we compare the Western monotheistic traditions with the Eastern traditions of Hinduism and Buddhism. In the Western worldview, time is linear. The universe had a beginning and will have an end, and each event happens just once. In the Eastern worldviews of Hinduism and Buddhism, on the other hand, time is cyclical. The universe has always existed, and it has been reshaped and destroyed millions of times. Each person, too, has been born, lived, and died countless times in the process known as reincarnation (metempsychosis).

Western and Eastern traditions also differ in how they think about ultimate reality. In Judaism, Christianity, and Islam, the ultimate reality is God – the creator of the universe, its king and its judge. God rules the universe by giving commands, will judge everyone after death based on how well they followed those commands, and will reward or punish them. In Hinduism, by contrast, the ultimate reality is *Brahman*, which is beyond all the gods. According to an ancient idea from the Hindu scriptures known as the Upanishads, Brahman is also the same as *atman* – the self or mind – so each person's consciousness is ultimate reality. Buddhism takes still a different view of ultimate reality. Its founder, Siddhartha Gautama, did not teach about gods, and he said that there is no Brahman and there is no atman. In fact, he taught that everything is constantly changing, so there are no enduring substances at all. What I think of as my self – the core of me that stays the same from day to day and year to year – is an illusion. For Buddhists, ultimate reality is not a god or Brahman, but a mental state called *nirvana*. It is blissful, but most notably for what is lacking. It is like dreamless sleep. You reach nirvana, they say, when you stop clinging to all the illusions that have kept you suffering and being reborn, such as the belief that you are an enduring substance. While the goal of life for most monotheists (Zoroastrians, Jews, Christians, Muslims, and Baha'is) is to reach heaven and be with God, the goal for Buddhists is to achieve nirvana. That is, while the monotheistic notion of heaven is having your desires fulfilled, nirvana is having them extinguished. Comparing desire to the flame of a candle, Buddhists say that nirvana is blowing out the candle. Hinduism might seem closer to Western religions than Buddhism because it has gods. But instead of the one God of monotheism, there are 330 000 000 gods – although that number is not meant to be taken literally – and they did not create the universe, they do not rule it, they do not preside at a Last Judgment, and they do not reward and punish people by sending them to heaven or hell.

Another topic on which the Western and Eastern traditions differ is life after death. In the Western religions, we are on earth just once, and we are here to do God's will. That is usually described as worshiping and obeying God. Disobeying God is sin, and it requires God's forgiveness. After death, we will be judged by God and then rewarded or punished in another world – heaven or hell, in most denominations – where we will be either with God or separated from God. So the Big Problem in life is separation from God through sin; and the Big Solution is getting back together with God, through what Christians call salvation or redemption. In both Hinduism and Buddhism, on the other hand, morality is not created by divine commandments, but is built into the universe as *karma* – the natural justice of the world. Good actions naturally lead to good consequences, and bad actions naturally lead to bad consequences. No god has to judge, reward, or punish. At death, we go on to a next life, but that life is on earth, not in heaven or hell. We are reincarnated.

So any assumption that all religions are similar is problematic. Not only do they differ in worldview and truth claims, they differ profoundly in purview – what aspects of life they deal with. While some traditions are characterized by belief in the supernatural and associated rituals and values, many traditions consider all of life as the domain of religion, including law, governance, and health sciences. Recognizing such diversity, the nineteenth-century German scholar credited with developing the scholarly study of religion (*Religionswissenschaft*, Religious Studies), Max Müller, cautioned against generalizing about religion based on one's own experience. He is often quoted as saying, "He who knows one, knows none."

In this chapter we will identify several common misbeliefs about the nature of religion, most of which stem from the tendency to generalize about all religions based on stereotypes drawn from one or a few.

Reference

Barrett, D., Kurian, G. and Johnson, T. (eds) (2001) *World Christian Encyclopedia*, 2nd edition, Oxford University Press, New York.

1. All Societies Have Religions

Not all religions share the same set of beliefs, but in one form or another, religion is found in all known human societies. (Ashley Crossman (online))

The phrase "World Religions" came into use when the first Parliament of the World's Religions was held in Chicago in 1893. Representation at the Parliament was not comprehensive. Naturally, Christians dominated the meeting, and Jews were represented. Muslims were represented by a single American Muslim. The enormously diverse traditions of India were represented by a single teacher, while three teachers represented the arguably more homogenous strains of Buddhist thought. The indigenous religions of the Americas and Africa were not represented. Nevertheless, since the convening of the Parliament, Judaism, Christianity, Islam, Hinduism, Buddhism, Confucianism, and Taoism have been commonly identified as World Religions. They are sometimes called the "Big Seven" in Religious Studies textbooks, and many generalizations about religion have been derived from them.

Increasingly, scholars are questioning that characterization. For one thing, it is based on questionable criteria regarding what makes the Big Seven count as World Religions. It can't be because they are followed by huge numbers of people; Judaism ranks far behind Shinto and Sikhism in that regard, and they aren't considered World Religions. Judaism could be counted as a World Religion because it is foundational to the two most widely followed religions in the world – Christianity and Islam – but if that were the criterion then Zoroastrianism should count too, because of its influence on Judaism, Christianity, and Islam. If we think of World Religions as those practiced by people in diverse regions around the world, then why are Confucianism and Taoism included? More importantly, though, "World Religions" seems to imply that all communities have something identifiable as religion, just as all communities have language. (In fact, language was exactly the counterpart that Müller used when he began the scholarly study of religion. He borrowed the phrase "He who knows one, knows none" from the study of languages.) Viewing religion in this way can make people more tolerant of other religions, although it is just as common for people to believe that their religion – alone among all the world's religions – is superior. Either way, the idea that what we think of as religion in our own culture has a counterpart in all other cultures is problematic in the view of many contemporary scholars.

Among the problems with the idea that all societies have religions is that it assumes, at the very least, that things or aspects of life categorized as "religious" can be distinguished from those that fall outside that category. That is, it assumes that there are aspects of life that are not involved in religion. Actually, however, this compartmentalization of religion is not found in all societies today, and was not found anywhere before 1500. Many languages do not even have a word equivalent to our word "religion," nor is such a word found in either the Bible or the Qur'an. And no indigenous tribe in the Americas, for example, talks about "religion" as something distinct from the rest of life.

According to many historians, the concept *religion* was first used in Europe in the 1500s as a way to distinguish between the domain of church authority and that of civil authorities. *Religion* was contrasted with *politics* by kings and emperors who wanted to command some of the loyalty and service that people devoted to bishops and the Pope. To build nation-states, for example, kings and emperors wanted a monopoly on the legitimate use of force or violence, and that required that church leaders give up their authority to create armies, as they had done in the Crusades. Eventually, kings and emperors demanded complete control over things involved in "this world" – the secular world (from the Latin *saeculum*, referring to things that exist in ordinary time). They wanted to create and enforce laws, collect taxes, and regulate trade, in addition to waging wars. They therefore wanted church officials to limit their activities to those things dealing with the "other" world – the eternal world. They wanted them to stay out of power politics and limit themselves to things like interpreting scripture, formulating doctrines, and conducting rituals. These would come to be characterized as "holy" or "sacred" and, for Christians, they became the proper sphere of religion.

But the word "religion" was not new in the 1500s. Ancient and medieval Western societies used the Latin term *religio*; it referred to the virtue of carrying out all one's social obligations – to family, neighbors, rulers, and God. To have *religio* was to be responsible in all areas of life. When *religio* came into English as *religion* around 1200, the *Oxford English Dictionary* tells us, it acquired a different meaning: "a state of life bound by monastic vows." Christians would then write of "the religions" of the Benedictine monks and the Franciscan and Dominican friars. (Cavanaugh, 2009: 64) Now the meaning of the term was shifting again: to mean just those aspects of life governed by church authorities.

To maximize their power, kings and emperors crafted agreements like the 1555 Peace of Augsburg, which established the principle *Cuius regio, eius religio* – a Latin phrase meaning that a ruler's religion would be the religion of the people he ruled. Such attempts to take power away from church leaders were never completely successful, as church authorities held on to considerable "political" power for centuries. Until 1870 the Pope retained the power of an absolute monarch in the Papal States of the Italian peninsula – an area twice the size of Massachusetts – as he still does today in the much smaller state called Vatican City. But the new idea of *religion* as something distinct from *politics* had taken root.

As European Christians colonized Asia and Africa, they applied "religion" with this new meaning to the societies there and, in the process, created new concepts like "Hinduism," "Buddhism," "Confucianism," and "Taoism." They categorized these, along with hundreds of smaller traditions, as species within the genus *religion*, just as lion (*panthera leo*) and tiger (*panthera tigris*) are species within the genus *panthera*. As scholars have been saying since Wilfred Cantwell Smith's landmark 1962 book *The Meaning and End of Religion*, imposing this European concept of religion on non-European cultures distorts what people in the rest of the world do and think. Before the British colonized India, for example, the people there had no concept "religion" and no concept "Hinduism." There was no word "Hindu" in classical India, and no one spoke of "Hinduism" until the 1800s.

Until the introduction of that term, Indians identified themselves by any number of criteria – family, trade or profession, or social level, and perhaps the scriptures they followed or the particular deity or deities upon whose care they relied in various contexts or to whom they were devoted. But these diverse identities were united, each an integral part of life; no part existed in a separate sphere identified as "religious." Nor were the diverse traditions lumped together under the term "Hinduism" unified by sharing such common features of religion as a single founder, creed, theology, or institutional organization. Perhaps the most salient characteristic they shared – besides the fact that they were from the Indian subcontinent (which is the core meaning of "Hindu") – was that they were not Jewish, Christian, or Muslim. In fact, the use of the term "Hindu" may be traced to the first systematic census of India, carried out by the British in 1871, which included religious identity among its statistics.

"Buddhism," similarly, is a European concept that aggregates what millions of people have done and thought over a period of 2500 years, and categorizes it as "religion." The acknowledged founder of the diverse practices known as Buddhism is Siddhartha Gautama, who came to be called the Buddha – the Awakened One. But he did not teach about God or gods, souls, heaven, hell, sin, redemption, or most of the other things associated with Western concepts of religion. His teaching centered on the prevalence of suffering and how to reduce it. Similar ideas in ancient Greece were called "Stoicism" and were classified as a philosophy. In universities today, Buddhism is sometimes taught in philosophy departments, and some of the Buddha's methods are classified as "self-help psychology." The core of his message was psychological. The Buddha's teaching is summarized in the Four Noble Truths:

> Life is full of suffering.
> The source of suffering is attachment (or craving).
> Suffering can be overcome by overcoming attachment (or craving).
> The way to do that is the Noble Eightfold Path.

Like the Four Noble Truths, the Noble Eightfold Path is not about other-worldly things, but about how human beings think and act in every aspect of their lives. The eight are: right understanding, right intention, right speech, right action, right livelihood, right effort, right mindfulness, and right contemplation. People should think carefully about their goals, set their minds to achieving them, speak and act in ways that promote them, choose careers that keep them on the right path, and remain focused on their goals in order to avoid distractions.

"Confucianism" is also often classified as a philosophy – of social relations and government. In fact, until the twentieth century, people seeking government jobs in China had to pass an exam on Confucian principles. Like the Buddha, Confucius did not teach about otherworldly things such as gods, souls, or afterlife. Instead, he systematized ancient Chinese ideas about social relations and government, all of which were considered to be part of the great cosmic system. The teachings of Confucius focus on practical ways to achieve balance and live in harmony with the universe. Again, this involves all aspects of life, including work, education, the arts, and governing.

Nonetheless, Christian missionaries and scholars created the category *Confucianism* as a species under the genus *religion*. They also lumped a miscellany of other traditional Chinese ideas and practices under the category *Taoism*, which they treated as another species under the genus *religion* when, in fact, Chinese people are generally not either Confucians or Taoists, but incorporate aspects of the teachings and rituals of both Confucian and Taoist traditions, as well as those of various Buddhist teachers in their daily lives. Confucian, Taoist, and Buddhist teachings are referred to as the "three teachings" (San Jiao) of China. The San Jiao are considered to be "harmonious as one," and, together help people lead successful lives.

So the modern notion of *religion* developed to help European kings distinguish their power from that of church authorities. But that segregation of life into secular and religious spheres is not shared in many other parts of the world. As a result, "religion" is not like "language" or "tool use"; it does not refer to some objective reality found around the world and throughout the centuries.

That helps explain why scholars of religion have not produced a satisfactory definition of the word that applies even to Christianity, Judaism, Islam, Hinduism, Buddhism, Confucianism, and Taoism, let alone the 10 000 other traditions they classify as "religions." In the nineteenth century, some tried to define "religion" as a relationship to God or gods, but that doesn't work for Theravada Buddhism, Confucianism, Taoism, and other traditions not based on gods. (Theravada Buddhism is the earliest kind of Buddhism, the kind closest to what the Buddha taught. Theravada doesn't have gods, but later kinds of Buddhism, such as forms of Mahayana Buddhism, do have gods.) Vaguer definitions of "religion" as a relationship to "the transcendent" failed for similar reasons. Theravada Buddhism doesn't seem to be about anything beyond or outside the universe, and the same is true of Confucianism. The ancient Greeks had gods but did not think of them as transcendent; Zeus and Hera were physical beings who looked like men and women and lived nearby on Mount Olympus.

In the twentieth century, scholars have struggled to find inclusive ways to describe "religion." Well-known religion scholar Ninian Smart (1999) identified seven aspects of religions: social identity, ethics, rituals, myths, doctrines, emotional experiences, and things and places manifesting the sacred. Theologian Paul Tillich (d. 1965) tried to go beyond definitions of "religion" that were slanted toward Western monotheism by analyzing religion as based on people's "ultimate concern." Many scholars have followed him, but that analysis seems to cover too much rather than too little. For some people, art, music, wealth, or even football is their ultimate concern, but few scholars of religion would want these to count as religions. Other scholars have given up on using the term "religion," many under the influence of the great twentieth-century pioneer of Religious Studies, Wilfred Cantwell Smith, who described the modern concept "religion" as a purely Western construct that reduced a vast range of human experience to a "system of observances or beliefs." (Smith, 1962: 29) Recognizing the vagueness and ambiguity of the term "religion," contemporary scholars generally use the term cautiously, often substituting the term "tradition" for "religion" when referring to religions other than Christianity. Some scholars have even suggested bypassing the denominational categories in favor of "modes of religiosity" or "modes of non-religiosity." Instead of identifying people as Jews, Christians, or Muslims, for example, these scholars suggest identifying them as dogmatic, fundamentalist, or skeptical, regardless of their denomination. This reflects the recognition that fundamentalist Jews, Christians, and Muslims, for instance, may have more in common with each other than they do with their more skeptical or progressive co-religionists. This is not likely to catch on, of course, given the complex psychological and social ramifications of religious identity, but it does demonstrate the importance of recognizing that "religion" is not a simple category.

References

Cavanaugh, W. (2009) *The Myth of Religious Violence*, Oxford University Press, New York.

Crossman, A. (online) *Sociology of Religion*. About.com, http://sociology.about.com/od/Disciplines/a/Sociology-Of-Religion.htm (accessed January 6, 2013).

Smart, N. (1999) *Worldviews: Crosscultural Explorations of Human Beliefs*, Scribner, New York.

Smith, W.C. (1962) *The Meaning and End of Religion*, Fortress, Minneapolis MN.

Further Reading

Masuzawa, T. (2005) *The Invention of World Religions: Or, How European Universalism Was Preserved in the Language of Pluralism*, University of Chicago Press, Chicago.

Morreall, J. and Sonn, T. (2011) *The Religion Toolkit: A Complete Guide to Religious Studies*, John Wiley & Sons, Ltd, Chichester.

Prothero, S. (2010) *God is Not One: The Eight Rival Religions that Run the World and Why Their Differences Matter*, HarperCollins, New York.

Teiser, S. (1996) The spirits of Chinese religion, in *Religions of China in Practice* (ed D. Lopez), Princeton University Press, Princeton.

Whitehouse, H. (2004) *Modes of Religiosity: A Cognitive Theory of Religious Transmission*, AltaMira Press, Walnut Creek, CA.

2.   Religion Is about the Spiritual

> I love you when you bow in your mosque, kneel in your temple, pray in your church. For you and I are sons of one religion, and it is the spirit. (Khalil Gibran, Lebanese artist and poet (Najjar, 2008: 150))

Closely related to the idea that religion can be separated from non-religious spheres of life is the notion that religion is about what is spiritual. This is another distinction that is prominent in some religions, but not in all, or even most.

Dictionaries tell us that the adjective "spiritual" is based on "spirit," and "spirit" is contrasted with what is material. As the first meaning of "spiritual," *Webster's Revised Unabridged Dictionary* has:

> Consisting of spirit; not material; incorporeal; as, a spiritual substance or being.

With that meaning of "spiritual," another way to express the claim made in this myth is to say that religions are about what is not material. To today's Christians, this idea looks familiar and fits with the distinction between the material body and the non-material spirit or soul. Christian preachers have often described their work as "saving souls," that is, saving the nonmaterial part of human beings that will spend eternity in heaven or hell.

It was in the Middle Ages that Western Christian theologians developed the distinction between the material body and the non-material spirit or soul. Thinkers such as Augustine of Hippo and Thomas Aquinas were influenced by Greek philosophers, especially Plato, for whom the soul was the center of consciousness and the core of a person's identity, while the body was not essential to the person. This view is called *dualism*, from the Latin word *duo*, meaning "two." Dualists believe that although our bodies – being material and part of the natural world – are subject to change, there is something nonmaterial that gives stability and consistency to our unique identity. Unlike the material body, Plato said, the soul is naturally immortal – it cannot die. Medieval theologians described not just the soul as spiritual, but God, angels, and demons.

With the spiritual/material distinction, Christians could then talk about their "spiritual lives" as distinct from their "material lives." By the seventeenth century, the *Oxford English Dictionary* tells us, the word "spirituality" had come to mean "attachment to or regard for things of the spirit as opposed to material or worldly interests."

But many religions do not have a distinction between the material and the spiritual. Hundreds of traditional religions of the Americas and Africa, for example, involve animism, the belief that all things are animated by souls or spirits. In these traditions, spirits are all around in objects such as trees and rocks; they are not part of some nonmaterial "spiritual" realm.

Traditional Chinese religions, too, aren't about "the spiritual." For 2500 years, Taoism and Confucianism have taught people how the universe is ordered, how society should be organized, and how people should treat each other, without talking about "the spiritual." Taoism teaches about the Tao, "the Way" that natural processes work and that we should follow. Taoists view life holistically without making a radical distinction between what is material and what is not material. The same is true of Confucianism. Confucius taught an ethical system in which people respect and care for each other. The central virtue in Taoism is *wu-wei*, living in accordance with the Way of the cosmos (the *tao*), rather than trying to control events. Confucianism and Taoism share a worldview in which Tao is all-pervasive; it is in the things and events all around us, not in a separate nonmaterial realm.

The distinction between what is spiritual and what is material is not even evident in early Biblical literature. Consider the descriptions of God in the Hebrew Bible. In Genesis, the Creator is male. He makes the world in six days and then rests from his work:

> The Lord God formed man from the dust of the ground, and breathed into his nostrils the breath of life; and the man became a living being. And the Lord God planted a garden in Eden, in the east; and there he put the man whom he had formed. (Genesis 2:7–8)

Describing Adam and Eve after they had eaten from the forbidden tree, Genesis 3:8–9 says that:

> They heard the sound of the Lord God walking in the garden at the time of the evening breeze, and the man and his wife hid themselves from the presence of the Lord God among the trees of the Garden. But the Lord God called to the man, and said to him, "Where are you?"

Here God is not "spiritual." He shapes dirt into a human form, breathes into its nostrils to bring it to life, plants a garden, and walks in the garden as the day cools off. In creating Adam and Eve, he said, "Let us make humankind in our image, according to our likeness" (Genesis 1:26).

Physical descriptions of God continue throughout the Bible. In Exodus 33:20–23, God tells Moses that he won't show him his face but will show him his back. In Psalm 18:8, God was angry and "smoke went up from his nostrils, and devouring fire from his mouth." Joshua 10:11 says that to help the Israelites do battle with the Amorites, "the Lord threw down huge stones from heaven on them." Heaven, God's abode, is a place above us but not a separate realm. It is often pictured as a city ruled by God, who sits on a throne, with the angels as his courtiers (Psalm 103:19–21; Job 1:6). Isaiah (63:15) asks God to "[l]ook down from heaven and see, from your holy and glorious habitation." God is "El Elyon," the Most High, living in the highest place. Being above the earth, heaven is an ideal place to watch human affairs. "The Lord looks down from heaven; he sees all humankind. From where he sits enthroned he watches all the inhabitants of the earth" (Psalm 33:14). Heaven is also a place from which God can do things to people. He sends down fire to show his acceptance of some sacrifices (I Chronicles 21:26; II Chronicles 7:1).

If God is not described as nonmaterial in the Bible, it's no surprise that angels or devils are not described as such, either. In the story of the three messengers from God visiting Abraham in Genesis 18–19, for instance, they are sometimes called "angels" and sometimes called "men." When they met Lot in Sodom, they ate dinner together and then "the men of the city . . . surrounded the house; and they called to Lot, 'Where are the men who came to you tonight? Bring them out to us, so that we may know [have sex with] them.'" (19:1–5). These are clearly not "spiritual" beings.

The New Testament, too, has passages that encourage us to think of angels and men as interchangeable. The four Gospels say that when Mary Magdalen and the other women went to the tomb of Jesus on Easter morning, they were told by someone that he had been raised. In Mark 16:5, it was "a young man, dressed in a white robe." Matthew 28:2–3 says it was "an angel of the Lord . . . whose appearance was like lightning, and his clothing white as snow." In Luke 24:4, it was "two men in dazzling clothes," and in John 20:12 "two angels in white."

Like angels, demons or "evil spirits" are described in the Bible as physical beings. When Jesus exorcises the "unclean spirits" in Luke 8:26–36, for example, "the demons came out of the man and entered the swine, and the herd rushed down the steep bank into the lake and was drowned." The spirits here are clearly physically located, and they change their location from being inside the man to being inside the pigs.

Besides God, angels, and demons, as we said, the other thing that Christian theologians have said is spiritual rather than material is the human soul. But that idea is not Biblical, either. In the Bible, the soul is what makes something be alive. The Bible's words for soul are the Hebrew *nefesh* and *ruah*, and the Greek *spirē* and *pneuma*. These words mean wind, breath – air that's moving. Remember how God made Adam come alive in Genesis 2 – by breathing into his nostrils. The soul is thought of in the Bible as a thinner, lighter kind of stuff than the arms and legs. It's what we now call a gas, rather than a solid, but it's still material.

Not only are there currently thousands of religions that are not about "the spiritual" as nonmaterial, then, but the religion that puts the most emphasis on "the spiritual" today – Christianity – started out with no concept of the nonmaterial, thinking of souls as a light kind of matter.

References

Najjar, A. (2008) *Kahlil Gibran: a Biography*, Saqi, Beirut.
Oxford English Dictionary (1989) Oxford University Press, Oxford.
Webster's Revised Unabridged Dictionary (1913) G. and C. Merriam, New York.

3. Religion Is about the Supernatural

Religion: the service and worship of God or the supernatural. (*Merriam-Webster Dictionary*)

People today often think of religion as being about "the supernatural" – a category that includes such things as God, miracles, angels, and demons. The Latin word *super* means "above," so what is supernatural is above the natural. While the natural world is explained by physics, chemistry, and biology, with formulas such as Newton's laws of gravity, the supernatural world is not bound by the laws of science. People often explain the appeal of religion by saying that science cannot explain everything, so they believe in the supernatural world as well as the natural world. One way to understand miracles, for example, is that they are God's breaking of scientific laws to reveal himself or to answer people's prayers.

While this description works well for many contemporary versions of Christianity, Judaism, and Islam, it doesn't work for thousands of religions throughout history, or even for Christianity, Judaism, and Islam before the birth of modern science around 1600. So it's inaccurate to say that religion in general is about the supernatural.

Of the world's 10 000 religions, most do not make the distinction between the natural and the supernatural; many do not even have a word for "nature" or "natural." In the tribal religions of Africa, Australia, and the Americas, for example, plants, animals, people, witches, gods, spirits, ghosts, and everything else are simply part of the world. There is no science explaining "natural" events, and so there are no "supernatural" events left unexplained by science. Gods and spirits may be thought of as having superhuman powers – powers greater than people have – but gods and spirits are not in a "supernatural" world distinct from the world of plants, animals, and people.

Many tribal religions involve animism, the belief that all things have souls or spirits, including rocks and rivers. In these religions, spirits are not in some supernatural realm distinct from a natural realm.

In the great religions of India and China, too, the distinction between natural and supernatural seldom applies. In Hinduism, for example, the cow is sacred, and Hanuman, a monkey, is the eleventh avatar of the god Shiva and a hero in the religious epic *Ramayana*. Are cows and Hanuman natural or supernatural? That question doesn't make sense in Hinduism.

A central belief in Hinduism is reincarnation, rebirth, but that is not seen as something "supernatural." It is just what has always happened to people when they die.

Siddhartha Gautama, the man who became the Buddha, The Awakened One, did not teach about gods and spirits or "the supernatural." As we have seen, the core of his message, the Four Noble Truths, are about how to live a contented life. The Eightfold Path prescribes how people should think and act in order to achieve that goal: correct understanding, intending, speaking, acting, making a living, persevering, focusing and contemplating. None of those is supernatural, nor are the essential virtues cultivated by Buddhists: compassion (*metta*), kindness (*karuna*), and sympathetic joy (*mudita*).

Buddhists do believe in a kind of rebirth, but, like Hindus, they do not consider it "supernatural." *Nirvana* – the bliss of no longer suffering and being reborn – is achieved by living according to the Noble Eightfold Path and practicing the essential virtues.

Similarly, the indigenous religions of China, Confucianism and Taoism are about how people should live and be happy. Confucius taught an ethical system in which people respect and care for each other. The central virtue in Taoism is *wu-wei*, living in accordance with the Way of the cosmos, rather than trying to force events in accordance with one's will or desires. In

Confucianism and Taoism, there is the idea of the Tao, the Way that things happen, but that Tao is in the things and events all around us, not above them. The spirits of the deceased may surround us, along with those of rivers and mountains, but again, they are part of the "natural" environment.

If we look at religions that are no longer practiced, like those of ancient Greece, Rome, and Northern Europe, we find gods like Zeus, Venus, and Thor, who are part of the single world in which humans live, not above that world. The Greek gods, for instance, were thought to live on Mount Olympus and visit people from time to time.

Even in European cultures, the modern notion of "the supernatural" as an adjective *supernatural* meaning "attributed to some force beyond scientific understanding or the laws of nature" (*Oxford English Dictionary*) is of relatively recent origin. To medieval Europeans, the word "supernatural" did not mean a realm distinct from the "natural" realm. It was used to describe someone acting in a way that they could not usually act. Most often it was applied to human beings acting with the help of God's grace. With that meaning, obviously, "supernatural" could never be applied to God himself. But as early modern thinkers developed the idea of nature as a physical system that can be explained by physics and the other "natural sciences," the "supernatural" came to mean a realm of beings that were not subject to the laws of nature – such as God, angels, demons, ghosts, and spirits.

Reference

Merriam-Webster Dictionary Online, www.merriam-webster.com/dictionary/religion (accessed January 10, 2014).

4. Religion Is about Faith or Belief

Question with boldness even the existence of God; because, if there be one, he must more approve of the homage of reason than that of blindfolded fear. (Thomas Jefferson, Letter to Peter Carr, 1787.)

In the English-speaking world today, "faith" is often used as a synonym for "religion," even by scholars of religion. The popular introduction to world religions titled *Many Peoples, Many Faiths*, by Robert Ellwood and Barbara McGraw (2013), for example, is in its 10th edition. There is also John Bowker's (2006) *World Religions: The Great Faiths Explored and Explained*.

And "faith" is often used as a synonym for "belief," so that religions are referred to as "belief systems." But, in fact, faith and belief are not equivalent terms, and "religion" is not reducible to either one.

The great pioneer of Religious Studies Wilfred Cantwell Smith (d. 2000) devoted a significant part of his research to distinguishing between "faith" and "belief." In biblical times, Smith argues, "faith" meant confidence (which comes from the same root as "faith," the Latin *fideo*) or trust, specifically expressed in a relationship to whatever it is one perceives as the transcendent. Whatever that transcendent is, Smith observed, commitment to it can be expressed in many forms, including ritual, art, ethical behavior, and commitment to community. It could also be expressed in rational explanations or doctrines about the transcendent; Smith (1998: 39) said this expression of commitment to the transcendent is "particularly characteristic of Christians." Belief, he continued, in today's usage, means intellectual assent to certain propositions for which there is no empirical proof. But Smith argues that that meaning does not occur in either the Bible or the Qur'an. What does occur, he claims, is belief as it was meant in pre-modern times (and still is meant in its German cognate *belieben*), "to hold dear," "to be loyal to," "to value highly," that is, "to love" (Smith, 1998: 41). Thus, for Smith, belief in God meant not simply accepting the existence of God but pledging commitment to living one's life in the service of God. In that sense, believing in God presupposed God's existence. Questioning God's existence was literally unthinkable in the biblical context. The real choice was between being loyal to God by living in accordance with one's perception of God's will, and refusing to do so. Belief, in other words, could only be expressed in actions. It could not be reduced to a set of statements.

Belief in the modern sense of accepting certain statements as true began its path toward centrality in Christianity when Christianity shifted from being the voluntary commitment of people inspired by their teachers, and became a requirement of citizenship in the Roman Empire. When Christianity was thus politicized, members of the community were identified by their affirmation of a list of specific claims.

The groundwork for making this sense of "belief" the defining feature of being a Christian was laid by Roman Emperor Constantine (d. 337). Christians had been considered a dissident sect by earlier emperors, but Constantine legalized Christianity, assuring Christians' loyalty to him. He even incorporated Christian leaders into his new administration. He supported bishops financially and gave them basilicas, Roman public buildings, to use as churches.

Constantine's goal was to reunify the Roman Empire, which, by that time, had split into several autonomous regions. Newly liberated Christians throughout these realms had the potential to help unify the Empire. But it soon became obvious that there were disagreements among various Christian authorities, disagreements focusing on just who Jesus was and what he did. Some said, for example, that Jesus was the uncreated Son of God, equal to the Father, while others said that Jesus was created by God and so was not equal to him. Constantine wanted Christians to resolve their disagreements and accept a uniform set of beliefs so that Christianity could be a single and, hopefully, unifying ideology. So in 325 the Emperor called Christian leaders together in the town of Nicaea, near his new imperial capital, Constantinople, and charged them with producing a set of teachings for all Christians.

As it turned out, this was not an easy task. At the Council of Nicaea, and then at subsequent councils, church authorities debated their diverse claims, hammering out sets of official teachings that started with the words "I believe" – *credo*, in Latin, the root of the term "creed." But diverse understandings of Christianity continued. Disagreements over the idea of the Trinity – that God is at once Father, Son, and Spirit – were paramount.

In 380, Roman rulers announced the Code of Theodosius, requiring everyone in the Roman Empire to believe in the Trinity. Those who did not were "foolish madmen." The edict continued: "They shall be branded with the ignominious name of heretics … They will suffer in the first place the chastisement of the divine condemnation and in the second the punishment of our authority which in accordance with the will of Heaven we shall decide to inflict" (Bettenson, 1943: 31). Within five years, the first "heretics" were beheaded – a bishop from Avila, Spain, named Priscillian, and six of his followers. All were executed not because of something they did, but because of something they believed – a chilling parallel to the reasons Christians were persecuted in pre-Christian Rome. When a particular religious ideology becomes the basis of political legitimacy, those who do not share it suffer.

Acceptance of the claims outlined in specific creeds continued to be the defining feature of Christianity. Questions regarding the source of the Holy Spirit – who came to be described by theologians as one of three "persons" of the single God – were central to the split of Western Christianity from Eastern Christianity in 1054. The split of Western Christianity into diverse denominations in the Protestant Reformation of the sixteenth century pivoted on the question of the relative merits of belief and good works. The formula settled upon by the Protestants was "faith alone" (*sola fide*), meaning that correct belief about God, rather than good works, is all that is necessary for salvation.

This is the origin of the modern meaning of belief and its equation to faith, and the reduction of "religion" to "faith" or "belief system." However, as Smith points out, Christianity is unusual in this regard. No other World Religion – not Judaism, Islam, Hinduism, Buddhism, Taoism, or Confucianism – sees itself as a system of beliefs.

How, then, do non-Christian religions understand themselves? Judaism and Islam, the two closest to Christianity, identify members of their communities on the basis of their following of divine law – Torah and Sharia, respectively. They stress *orthopraxy*, which means correct action, rather than *orthodoxy*, correct teaching.

As we move to the religions of South and East Asia, thinking of them as belief systems is even less accurate. In Hinduism, there are countless gods – 330 000 000, it is sometimes said. Some people are devoted to one of them – Shiva or Vishnu, for example. Others venerate some of the major gods and turn to minor gods for help in specific matters. And some follow an ancient tradition centered on Brahman, Ultimate Reality, which is described as beyond the gods. Being devoted to one or more gods, or to none, does not mean that one rejects the existence of other gods. And whatever gods a Hindu is devoted to, there are no associated official doctrines comparable to the statements about Jesus in Christian creeds.

Like Hinduism, Buddhism is pluralist – it accepts many worldviews and many ways of life. Siddhartha Gautama, the founder of the tradition, started out as what we now call Hindu, but he did not teach about the gods. His concern was with overcoming suffering. As we saw above, he taught that people should practice the Eightfold Path (right understanding, right intention, right speech, right action, right livelihood, right effort, right mindfulness, and right contemplation) and the essential virtues of kindness, compassion, and sympathetic joy. Siddhartha is revered as the Buddha, the Awakened One, not because he is a god or because these truths are divinely revealed, but because the method he taught has been effective in dealing with suffering and achieving happiness for millions of people over the centuries. The Eightfold Path and the essential virtues are not doctrines to be accepted on faith, but techniques that many people find useful.

Confucianism, like Buddhism, is about human problems rather than gods or beliefs. Growing up in China at a time of war and social breakdown, Confucius asked how society could restore the social harmony of earlier centuries. He didn't claim that his ideas were divinely revealed or that they had to be accepted as absolutely and uniquely true, based on faith.

Rather, he looked back through Chinese literature and found human wisdom that had effectively guided people toward social harmony in the past. This was based on the model of treating others with the respect, obedience, and care that good children show their parents.

Confucianism spread across China to become its most influential tradition, but it exists in harmony with other traditions, as well. Taoism arose in China about the same time as Confucianism, but it took a different approach to what people needed to do to be happy. Its focus was not on social relationships based on respectful submission, but on people's fitting into the patterns and rhythms of the natural order of the universe, the Tao. The main virtue in Taoism, as we saw, is *wu-wei*, living in harmony with the Way, rather than trying to force events in accordance with our desires.

In China, as in India, there is no central authority like an emperor or pope telling people what they must believe. And so there are no heretics. Different traditions coexist not just in villages but in individual people. One temple may have Taoist priests and Buddhist monks; one person may have a Taoist wedding and a Buddhist funeral. People may follow Confucian principles of social respect, marry in a Taoist temple, and practice Buddhist methods of meditation. There are also rituals for household gods and village gods that predate Taoism and Buddhism. So while beliefs are undoubtedly involved in Indian and Chinese religions, the emphasis is on practice, making the term "faith" an insufficient descriptor, as it is for Judaism and Islam, as well.

References

Bettenson, H. (ed) (1943) *Codex Theodosianus. Documents of the Christian Church*, Oxford University Press, Oxford.

Bowker, J. (2006) *World Religions: The Great Faiths Explored and Explained*, DK, London.

Ellwood R. and McGraw, B. (2013) *Many Peoples, Many Faiths*, Pearson, New York.

Jefferson, T. (1787) Letter to Peter Carr, August 19, www.let.rug.nl/usa/presidents/thomas-jefferson/letters-of-thomas-jefferson/jefl61.php (accessed January 10, 2014).

Smith, W.C. (1998) *Believing – An Historical Perspective*, Oneworld, Oxford.

Further Reading

Smith, W.C. (1998) *Faith and Belief: The Difference between Them*, 2nd edition, Oneworld, Oxford.

5. Worship Is an Essential Part of Religion

> Human beings by their very nature are worshipers. Worship is not something
> we do; it defines who we are. You cannot divide human beings into those who
> worship and those who don't. Everybody worships; it's just a matter of what,
> or whom, we serve. (Paul David Tripp (2002: 16))

The 1950s, under the impact of the Cold War, saw the emergence in the
United States of a widespread fear of Communism, which was officially
atheist. In an effort to combat it, the American Advertising Council, with
the support of President Eisenhower, developed a public campaign to
encourage religion, complete with national advertising. Thousands of billboards featured pictures of happy families with the words, "Worship together
this week" (Spring, 2011: 94).

The Advertising Council's campaign reflects the common perception
that to practice religion means essentially "to worship" – as in: show devotion to and acknowledge the supreme value of something. This can be seen
in the titles of many introductions to world religions, such as Mary Pope
Osborne's (1996) *One World, Many Religions: The Ways We Worship*. It is
also reflected in the generic term devised for gatherings of diverse religious
communities. Churches, temples, and synagogues are grouped together as
"houses of worship" or as "worship centers."

The association of religion with worship is understandable in the
Western monotheistic religions – those that believe in one God. Judaism,
Christianity, and Islam developed in areas where there were powerful kingdoms with absolute rulers. Pharaohs had ruled nearby Egypt since the third
millennium BCE. To the east, leaders like Hammurabi and Nebuchadnezzar
had ruled Babylon since the early second millennium. Once they had settled in Canaan, the Israelites wanted to "be like other nations." They wanted
to be ruled not by tribal elders or judges, as they had been, but by kings
(1 Samuel 8:20). (Samuel, the last of the judges, warned them that this was
a bad idea, but that is another story.) As God remained their ultimate ruler,
it was natural to view God as the ultimate king – or even "King of Kings," as
powerful ancient rulers were called. They also referred to God as Lord
(Adonai), on the model of a great landowner. Biblical passages refer to
God's throne and his heavenly court. Just as kings, pharaohs, and emperors
governed various areas of the earth, Yahweh was believed to govern
the whole world. That's why many Jewish prayers begin with the words
"Barukh atah Adonai Eloheinu, melekh ha'olam" ("Blessed are You, Lord,

our God, King of the Universe"). Because kings and emperors maintained their power through military conquest, too, God was described as "Lord of Hosts" (armies), leading Israel in battle against neighboring tribes (for example, 1 Samuel 17:45).

As a Jew, Jesus inherited the idea of God as king, though he taught about a kingdom "not of this world" (John 18:36), rather than of a great earthly realm. Still, the goal of his preaching was to establish the Kingdom of God – the rule of God. In the prayer he taught his followers, Jesus asks that "Your kingdom come, your will be done, on earth as it is in heaven" (Matthew 6:10). After the early church declared that Jesus was God, it was natural for Christians to picture him as a patriarch, too. Some early Christian paintings and mosaics portray Jesus as *Pantokrator*, Greek for "Ruler over All." That idea was strengthened in the Middle Ages and so today many Catholic churches are named "Christ the King," and references to Jesus as "Lord" remain common.

When Islam arose in the seventh century, it also had as its goal the Kingdom of God on earth. The word *Islam* itself means "submission," submission to God's rule. The opening chapter of the Qur'an, recited daily by Muslims, begins:

> In the name of God, the most merciful and compassionate:
> All praise to God, Lord of the worlds,
> The most merciful and compassionate,
> King of the Day of Judgment . . .

Within this Western monotheistic understanding of the relationship between God and human beings, it is easy to see how people could think of worship as the essence of religion. To worship God is to express the highest degree of reverence for and submission to God, and that is the ultimate version of what the subjects of any ruler do when they publicly acknowledge his greatness and power. It is demonstrated in postures like lowering oneself in relation to the ruler, by bowing, kneeling, or lying prostrate on the floor.

Associated practices include proclaiming the ruler's greatness (glorifying him), and acknowledging one's humility and failings (sins). This may include undertaking penances, such as fasting. Monotheistic worship also reflects the secular model of submission to authority by including expressions of gratitude for all they have done, asking for their continued favor – mentioning, perhaps, specific requests – and showing some reciprocity by presenting something of value (presenting them with gifts).

However strong the linkage between religion and worship in Judaism, Christianity, and Islam, it is not dominant in many other religions. Three examples are Theravada Buddhism in South and Southeast Asia, and Confucianism and Taoism in China. All three developed several centuries before Christianity, and in them there is no Creator God to glorify, thank, petition, or ask for forgiveness.

Theravada is the form of Buddhism considered to be most similar to what the Buddha taught, which was about how to reduce suffering and live a balanced life. The basic goal is to stop craving things. This goal is often called "non-attachment." There are no gods to worship. The ultimate goal is not to glorify God forever in heaven, but to reach *nirvana*, the blissful condition that comes with the cessation of desire.

Confucius lived at a time of political strife in China, a time called the Period of Warring States. His goal was to reestablish a peaceful, just society based on mutual respect and concern for the common good. To do that, he looked to great leaders of earlier centuries, especially the Duke of Zhou, as role models. With the leader as a moral exemplar, Confucius said, the people will be virtuous too. The virtues he emphasized were humaneness, justice, propriety, knowledge, and integrity, and he saw these virtues as developing from five basic relationships. The primary one is father and son. The others are modeled on it: ruler and subject, older brother and younger brother, husband and wife, and friend and friend. The ideal son shows *hsaio*, respect and concern for his parents, and that is the model for other social relationships. All members of society are called upon to behave humanely, including the ruler.

Unlike the Buddha, Confucius did talk about the gods, but they were neither universal sovereigns nor his main concern. Devotion to the gods, he said, should be modeled on *hsaio* like other social relationships.

Taoism is the other great tradition indigenous to China. Unlike Confucianism, it is suspicious of leaders, governments, and social structures in general. Its focus is not on God or gods but on the *Tao*, "the Way," which is the system that regulates every thing and process. As we saw above, for Taoists the main virtue is *wu-wei*, living simply and effectively, in accordance with the Way of the cosmos. Taoism also stresses the virtues of humility and compassion. Taoists do talk about gods, but again, they are not sovereign rulers to be obeyed at all costs. They are part of the universe and, like humans, are governed by the Tao.

Theravada Buddhist, Confucian, and Taoist temples are not, therefore, strictly "houses of worship," as synagogues, churches, and mosques are.

Theravada Buddhist temples may contain relics and images of the Buddha or his disciples, and people may present offerings in hopes of receiving blessings, but temples are primarily places where teaching and meditation take place. Taoist temples serve as locations for religious functions, such as weddings and funerals. Confucius, like the Buddha, has never been considered a god, although there are temples dedicated to him and people may even make offerings. But the temples are primarily described as places to honor the teachings, rather than the person, of Confucius.

References

Osborne, M.P. (1996) *One World, Many Religions: The Ways We Worship*, Random House, New York.

Spring, D. (2011) *Advertising in the Age of Persuasion: Building Brand America, 1941–1961*, Palgrave Macmillan, New York.

Tripp, P.D. (2002) *Instruments in the Redeemer's Hands: People in Need of Change Helping People in Need of Change*, P&R Publishing, Phillipsburg NJ.

6.   Religion Is a Personal Matter

> I believe in a president whose religious views are his own private affair, neither imposed by him upon the nation, or imposed by the nation upon him as a condition to holding that office. (John F. Kennedy (1960))

Modern Europeans and Americans often make a distinction between religion and the rest of life. Religion is about the sacred, said pioneer sociologist Émile Durkheim (1995), and that is distinct from things like politics, business, and sport. Those things are "secular." Many people go further and claim that, unlike what is secular, religion is a personal matter – between an individual and God. A century ago, Harvard philosopher William James (2008: 31) wrote that religion is "the feelings, acts, and experiences of individual men in their solitude, so far as they apprehend themselves to stand in relation to whatever they may consider divine."

This idea that religion is a personal or private matter is reflected in the modern separation of religion from politics. In the United States, for example, the early states, like European countries, had linked their governments to particular Christian denominations, and thus discriminated against those who were not members of the designated denomination. "Founding Father" and third president Thomas Jefferson wanted the new state governments and the federal government to cease this practice. His own state, Virginia, had given many benefits to Anglicans and had discriminated against non-Anglicans. Jefferson's 1786 Virginia Statute of Religious Freedom declared that no one:

> shall be compelled to frequent or support any religious worship, place, or ministry whatsoever, nor shall be enforced, restrained, molested, or burthened in his body or goods, nor shall otherwise suffer on account of his religious opinions or belief; but that all men shall be free to profess, and by argument to maintain, their opinion in matters of religion, and that the same shall in no wise diminish, enlarge, or affect their civil capacities.

A few years later, when the US Constitution was written, these ideas were included in the First Amendment: "Congress shall make no law respecting an establishment of religion, or prohibiting the free exercise thereof." Writing to a group of Baptists in the state of Connecticut who had expressed concerns about the establishment of official religions, Jefferson expressed agreement with them that religion "is a matter which lies solely between Man and his God, that he owes account to none other for his faith or his worship" (Padover, 1943: 518–519).

Over the next two centuries, the United States became famous for its separation of church and state. In 1960, it was central to the presidential campaign of John F. Kennedy. Kennedy was Catholic, and there was lingering suspicion that Catholics were ultimately bound by obedience to the Vatican and were incapable of separating religion from politics. This prejudice against Catholics was promoted by groups like the Ku Klux Klan. Rumors spread that Kennedy would take orders from the Pope and channel federal money to Catholic schools. So on September 12, 1960, he delivered a major address to the Greater Houston Ministerial Association, which included this line: "I believe in a president whose religious views are his own private affair, neither imposed by him upon the nation, or imposed by the nation upon him as a condition to holding that office."

This understanding of religion makes each person's religion his or her own business. Like their personal preferences regarding music or poetry, for example, it's a private matter. They may want to tell other people about it, but they don't have to.

The claim that religion is a personal matter confuses two things. The first is freedom of religion – the right of a person to follow any religion or none – and the second is the nature of religion. Personal freedom to choose one's religion is highly valued, particularly in the modern world. But saying that a person should have the freedom to choose any or no religion does not imply that the religions among which they choose are strictly "a personal matter." Indeed, few things are as intensely social as religion. The renowned twentieth-century religion scholar Ninian Smart (1999) identified seven aspects of religions: social identity, ethics, rituals, myths, doctrines, emotional experiences, and things and places manifesting the sacred. Of these, the first six are clearly social. The social identity conferred by a religion locates people within a group. Ethics is the rules for how people treat each other. Rituals may be performed solo but are usually social actions. Myths (in the scholar's sense of stories that explain important aspects of life) are handed down from generation to generation within groups. Doctrines are official teachings of a group announced by religious leaders who got their authority from that group. Even things and places of religious significance usually have that significance conferred on them by groups.

As we have seen, in the Hebrew Bible, or Old Testament, for example, there was no distinction between religion and the rest of social life. There isn't a word for "religion" in the Hebrew Bible. The Laws of Moses were the civil and religious laws of the people of Israel, and God dealt with the people of Israel as a group, through representatives called prophets.

Christianity, too, began as a social movement. It was Jesus' attempt to bring about the Kingdom of God on earth – that is, to get everyone to live as God wanted them to live. When Christianity was made the official religion of the Roman Empire in the fourth century, it became even more socially structured. Many Christians today say that the essence of their religion is a personal acceptance of Jesus Christ as their Savior. But when Jesus described the Last Judgment in Matthew 25, the criterion was not how much of a personal relationship people had developed with him as their Savior, but how well they had met the needs of other people for food, clothing, shelter, and companionship.

If we look beyond the Western monotheistic religions, the social nature of religion is still more obvious. Confucianism, for example, the great tradition that governed China for millennia, is basically a set of guidelines for social and political organization.

Like Thomas Jefferson, we may well object to the ways people have manipulated various religions for their own benefits, and that may prompt us to defend the First Amendment of the US Constitution. But the very possibility of groups using religion to benefit themselves shows that religion is essentially a social and not a personal matter.

The social dimension of religion also calls into question the idea made popular by John F. Kennedy that a candidate's religion is strictly a private matter. In the US presidential primaries of 2012, Rick Santorum made his conservative Roman Catholic moral views part of his campaign. The Constitution should be amended, he said, to ban abortion and gay marriage; he added that the 1965 Supreme Court ruling that Americans have a right to privacy that includes the use of contraceptives was a mistake. As he hoped, these statements got him a lot of votes from conservative Christians. But it was also reasonable for people who did not share his religious beliefs not to vote for him based on those beliefs. They were not merely a personal matter.

References

Durkheim, É. (1995) *The Elementary Forms of Religious Life*, translated by Karen Fields, Free Press, New York.

James, W. (2008) *The Varieties of Religious Experience*, Arc Manor, Rockville MD.

Kennedy, J.F. (1960) Speech to the Greater Houston Ministerial Association, September 12.

Padover, S. (ed) (1943) *The Complete Jefferson*, Tudor, New York.

Smart, N. (1999) *Worldviews: Crosscultural Explorations of Human Beliefs*, Scribner, New York.

7. Science Will Eventually Replace Religion

> It is time that scientists and other public intellectuals observed that the contest between faith and reason is zero-sum … There is simply no good reason to believe [the sorts of things that religious dogmatists believe], and scientists should stop hiding their light under a bushel and make this emphatically obvious to everyone. (Sam Harris (2005))

In the past two centuries, there have been huge changes in society, as modern physics, chemistry, and biology developed, along with psychology and the social sciences. Modern science, in turn, made possible the Industrial Revolution, which saw the creation of railroads, automobiles, airplanes and spacecraft, synthetic materials, electronics, computers, and the other technological marvels that shape our lives today.

How have modern science and technology affected traditional religions? One popular idea that took shape in the first half of the nineteenth century is that as science and technology gain importance in people's lives, the importance of religion diminishes. Pioneering sociologist Auguste Comte (d. 1857), for example, along with Karl Marx (d. 1883) and Sigmund Freud (d. 1939), said that religion began at a very early stage of the human race, when people knew little about the physical world and about themselves. They did not think logically and were highly superstitious, so they used magic and sacrifices to try to ensure a good hunt or a plentiful harvest, and to make diseases go away. As humans have learned more about how the universe and their own bodies and minds actually work, these thinkers argued, we have had less need for religion. While people once thought of lightning and thunder as the actions of gods in the sky, for example, science has taught us that lightning is a discharge of static electricity and thunder is the acoustic effect of that discharge. Countless generations of humans thought of plagues as divine punishments, but science has taught that they are caused by microorganisms such as bacteria and viruses. Scientific knowledge has thus demystified the world and given us the tools to understand the causes of our problems, and therefore to solve them.

As science and technology continue to develop, Comte, Marx, Freud, and many others thought, people will eventually be able to explain and control the world around them without appealing to any supernatural forces or gods. That will leave nothing for religion to do, and so it will wither and die. This viewpoint is captured in a quotation widely attributed to the philosopher Bertrand Russell: "Religion is something left over from the infancy of our intelligence; it will fade away as we adopt reason and science as our guidelines."

In the last few years, four prominent atheists have presented similar ideas – Daniel Dennett, Sam Harris (quoted above), Richard Dawkins, and Christopher Hitchens. In *Breaking the Spell: Religion as a Natural Phenomenon*, American philosopher Daniel Dennett (2007) argues that religion gave early humans the reassuring feeling that they could control the world around them. That feeling, however, was based on false beliefs about gods and spirits, and so the reassurance was illusory. Religion is based on wishful thinking, and should be replaced by science.

American neuroscientist Sam Harris has written two books advocating that we replace religion with science: *The End of Faith: Religion, Terror, and the Future of Reason* (2004) and *Letter to a Christian Nation* (2008). Not only did early humans misunderstand the world, he says, but their false beliefs led to barbaric customs such as sacrificing children to the gods. God's commanding of Abraham to sacrifice his son in the Bible shows how that practice was familiar to the ancient Israelites. We need to replace religion with science, Harris says, not only to understand the world better, but to treat each other better.

The title of British evolutionary biologist Richard Dawkins' book, *The God Delusion* (2006), shows his similarity to the other three in this group. In explaining the universe and the origin of living things, he says, the Big Bang Theory and the theory of evolution are more rational and credible than religious explanations. Dawkins insists that substituting religious myths for rational explanations of life deprives people of the tools necessary for leading successful, independent lives. He goes further, arguing that training children through unsubstantiated threats of violence and promises of reward is a form of child abuse (2006).

British-American essayist Christopher Hitchens (2007) presents some of the strongest attacks on religion. In *God Is Not Great: How Religion Poisons Everything*, he devotes an entire chapter (16) to religion as child abuse. Religion, he claims, is "violent, irrational, intolerant, allied to racism and tribalism and bigotry, invested in ignorance and hostile to free inquiry, contemptuous of women and coercive toward children" (2007: 56).

If such arguments are correct, then we should expect that religion will gradually disappear as science explains more and more about our world. Fifty years ago, some scholars predicted that by 2000, Europe and North America would be thoroughly secular, as people largely dropped religion. People's beliefs about the natural world and about themselves would be scientific beliefs, and values and social norms would be based on science. That was expected not only by atheists, but also by many religious believers. Professor Harvey Cox of Harvard Divinity School, for instance, celebrated such changes in his best-selling book *The Secular City* (1965).

Predictions about the decline of religion have largely come true in Europe over the last four decades. Sweden, for example, is often described as the least religious country in the world. Until the late 1800s, it had a state church to which everyone automatically belonged. But gradually over the twentieth century, Swedes separated their government from that church. The vast majority are still members of the Church of Sweden, where they are baptized, married, and buried, but that's the extent of their "religion." About 95% of them say they "seldom or never" attend church services. The Church itself estimates that less than 2% attend regularly. Only 15% believe in a personal God, and only 19% believe in life after death.

But the opposite happened in the United States. There, as science and technology have continued to flourish, so has religion, especially among evangelical Protestants. The Evangelical Free Church of America, for instance, was six times larger in 2000 than in 1960; the Church of God in Christ was thirteen times larger. In 1970 there were fifty megachurches – churches with weekly attendance of 2000 or more – in the United States; now there are 1300. The largest, Lakewood Church in Houston, Texas, draws 45 000 people each week. The United States is the most religious country in the industrialized world, with 76% identifying themselves as Christians in the US Census. It is the only developed country where a majority say that religion plays a "very important" role in their lives. In a 2012 survey by the Pew Forum on Religion and Public Life, 36% of Americans said that they attend religious services at least once a week.

How could the scholarly predictions of the demise of religion have been so mistaken? The claim that the more scientifically and technologically advanced a society is, the less religious it is rests on two fundamental misconceptions about religion. The first is that when people explain things by appealing to God, they think of God as directly causing those things in the same way as, for example, kicking a football causes it to fly into the air. It is true that before the microscope allowed scientists to see the microbes that cause disease, many religious people thought of God as the cause of disease. But the discovery of microbes did not make people eliminate God from their explanation of disease. It certainly did not turn believers into atheists. Most people maintained their belief in God as the cause of everything – including disease-causing microbes – and added a new fact to their worldview: that microbes are the *direct* causes of many diseases. They still thought of God as the creator of all things, who keeps them in existence from moment to moment. For them, God was still the *ultimate* cause of all things and all events, including microbes making people sick. And so thousands of believers have studied science and remained believers. Today, when most people pray to God to cure them of an infection, for example, they are well aware that the direct cause of that infection is pernicious microorganisms. But they are appealing for help to God as the ultimate cause of all things and events, including the bacteria and viruses.

The second mistaken assumption in the myth that as science grows, religion shrinks, is that the main function of religion is to explain things. While religions certainly do that, they do much more. As we saw above, religion scholar Ninian Smart (1999) has identified seven aspects of religion: social identity, ethics, rituals, myths, doctrines, emotional experiences, and things and places associated with the sacred. Of these, only myths and doctrines involve explaining things, and any of the other five could be more valuable to someone than having explanations. People may even ignore the explanations provided by their religion's doctrines, but remain members of that religion because they value the sense of identity and community it provides, the rituals and other traditions, the moral code, the people in the group, and the places where they meet. Even clergy can reject doctrine, including the fundamental doctrine of God's existence. One of the most famous, Rabbi Mordechai Kaplan, for example, taught at the Jewish Theological Seminary in New York for fifty years, and started his own atheistic branch of the religion, Reconstructionist Judaism. Rabbi Richard L. Rubenstein, a student of Kaplan, is famous for his book *After Auschwitz: History, Theology, and Contemporary Judaism* (1992), which denies the existence of God. Similarly, Anglican bishops John Robinson, author of the best-selling *Honest to God* (1963) and John Shelby Spong, author of *A New Christianity for a New World* (2002) are atheists who reject many traditional Christian beliefs. But all remained clergy because of the many valuable things in their traditions.

Teachings about the origin and nature of the world, therefore, are not the sole purpose of religion. Nor, as we saw in Chapter 1, are religious myths meant as literal science. Religions have been with us since time immemorial and, despite the predictions of skeptics, they are likely to be with us for the duration.

References

Cox, H. (1965) *The Secular City*, Collier, New York.

Dawkins, R. (2006) *The God Delusion*, Mariner Books, Boston.

Dennett, D. (2007) *Breaking the Spell: Religion as a Natural Phenomenon*, Penguin, New York.

Harris, S. (2004) *The End of Faith: Religion, Terror, and the Future of Reason*, Norton, New York.

Harris, S. (2005) The Politics of Ignorance, *Huffington Post*, August 2, www.samharris.org/site/full_text/the-huffington-post-aug-2-2005 (accessed January 6, 2013).

Harris, S. (2008) *Letter to a Christian Nation*, Vintage, New York.

Hitchens, C. (2007) *God Is Not Great: How Religion Poisons Everything*, Twelve, New York.

Pew Forum on Religion and Public Life (2012) Summary of key findings, *US Religious Landscape Survey*, http://religions.pewforum.org/pdf/report2religious-landscape-study-key-findings.pdf (accessed Janury 10, 2014).

Robinson, J. (1963) *Honest to God*, Westminster John Knox, Philadelphia.

Rubenstein, R. (1992) *After Auschwitz: History, Theology, and Contemporary Judaism*, Johns Hopkins University Press, Baltimore and London.

Smart, N. (1999). *Worldviews: Crosscultural Explorations of Human Beliefs*, Scribner, New York.

Spong, J.S. (2002) *A New Christianity for a New World: Why Traditional Faith Is Dying and How a New Faith Is Being Born*, HarperOne, San Francisco.

8. Religion Causes Violence

Something about us ... tempts us to do wrong. It's pretty easily explained, I think. We are primates, high primates, but primates. We're half a chromosome away from chimpanzees and it shows. It especially shows in the number of religions we invent to console ourselves or to give us things to quarrel with other primates about. If anything demonstrates that God is man-made, not man God-made, surely it is the religions erected by this quasi-chimpanzee species and the harm that they're willing to inflict on that basis." (Christopher Hitchens (2007a))

Each day the international news seems to have at least one story about religious violence. The attacks by Muslim terrorists in the United States on September 11, 2001 and the United Kingdom on July 7, 2005 quickly come to mind. In the early 1990s in the former Yugoslavia, fighting between Orthodox Serbs, Catholic Croats, and Muslim Bosnians left more than 200 000 Muslims dead. European history, too, is full of violence associated with religion. The Thirty Years' War (1618–1648) between Catholics and Protestants is estimated to have killed 15 – 30% of the people in the German states, including almost half the males. In Ireland, Roman Catholics and Anglicans battled throughout the nineteenth and twentieth centuries and even now enjoy only an uneasy peace. And Western monotheistic religions aren't the only ones associated with violence. Even Buddhism, often thought of as a religion of compassion, has its share of violence. Sri Lanka, the island nation south of India whose constitution commits it to "foster and protect Buddhism," consists of a Buddhist majority and a Hindu Tamil minority. In the 1980s, when the Tamils pushed for independence from Sri Lanka, the government carried out a brutal campaign to suppress them, which the Buddhist majority enthusiastically supported. In the civil war that followed, 80 000–100 000 people were killed. And that was not an isolated incident in the history of Buddhism, as Michael Jerryson and Mark Juergensmeyer show in their book *Buddhist Warfare* (2010). The conclusion that some people draw from all this killing is that religion is inherently violent. Belonging to a religion makes people have negative feelings toward non-members and act aggressively toward them. In Christopher Hitchens' book *God Is Not Great: How Religion Poisons Everything* (2007b), the chapter "Religion Kills" offers many purported examples. In 2001, Hitchens writes, he was on a panel with a religious broadcaster who engaged him in a thought experiment. Suppose, the man said, you were in a strange city as night was falling, and you saw a large group of men approaching. Would you feel safer, or less safe, if you learned that they were coming from a prayer meeting? Hitchens answered with a confident "Less safe."

> Just to stay within the letter 'B,' I have actually had that experience in Belfast, Beirut, Bombay, Belgrade, Bethlehem, and Baghdad. In each case I can say absolutely, and can give my reason, why I would feel immediately threatened if I thought that the group of men approaching me in the dusk were coming from a religious observance. (2007b: 18)

Many religious people, including scholars of religion who are ordained ministers, agree with Hitchens that religion is especially prone to violence. Charles Kimball, a scholar and Southern Baptist minister, begins his book *When Religion Becomes Evil* (2002: 1) this way: "It is somewhat trite, but nevertheless sadly true, to say that more wars have been waged, more people killed, and these days more evil perpetrated in the name of religion than by any other institutional force in human history." According to Kimball, religion naturally causes violence because it is absolutist – it looks at the world in black-and-white, mutually exclusive terms such as "good" and "evil," "us" and "them." Richard E. Wentz, a minister in the United Church of Christ and author of *Why People Do Bad Things in the Name of Religion* (1993), agrees, as does Martin Marty, a Lutheran minister and professor at the University of Chicago. "Once a particular group considers itself as divinely chosen and draws sharp boundaries between itself and others," Marty (2000: 28) writes, "the enemy has been clearly identified, and violence can become actual."

Dozens of other scholars, too, from religious studies, sociology, political science, and history, have written about how, throughout history and across cultures, there has been a special link between religion and violence. In *Terror in the Mind of God: The Global Rise of Religious Violence*, Mark Juergensmeyer (2000: xi) says simply, "Religion seems to be connected with violence virtually everywhere."

Could the claims of these august scholars, with all their examples of violence around the world and throughout history, be conclusive?

It is certainly true that throughout history and across cultures, millions of people have killed millions of other people. But saying that is quite different from saying that something called "religion," as opposed to something called "politics" or "ethnic identity" or "class conflict," caused that violence. To pin the blame on "religion," we would have to distinguish religion from these other things and show that religion is more likely than they are to motivate violence. The problem with these claims is that not one of the scholars who say that religion is especially violent has a definition of "religion" that clearly distinguishes it from other social phenomena, especially from politics. Without such a definition, it is not clear just what these scholars are blaming the violence on.

Religion is notoriously difficult to define. A suitable definition could not include belief in God or gods, as we have seen, because several religions are not based on gods. Nor can religion be defined in terms of "the transcendent" or "the supernatural," for the same reason. Marty acknowledges the problem with defining "religion," but offers "five features that can help point to and put boundaries around the term" *religion*: it "focuses our ultimate concern," "builds community," "appeals to myth and symbol," "is reinforced through rites and ceremonies," and "demands certain behaviors from its adherents" (Marty, 2000: 10–14).

But these characteristics can be found in many other things, especially political ideologies such as Marxism, nationalism, and patriotism. Curiously, Marty notes that politics often shares these features. This becomes obvious in a survey of examples of wars that are allegedly caused by religion. The one cited most often, perhaps, is the Thirty Years' War (1618–1648), part of the century and a half of violence following the Protestant Reformation. This period saw a series of conflicts, often called the "Wars of Religion," after Lutherans, Calvinists, Huguenots, and other Protestants broke away from the Catholic Church. Differences in belief and practice created hostility between the various groups, and their disagreements grew into armed conflict. The trouble with calling this violence "religious" is that it is just as plausible to identify it as political or economic, or even social, as William Cavanaugh has shown in *The Myth of Religious Violence* (2009).

In France, for example, most of what the Protestant Huguenots were fighting against was not Catholic beliefs, rituals, or morality, but two political phenomena. One was the (Catholic) King's attempts to take power away from the nobles. In this struggle, Protestant nobles often joined forces with

Catholic nobles. In 1573, for example, the Catholic Duke of Bouillon led Huguenot forces against the Crown (Cavanaugh, 2009: 144). In France, as elsewhere, much of the fighting in the whole period involved local nobles resisting the attempts of kings and emperors to concentrate power in centralized states. (Cavanaugh, 2009: 163). That resistance began before the Protestant Reformation, with Catholic nobles opposing Catholic kings. French Protestants also opposed the corruption of kings and bishops. Starting in 1516, French (Catholic) kings had the right to appoint bishops and abbots. King Francis I gave these positions to his cronies, mostly nobles with no training in church affairs. Cardinal de Tournon, for instance, held simultaneous positions of provincial governor; financier of the Crown; archbishop of Auch, Bourges, Embrun, and Lyon; and abbot of over a dozen monasteries (Cavanaugh, 2009: 167).

If these really were "religious" wars, then fighting would not be between soldiers of the same religion, and armies of different religions would not be allied. But both were common. Catholic France allied with the Muslim Turks against the Catholic Holy Roman Emperor Charles V. Most of Charles' troops were mercenaries, many of them Protestants; so, on the battlefield it was often Protestants against Protestants. The second half of the Thirty Years' War was predominantly between the two great Catholic dynasties of Europe, the Habsburgs and the Bourbons. In the 1630s, Cardinal Richelieu brought France into the Thirty Years' War on the side of Lutheran Sweden against the (Catholic) Holy Roman Emperor Ferdinand II. In 1635 Catholic France declared war on Catholic Spain, a war that lasted until 1659. In 1643, Lutheran Sweden attacked Lutheran Denmark; the (Catholic) Holy Roman Emperor Ferdinand III came to Denmark's aid.

Cavanaugh presents another three dozen examples in which combatants were not opposed to each other based on religious difference. The primary cause of the violence was not "religion, as opposed to merely political, economic, or social causes," and "it is impossible to separate religious motives from political, economic, and social causes." (Cavanaugh, 2009: 177) So, the "Wars of Religion" are misnamed. At most we might call them "Wars of Religion, Politics, Economics, and Social Issues."

If we examine in detail the other examples of violence mentioned at the beginning of this discussion, we find similar reasons to question their designation as religious. It's not that religious differences play no role at all in these conflicts, but political, economic, and social factors are also involved, and there is no way to single out religious differences as the primary cause of the violence. The conflict in Sri Lanka, for instance, is between the dominant Sinhalese Sri Lankans and the minority Tamils. These are ethnic distinctions, not religious. In fact, while the Sinhalese are predominantly Therevadan Buddhist, they include a Christian minority. The Tamils are predominantly Hindu, but with significant Muslim and Christian minorities.

In the conflict between Roman Catholics and Anglicans in Ireland, similarly, differences in theology, ritual, and moral laws are minimal and never cited in the hostilities. Some Anglicans in Ireland, as elsewhere, even call themselves Anglo-Catholics. What the two groups have fought about are political, economic, and social issues, especially the domination of Ireland by the English starting in the twelfth century. Today, Anglicanism is seen by Roman Catholics as evidence of the continued influence of England over Northern Ireland, while Catholicism has always been the religion of the Irish poor and those who resisted English rule.

The fighting in Bosnia in the 1990s was also basically political. Bosnia was created by the break-up of Yugoslavia into three rival ethnic groups – Serbs, who are Orthodox; Croats, who are Roman Catholic; and Bosniaks, who are Muslim. After the death of the strong Communist leader Josip Tito in 1980, Yugoslavia descended into political chaos. By the late 1980s, a new leader had emerged, Slobodan Milosevic, a Serbian who inflamed old ethnic tensions for political gain. In 1991, his forces invaded Croatia to "protect" the 12% Serbian minority there. They besieged the city of Vukovar, and after destroying it, killed hundreds of Croat men and buried them in mass graves. In April 1992, the United States and the European Community recognized the independence of Bosnia, which was mostly Muslim but one-third Serbian. Milosevic soon attacked Bosnia's capital, Sarajevo. Serb snipers shot thousands of civilians in the streets, including 3500 children. Meeting weak resistance from the Muslims, the Serbs began rounding up men and boys, executing them by the hundreds, and raping women and girls. They called this violence "ethnic cleansing." Eventually, the United States and NATO stopped the mass murder (commonly referred to as genocide), but not before the Serbs had slaughtered another 8000 men and boys in Srebrenica in the worst genocide in Europe since World War II. The violence of the Serbs against the Muslim Bosnians, like their violence against the Catholic Croats, was not in opposition to their religious beliefs and practices. It was a way to increase Serb political power and territory.

In the cases of the terrorist attacks of September 11, 2001 in the United States and July 7, 2005 in the United Kingdom, unlike our other examples, the perpetrators cited religious motivations, by calling it *jihad*. They claimed a moral duty to kill Americans and Britons because of such offenses as the stationing of American and British troops in Saudi Arabia, the birthplace of their religion, Islam, during the First Gulf War. More broadly, they complained of Western imperialism and colonization, especially the attempt to take over Muslim lands by undermining Islamic law there. So we can talk about a religious rationale in these attacks. However, for the perpetrators of these acts, there is no distinction between religion and politics, so these attacks were just as much "political" as "religious" violence. It is also important to note that despite what they thought they were doing, the terrorists in these attacks were not acting with religious authority. Muslim authorities around the world condemned those actions. As we'll see in Chapter 5, both suicide and terrorism are grave sins in Islam. So it was not the Qur'an or Islam that helped prompt this terrorism, but misinterpretations of the Qur'an and Islam. Again, nothing here shows that religion is especially prone to causing violence.

References

Cavanaugh, W. (2009) *The Myth of Religious Violence*, Oxford University Press, Oxford.

Hitchens, C. (2007a) "Poison or Cure? Religious Belief in the Modern World", Debate with theologian Alister McGrath, Georgetown University, October 11, www.youtube.com/watch?v=xq-KiDdYvsY&t=54m47s (accessed January 7, 2014).

Hitchens, C. (2007b) *God Is Not Great: How Religion Poisons Everything*, Twelve, New York.

Jerryson, M. and Juergensmeyer, M. (2010) *Buddhist Warfare*, Oxford University Press, Oxford.

Juergensmeyer, M. (2000) *Terror in the Mind of God: The Global Rise of Religious Violence*, University of California Press, Berkeley.

Kimball, C. (2002) *When Religion Becomes Evil*, HarperSanFrancisco, San Francisco.

Marty, M., with Moore, J. (2000) *Politics, Religion, and the Common Good*, Jossey-Bass, San Francisco.

Wentz, R. (1993) *Why People Do Bad Things in the Name of Religion*, Mercer University Press, Macon GA.

3

Myths About Judaism, Jews, and Jewish Scripture

1. The Ancient Israelites Believed in One God
2. Moses Wrote the First Five Books of the Bible
3. The Book of Genesis Is Incompatible with the Theory of Evolution
4. Jews Believe They Were Chosen by God to Receive Special Privileges
5. The Jews Killed Jesus
6. Blood Libel: Jews Use Christian Blood in Their Rituals
7. Benjamin Franklin Advised the US Government to Expel Jews
8. *The Protocols of the Learned Elders of Zion*: Jewish Leaders Plot Global Takeover
9. Hannukah Is for Jews What Christmas Is for Christians

Introduction

The popular misconceptions about Jews and Judaism described in this chapter are of three kinds. Some reflect traditional understandings that have been changed through scholarly research, such as the belief that Moses wrote the first five books of the Bible. Some reflect interpretations that are considered correct but are not shared by others, such as the claim that believers must choose between the creation story in the Book of Genesis and the theory of evolution. This is an example of distinctions between reading scriptural stories as literal scientific and historic truth, and reading scriptural stories as metaphors for metaphysical truth. Most misconceptions are of the xenophobic variety described in Chapter 1, generated by people who distrust, fear, and even despise people outside their group.

50 Great Myths About Religions, First Edition. John Morreall and Tamara Sonn.
© 2014 John Wiley & Sons, Ltd. Published 2014 by John Wiley & Sons, Ltd.

1.   The Ancient Israelites Believed in One God

> The ancient Israelites wanted their own land where they could worship their
> god. In the Mediterranean world, most people believed in many gods. There
> were gods of death, sun, and rain. The ancient Israelites believed in one god,
> Yahweh. (Mediterranean Kingdoms (online))

Jews, Christians, Muslims, and Baha'is trace their religions to the ancient
patriarch Abraham (who lived around 1800 BCE), with whom God
established a covenant. That agreement was reaffirmed and deepened when
God gave the Law to Moses on Mount Sinai around 1450 BCE, and it has
bound monotheists – those who believe in just one God – ever since.
Surrounded by tribes and empires who worshipped many gods, the story
goes, the people of Israel remained faithful to just one – Yahweh.

In the last two centuries, Biblical scholars have found persuasive evidence
that this description of ancient Israel was created sometime after 621 BCE,
when King Josiah in Jerusalem banned the worship of all gods but Yahweh.

Evidence that the Israelites were not strictly monotheistic before 621
BCE comes from two main sources – the Hebrew Bible and archaeology. The
Second Book of Kings, Chapter 23, describes King Josiah's campaign to
eliminate worship of all gods but Yahweh. Verses 4–7 tell us that:

> The king commanded the high priest Hilkiah, the priests of the second order,
> and the guardians of the threshold, to bring out of the temple of the Lord all
> the vessels made for Baal, for Asherah, and for all the host of heaven; he
> burned them outside Jerusalem in the fields of the Kidron, and carried their
> ashes to Bethel. He deposed the idolatrous priests whom the kings of Judah
> had ordained to make offerings in the high places at the cities of Judah and
> around Jerusalem; those also who made offerings to Baal, to the sun, the
> moon, the constellations, and all the host of the heavens. He brought out the
> image of Asherah from the house of the Lord, outside Jerusalem, to the Wadi
> Kidron, burned it at the Wadi Kidron, beat it to dust and threw the dust of it
> upon the graves of the common people. He broke down the houses of the
> male temple prostitutes that were in the house of the Lord, where the women
> did weaving for Asherah.

The "temple of the Lord" is the great Temple in Jerusalem that had been
built by Solomon. Who were Baal, Asherah, and "all the host of heaven"?
Baal was a fertility god, often represented as a young man with wings.
Asherah was a fertility goddess, often represented as having the upper part

of a woman's body and the lower part of a tree. "Host" means a "large group." The host of heaven were the large group of divine beings thought to live in the sky.

The story above from the Second Book of Kings 23 continues in verses 13–20 with Josiah's destruction of religious shrines outside Jerusalem:

> The king defiled the high places that were east of Jerusalem, to the south of the Mount of Destruction, which King Solomon of Israel had built for Astarte [Asherah] the abomination of the Sidonians, for Chemosh the abomination of Moab, and for Milcom the abomination of the Ammonites. ... [At Bethel and in the cities of Samaria] he slaughtered on the altars all the priests of the high places who were there.

In his campaign, then, King Josiah not only destroyed shrines built by King Solomon for the divinities Astarte, Chemosh, and Milcom, but slaughtered the priests who led worship at some shrines. Before this campaign, obviously, at least some Israelites worshipped gods other than Yahweh.

"The host of heaven," the group of gods who live in the sky, appear elsewhere in the Bible. Psalm 82 describes Yahweh taking his place at a council of gods, where he criticizes them for protecting evil people while neglecting people in need. In the quotation below (from the New Revised Standard Version (NRSV) of the Bible) the quotation marks are around what Yahweh says to the other gods assembled at the heavenly meeting.

> "God has taken his place in the divine council; in the midst of the gods he holds judgment: How long will you judge unjustly and show partiality to the wicked? Give justice to the weak and the orphan; maintain the right of the lowly and the destitute. Rescue the weak and the needy; deliver them from the hand of the wicked."
>
> They have neither knowledge nor understanding, they walk around in darkness; all the foundations of the earth are shaken.
>
> I say, "You are gods, children of the Most High, all of you; nevertheless, you shall die like mortals, and fall like any prince."

The two gods mentioned most often as competing with Yahweh are Baal and Asherah. The First Book of Kings, Chapter 18, provides evidence of the extent of Baal and Asherah in the ninth century BCE. There Elijah, a prophet of the Lord, confronts Ahab, King of Israel, charging that he has "forsaken the commandments of the Lord and followed the Baals" (1 Kings 18:18).

Elijah tells the king to arrange a contest between him and the prophets of Baal and Asherah:

> "Now therefore have all Israel assemble for me at Mount Carmel, with the four hundred fifty prophets of Baal and the four hundred prophets of Asherah, who eat at Jezebel's table." So Ahab sent to all the Israelites, and assembled the prophets at Mount Carmel … Then Elijah said to the people, "I, even I only, am left a prophet of the Lord; but Baal's prophets number four hundred fifty. Let two bulls be given to us; let them choose one bull for themselves, cut it in pieces, and lay it on the wood, but put no fire to it; I will prepare the other bull and lay it on the wood, but put no fire to it. Then you call on the name of your god and I will call on the name of the Lord; the god who answers by fire is indeed God." All the people answered, "Well spoken!" (19–24)

When the prophets of Baal called on him to light their fire, nothing happened. So "at noon Elijah mocked them, saying, 'Cry aloud! Surely he is a god; either he is meditating, or he has wandered away, or he is on a journey, or perhaps he is asleep and must be awakened.'" (27) But when Elijah prayed to Yahweh,

> the fire of the Lord fell and consumed the burnt offering, the wood, the stones, and the dust, and even licked up the water that was in the trench. When all the people saw it, they fell on their faces and said, "The Lord indeed is God; the Lord indeed is God." Elijah said to them, "Seize the prophets of Baal; do not let one of them escape." Then they seized them; and Elijah brought them down to the Wadi Kishon, and killed them there. (38–40)

According to the Bible, then, there were at least 950 prophets of Baal and Asherah in ninth century BCE Israel. If each prophet had a following of just a dozen people, the number who worshipped Baal or Asherah was more than 10 000.

Archaeological evidence confirms the widespread worship of gods among ancient Israelites. Hundreds of small carved figures of Asherah have been found from the centuries before King Josiah. Excavations in the Sinai Desert done by scholars from the University of Tel Aviv in 1975–1976 uncovered the remains of an inn from the first half of the eighth century BCE. In it were line drawings and inscriptions on the walls and on two large storage jars. The most intriguing inscription is translated by some scholars as "Yahweh and his Asherah." There has been debate about that translation for decades, but if it's accurate, then the writer of this inscription probably thought of Asherah as the companion or consort of Yahweh.

The obvious conclusion is that monotheism did not start in ancient Israel with Abraham and Moses. It developed centuries after them, and was politically imposed on people who had believed in many gods. As Old Testament scholar Bernhard Lang (1981) summarizes current scholarly opinion:

> In the four and a half centuries during which there were one or two Israelite monarchies (c. 1020–586 BC), there was a dominant polytheistic religion that was indistinguishable from that of neighboring peoples. Insofar as there were differences between the Ammonite, Moabite, Edomite, Tyrian, etc. versions of religion, these beliefs stayed within the framework of Near Eastern polytheism, and each should be interpreted as a local variant of the same basic pattern. The Israelites … venerated their own protector god who was there to provide for health and family. But they venerated Yahweh as well, the regional and national god, whose special domain dealt with war and peace issues. Finally, they worshipped gods who performed specific functions, those that were responsible for various special needs: weather, rain, women's fertility, etc.

People familiar with the story of Moses returning from Mount Sinai to find his people worshipping a Golden Calf (Exodus 3:24) will not be surprised to find that the ancient Israelites were not always strictly monotheistic. Indeed, in theological perspective, among the many challenges of the prophets was to remind their communities of the need to recognize and obey a single God. Scrutiny of the Baal and Asherah stories provides a good example of how biblical scholarship and archaeological evidence can supplement theological positions, providing a rich picture of just how challenging the transition to monotheism was.

References

Lang, B. (1981) Die Jahwe-allein-bewegung, quoted in O. Keel and C. Uehlinger (1998) *Gods, Goddesses, and Images of God in Ancient Israel*, Fortress, Minneapolis, p. 2.

Mediterranean Kingdoms (online) *The Ancient Israelites: Under One God*, https://sites.google.com/site/mediterranean12345/articles-to-read/the-ancient-israelites-under-one-god (accessed January 7, 2014).

Further Reading

Coogan, M. (1987) Canaanite origins and lineage: reflections on the lineage of ancient Israel, in *Ancient Israelite Religion: Essays in Honor of Frank Moore Cross* (eds P.D. Miller, P.D. Hanson and S.D. McBride), Fortress, Philadelphia, pp 115–126.

Hadley, J. (2000) *The Cult of Asherah in Ancient Israel and Judah*, Cambridge University Press, Cambridge.

Keel, O. and Uehlinger, C. (1998) *Gods, Goddesses, and Images of God in Ancient Israel*, Fortress, Minneapolis.

Mayes, A. (1989) Sociology and the Old Testament, in *The World of Ancient Israel: Sociological, Anthropological and Political Perspectives* (ed R.E. Clements), Cambridge University Press, Cambridge, pp. 39–63.

2.   Moses Wrote the First Five Books of the Bible

Not only does the internal evidence of the Scriptures make it clear that Moses wrote the Pentateuch [first five books of the Bible], but other Old Testament books make Mosaic authorship clear. (Josh.org (website))

The writings that would eventually be grouped together as the Hebrew Bible (Christians' Old Testament) began to be written down around 2500 years ago. The Bible's first five books – Genesis, Exodus, Leviticus, Numbers, and Deuteronomy – are called Torah (in the narrow sense) in Judaism, or "teaching," since they contain the core of Jewish tradition. They are also called the Pentateuch, from the Greek words for "five" and "volumes." As in Judaism itself, the most important figure in these books is Moses. The book of Exodus tells how he led the people of Israel from slavery in Egypt toward the Promised Land in Canaan. At Mount Sinai he met God in person and received tablets containing the core of the Law that has governed Jewish life ever since. The exodus from Egypt and the receipt of the tablets at Mount Sinai are the two most important events in Judaism. The book of Leviticus is a collection of laws dealing with sacrifices and other rituals, clean and unclean foods, and daily life. Almost every law is presented with the words, "The Lord spoke to Moses...". As in Exodus, laws come from God through Moses to the people of Israel. In the book of Numbers, too, Moses is the central figure. For 40 years he leads the people of Israel – as Jews were called, referring not to a country but to Jews' ancestral tribal leader, Jacob, whose name was changed to Israel – across the desert toward the Promised Land. The book of Deuteronomy consists of several speeches by Moses to the Israelites (another term for the people of Israel) before they cross the Jordan River to enter the Promised Land.

Given the importance of Moses in these books, the laws in them have come to be called the Mosaic Law, and the books themselves called the Books of Moses. "Books of Moses" could simply mean books *about* Moses, but over the centuries a stronger meaning developed. It became common to say that – under divine inspiration – Moses *wrote* these five books. According to the Babylonian Talmud (authoritative "teaching" of Judaism) of around 600 CE, God dictated these books to Moses. That is not something claimed by the Bible itself, but it became a standard belief in both Judaism and in Christianity. Even today, it is still accepted by millions of people. In a typical example, P. N. Benware writes in his *Survey of the Old Testament* (1993: 27) that "Moses was the human author of Genesis and the other books of the Pentateuch … These five 'books of the law' were written by Moses alone, with the exception of Deuteronomy 34, which records the death of Moses."

Benware's exception of Deuteronomy 34 reflects a critique of the traditional belief that Moses wrote the five books of the Pentateuch, which was first made by seventeenth-century scholar Baruch Spinoza. Spinoza noted that Deuteronomy 34 describes the funeral of Moses:

> Then Moses, the servant of the Lord, died there in the land of Moab, at the Lord's command. He was buried in a valley in the land of Moab, opposite Beth-peor, but no one knows his burial place to this day. Moses was one hundred twenty years old when he died; his sight was unimpaired and his vigor had not abated. The Israelites wept for Moses in the plains of Moab thirty days … Never since has there arisen a prophet in Israel like Moses, whom the Lord knew face to face" (Deuteronomy 34:5–8, 10).

How could Moses have written about his own funeral? Spinoza concluded that he did not.

There are several other arguments against the claim that Moses wrote all of Genesis, Exodus, Leviticus, Numbers, and Deuteronomy. Spinoza (1670) provided a dozen, including:

1. The passage from Deuteronomy above says, "Never since has there arisen a prophet in Israel like Moses." Only someone who lived after prophets appeared in Israel could make this comparison, and prophets didn't appear until centuries after Moses died.
2. Many place names that appear in the Pentateuch were not in use during Moses' lifetime. For example, Genesis 14:14 says that Abraham pursued his enemies "as far as Dan." But that place was not called "Dan" until long after the death of Joshua, according to the Book of Judges 18:29. And Joshua came after Moses, so whoever wrote Genesis 14:14 and similar passages lived long after Moses.

3. Similarly, in Genesis 22:14, the place where Abraham prepares to sacrifice his son Isaac, Mount Moriah, is called "the Mount of God," a title it did not have until after the building of the First Temple, centuries after Moses.
4. Genesis 36:31 says, "These are the kings who reigned in the land of Edom before any king reigned over the Israelites." Whoever wrote this had to live after Israel had at least its first king, Saul, who ruled around 1000 BCE, long after Moses.
5. In Genesis 12:6, the author says that Abraham journeyed through the land of Canaan, and adds, "At that time the Canaanites were in the land." This implies that at the time Genesis 12:6 was written, the Canaanites were no longer in the land. That would be because the people of Israel had taken over the land of Canaan as their Promised Land. But during Moses' lifetime, the Canaanites still lived in Canaan, so Moses could not have written the passage above.
6. The writer of the five books speaks of Moses in the third person, saying things such as "Moses talked with God," and "The Lord spoke with Moses face to face." But in these five books, when Moses speaks about his own deeds, he naturally speaks in the first person. In Deuteronomy 2:2, for example, Moses says, "The Lord said to me" and in Deuteronomy 2:17, "The Lord spoke to me." If Moses had written all the accounts of his deeds in the Pentateuch, then he would have used the first person rather than the third person throughout.

Spinoza (1670: Part II, Chapter 8) concludes, "From what has been said, it is thus clearer than the sun at noonday that the Pentateuch was not written by Moses, but by someone who lived long after Moses."

As scholars have studied the five books in more depth, they have analyzed word choices (especially the use of different names for God), literary styles, and theological viewpoints. Many have concluded that the Pentateuch comes not from one author, but from several. According to a widely accepted theory developed by German scholar Julius Wellhausen (1885), known as the Documentary Hypothesis, the Pentateuch was written by four authors who lived in various parts of Palestine over a period of centuries. Scholars refer to these four with the initials J, E, D, and P. J was a writer who used "YHWH" as "the unpronounceable name of God." In English that is written as "Yahweh," sometimes as "Jehovah." The writer E, by contrast, does not call God "YHWH," but "Elohim." D is the author of the book of Deuteronomy, and P is a writer who added material about the priesthood among the Israelites. Besides all these four, the Documentary Hypothesis says there was R, a redactor or editor, who shaped the writings of J, E, P, and D into what is now the Pentateuch.

Nothing in the critical study of the Pentateuch takes away from the greatness of Moses, of course. He remains the most important figure in Judaism – the liberator of the Hebrew people from slavery in Egypt, and the one who received the Law from God at Sinai. Adding the writing of the Pentateuch to these deeds was the traditional way of acknowledging Moses' greatness, but, as modern scholarship has demonstrated, a careful reading of these books reveals that Moses was long dead when they were recorded.

References

Benware, P.N. (1993) *Survey of the Old Testament*, Moody Press, Chicago.

Josh.org (website) *Did Moses Write the First Five Books?* Josh McDowell Ministry, www.josh.org/resources/study-research/answers-to-skeptics-questions/did-moses-write-the-first-five-books (accessed January 7, 2014).

Spinoza, B. (1670) *Theologico-Political Treatise*, published anonymously.

3. The Book of Genesis Is Incompatible with the Theory of Evolution

There may not be any fossil evidence showing dinosaurs and people in the same place at the same time. But it is clearly written [in the Bible] that they were alive at the same time. (Mark Looy, spokesman for the Creation Museum in Petersburg, Kentucky (Slack, 2007))

For more than a century, fundamentalist Christian groups, particularly in the United States, have argued that Christians must reject the theory of evolution because it contradicts the Bible's description of how God created all the species of plants and animals within just a few days. After the sixth day of creation, they say, God had made all the kinds of living things that would ever exist – all the plants and animals we know today, along with ones that later became extinct, such as dinosaurs. At the Creation Museum in Petersburg, Kentucky, exhibits show humans and dinosaurs living side by side; Noah's ark has a triceratops and a stegosaurus. Though the Book of Genesis doesn't mention dinosaurs, museum staff say, archaeological evidence shows that they did exist. But they must have co-existed with humans, and with all other kinds of living things, in the earliest days of creation because scripture reveals that all species were created together.

If all the kinds of plants and animals were created in the first week of the universe, it must be the case that no kinds arose later. So, the argument goes, biologists must be wrong when they say, for example, that over millions of years, birds evolved from dinosaurs, and humans evolved from apes.

Christian fundamentalists who deny evolution admit they can't prove the story of creation in Genesis, but, they point out, those who believe in evolution can't prove their theory either. Both explanations are taken on faith, they say. That means that our choice of what to believe is between the Word of God, on the one hand, and something thought up by Charles Darwin and later scientists, on the other. Should we put our faith in God, the creator of the universe, they ask, or in human beings? For them, the answer is obvious.

Arguments like these were first formulated by certain American Christians in the late 1800s. Opposition to the theory of evolution then became central among fundamentalists – people named after *The Fundamentals*, a 12-volume work published in 1910–1915 by the Bible Institute of Los Angeles. Distributed widely among Protestant ministers and teachers, the essays were meant to defend fundamentalists' interpretation of the Bible from perceived attacks emanating from an array of modern developments including liberalism and atheism (as well their old nemesis, Catholicism). In 1919, the World's Christian Fundamentals Association was founded by Baptist minister William Bell Riley. Among the Fundamentals – the core beliefs – was the literal truth of the Bible. By that, they meant that every verse of the Bible is historically and scientifically accurate. Since the story in Genesis says that world was created in six days, the fundamentalists said, the theory of evolution must be false.

In the 1920s, American fundamentalists openly fought against the theory of evolution by passing state laws banning the teaching of evolution in public schools. In the 1925 Scopes Trial, a high school teacher was convicted of teaching evolution in a school in Tennessee and fined $100. (Helping the local prosecutor was William Jennings Bryan, three times the Democratic candidate for US President, and Secretary of State under Woodrow Wilson.)

Today, the argument that the theory of evolution must be false because the Bible is true, is still convincing to almost half of Americans. In a 2012 Gallup poll (Newport, 2012), 46% of respondents agreed with this statement: "God created human beings pretty much in their present form at one time within the last 10 000 years or so."

Fundamentalist Christians regard those who believe in evolution as suspect, so many politicians seeking conservative Christian votes in US elections express doubt about the theory. Among the contenders for the 2012 Republican nomination for President, only Mitt Romney and Jon Huntsman admitted to accepting the theory of evolution; and on a Tweet, Huntsman prefaced his admission, saying, "Call me crazy, but …" Rick Perry, Governor of Texas, declared many times that evolution is just "a theory that's out there," which he rejected. Ron Paul, a medical doctor running for president, also rejected the theory. Newt Gingrich, former Speaker of the House of Representatives, insisted that the United States was founded on Christian principles and that creationism – the idea that God created the world and everything in it in six days, just as the Bible says – should be put back in schools. Representative Michele Bachman and former Senator Rick Santorum rejected evolution and said that intelligent design – a version of creationism that insists the universe is too complex to be explained by anything other than God – should be taught instead.

Even by Darwin's time, scholars studying the Book of Genesis were saying that its story wasn't as simple as many Christians thought. The second chapter, for example, has a different story of creation from the first chapter. In it, God makes humans *before* he makes trees. Such inconsistencies led some nineteenth-century scholars to suggest that Genesis 1 and Genesis 2 were written by different people at different times, an idea now accepted by the majority of Bible scholars. Those inconsistencies also make it impossible to read the text both literally and rationally. How could the first human be created both before and after trees are created? And what about "the firmament" mentioned in Genesis 1:6–8, a vault over the earth "to separate water from water," which God called "heaven"? This description reflects the ancient worldview in which the earth is flat and the sky is a dome over the earth. Those who have flown in jets and watched space flights might wonder just where this dome is, but fundamentalists know it is there.

Among the more intriguing challenges associated with reading Genesis literally is that it describes God as creating the sun, moon, and stars on the "fourth day" (1:14–19). What could "day" have meant before there was a sun? Earlier in Genesis 1, verses 3–4 say that God made light "and he separated light from darkness. He called the light day, and the darkness night." But what light could that be, three "days" before the sun, moon, and stars existed?

Still another problem is that several passages in Genesis describe God as a limited, physical being – like a man, only more powerful. Genesis 2:2

describes God as resting "from all the work that he had done." This way of thinking about God is inconsistent with the belief that God is not limited by material form, is all-powerful ("almighty") and perfect. Yet a truly literal reading of Genesis commits one to belief in a physical God who works, gets tired, and needs rest.

Anthropomorphic ("human-shaped") descriptions of God appear as well in stories of God interacting with Adam and Eve. For example:

> The man and his wife heard the sound of the Lord God walking in the garden
> at the time of the evening breeze and hid from the Lord God among the trees
> of the garden. But the Lord God called to the man and said to him, "Where
> are you?" (Genesis 3:8–9)

It is hard to escape questions about God's size and appearance, for example, if one reads this passage literally. Was God the size of a regular man or, as the Monty Python parody puts it, "absolutely huge?" A more troubling question concerns the limitations on God's knowledge. Monotheists (Zoroastrians, Jews, Christians, Muslims, and Baha'is) usually think of God as omniscient – all-knowing. Why was God unaware of the whereabouts of Adam and Eve?

In view of such questions, many Bible scholars over the last two centuries have dealt with the question of literalism in the creation story, and pointed out that our modern methods of writing history and doing science did not exist in the ancient world. As we saw in the Introduction, many contend that the stories were not intended as empirically verifiable accounts of history and science, but that they nonetheless convey key truths. Included among them is that God created the universe and everything in it, one way or another. Scripture is not required to explain the precise means by which that creation took place; one can believe in scientific evidence for a gradual process of evolution taking place over millions of years, and still accept the Biblical teaching that nothing would exist if not for God.

While some Orthodox rabbis reject evolution and insist on reading Genesis as science and history, many others accept that the Genesis creation story does not preclude the gradual evolution of life forms. Rather, the gradual evolution of life forms demonstrated by scientific research is simply a part of the overall divine creation plan. God is the origin; evolution is the instrument. This is the position presented in books like Gerald Schroeder's (1991) *Genesis and the Big Bang: The Discovery of Harmony Between Modern Science and the Bible*. Conservative and Reform rabbis likewise insist on the divine origin of the world but also support scientific exploration and understanding of the way that life evolved. Rabbi Michael Schwab (2005), for example, insists that "Judaism, as a religion, and certainly Conservative Judaism, sees creation as a purposeful process directed by God … What Darwin sees as random, we see as the miraculous and natural unfolding of God's subtle and beautiful plan." That is, instead of reading Genesis as literal science and history, Schwab says, it is possible to maintain its truth and the credibility of scientific discoveries by reading it as an allegory. Similarly, voices of Reform Judaism hold that the science of evolution and natural selection are compatible with the divine origin and guidance of the development of the world in all its diverse forms. Thus, while Judaism is not a religion of creeds but a tradition concerned with how people act, and there is therefore no single teaching regarding the truth claims of creation, there is certainly a preponderance of opinion among Jewish authorities that evolution is not inconsistent with belief in the Bible.

The Roman Catholic Church has adopted a similar position. In 1950, Pope Pius XII issued an encyclical (authoritative message) titled *Humani generis* dealing with a number of issues in modern thought, including the theory of evolution. The encyclical states that nothing in the theory of evolution necessarily contradicts Catholic doctrine, so that studying it is permitted, although caution is necessary:

> The Teaching Authority of the Church does not forbid that, in conformity with the present state of human sciences and sacred theology, research and discussions, on the part of men experienced in both fields, take place with regard to the doctrine of evolution, in as far as it inquires into the origin of the human body as coming from pre-existent and living matter—for the Catholic faith obliges us to hold that souls are immediately created by God. However, this must be done in such a way that the reasons for both opinions, that is, those favorable and those unfavorable to evolution, be weighed and judged with the necessary seriousness, moderation and measure, and provided that all are prepared to submit to the judgment of the Church, to whom Christ has given the mission of interpreting authentically the Sacred Scriptures and of defending the dogmas of faith.

More recently, Pope John Paul II (1996) went further. Referring to Pius XII's encyclical, he said:

> Today, almost half a century after the publication of the Encyclical, new knowledge has led to the recognition of more than one hypothesis in the

theory of evolution. It is indeed remarkable that this theory has been progressively accepted by researchers, following a series of discoveries in various
fields of knowledge. The convergence, neither sought nor fabricated, of the
results of work that was conducted independently is in itself a significant
argument in favor of this theory.

Similarly, the Presbyterian Church USA (1969) issued a statement on
evolution, declaring, "Neither Scripture, our Confession of Faith, nor our
Catechisms, teach the Creation of man by the direct and immediate acts of
God so as to exclude the possibility of evolution as a scientific theory." The
statement acknowledges that their forebears may have understood such
scriptural phrases as "six days," "of the dust of the ground," and "the rib of
man" literally, but those understandings are not binding. Calling on the
authority of John Calvin himself, the statement continues, "The Bible is not
a book of science." Thus, "We conclude that the true relation between the
evolutionary theory and the Bible is that of non-contradiction...."

The Episcopal Church noted in its *Catechism of Creation* (Church of
England, 2005) that it has no official position on evolution. "However," the
Catechism says, "clergy and scientists from both the Catholic and Evangelical
traditions of Anglicanism have accepted evolution from Darwin's time to the
present. In a resolution passed by General Convention in 1982, the Church
affirmed the ability of God to create in any form and fashion, which would
include evolution." Furthermore, the Catechism notes, "The Bible, including
Genesis, is not a divinely dictated scientific textbook." Therefore, although
evolution is a "web of theories," they are "strongly supported by observations
and experiments" (which the Catechism describes), and do not contradict
scripture. The Biblical description of creation affirms that humans were
bestowed with the "divine gift of unconditional love and compassion, our
reason and imagination, our moral and ethical capacities, our freedom, or
our creativity." It does not describe the precise means by which God created.

Likewise, the United Methodist Church (2012) issued an official statement on evolution that begins, "We recognize science as a legitimate
interpretation of God's natural world." Segregating theological issues from
the scientific, the statement claims, "We find that science's descriptions of
cosmological, geological, and biological evolution are not in conflict with
theology." Indeed, the Church asserts, "We find that as science expands
human understanding of the natural world, our understanding of the
mysteries of God's creation and word are enhanced."

There are, of course, groups insisting that the Bible's creation story
contradicts and precludes acceptance of theories of evolution. These

include the Lutheran Church-Missouri Synod, the Southern Baptist Convention, and some conservative Muslims. However, this position is supported by neither mainstream Jewish and Christian authorities nor progressive Muslims, and cannot be considered definitive.

References

Bible Institute of Los Angeles (1910–1915) *The Fundamentals* (12-volumes), Bible Institute of Los Angeles, Los Angeles.

Church of England (2005) *Catechism of Creation: Creation and Science*, http://episcopalscience.org/creation-science (accessed January 7, 2014).

John Paul II (1996) Message to the Pontifical Academy of Sciences: On evolution, October 22, www.ewtn.com/library/papaldoc/jp961022.htm (accessed January 7, 2014).

Newport, F. (2012) In U.S., 46% Hold Creationist View of Human Origins, *GALLUP Politics*, June 1, www.gallup.com/poll/155003/Hold-Creationist-View-Human-Origins.aspx (accessed January 7, 2014).

Pius XII (1950) *Humani Generis*, 36, www.vatican.va/holy_father/pius_xii/encyclicals/documents/hf_p-xii_enc_12081950_humani-generis_en.html (accessed January 7, 2014).

Presbyterian Church USA (1969) Evolution and the Bible, www.presbyterian-mission.org/ministries/theologyandworship/evolution (accessed January 7, 2014).

Schroeder, G. (1991) *Genesis and the Big Bang: The Discovery of Harmony Between Modern Science and the Bible*, Bantam, New York.

Schwab, M. (2005). *How Did We Get Here?* November 4, Jewish Virtual Library, www.jewishvirtuallibrary.org/jsource/Judaism/jewsevolution.html (accessed January 7, 2014).

Slack, G. (2007) *Inside the Creation Museum*. Salon.com, May 31, www.salon.com/2007/05/31/creation_museum (accessed January 7, 2014).

United Methodist Church (2012) Science and technology, in *The Book of Discipline of the United Methodist Church*, United Methodist Publishing House, paragraph 160 F.

Further Reading

Marsden, G. (2006) *Fundamentalism and American Culture*, Oxford University Press, Oxford.

Numbers, R. (2006) *The Creationists: From Scientific Creationism to Intelligent Design*, Harvard University Press, Cambridge MA.

4.   Jews Believe They Were Chosen by God to Receive Special Privileges

Few Jewish beliefs have been subject to as much misunderstanding as the "Chosen People" doctrine. (The Jewish Theological Seminary of America (1988))

The notion of being a people chosen by God is central to Jewish tradition, but it is the interpretation of this concept that has been open to misinterpretation. For centuries, Christians understood it to mean that Jews believe they alone were chosen by God to receive the gift of revelation, which provides the guidance necessary to attain eternal life in the World to Come. In other words, according to this myth, Jews believe that only Jews have access to eternal reward. Some Christian thinkers even taught that Christians had inherited God's promises when Jews rejected Jesus as the Messiah. Thus the Christians became God's chosen people, and it is they – rather than Jews – who hold the keys to the Kingdom of God. This view is associated with third-century theologian Origen and Martin Luther, for example. Another, perhaps more problematic, misperception is that Jews believe they have a God-given right to the land that became the state of Israel and are commanded to annihilate anyone who resists their claim.

That Jews are God's chosen people is based on scripture. "For you are a holy people…and God has chosen you to be his treasured people from all nations on the face of the earth," says Deuteronomy 14:2. The book of the prophet Amos quotes God telling the Israelites, "You only have I known of all the families on earth…" (Amos 3:2, NRSV).

But the notion of Jews as God's chosen people is not interpreted by Jewish authorities as meaning that they alone can achieve eternal reward. Instead, it is usually interpreted as meaning that God chose Jews for special responsibilities and will hold them accountable for carrying out those responsibilities. In fact, as the Amos quote continues: "You only have I known of all the families on earth; therefore I will punish you for all your iniquities." In Judaic tradition, the Jews were indeed chosen by God to receive revelation, the Torah. The Torah teaches them how to be good people, and observing the Torah is their exclusive obligation. Other people are not expected to observe the Torah, but that does not mean that they will have no share in the afterlife. The Talmud – the body of wisdom developed by Jewish scholars over the centuries – teaches that the afterlife is open to all righteous people. For Jews, the route to the afterlife is observance of the Torah. For non-Jews, the route to eternal life is living justly.

If observing the Torah is the core of the covenant between God and the Jews, what about the land? The first book of the Hebrew Bible records God telling Abraham, "To your descendants I give this land, from the valley of Egypt to the great river Euphrates..." (15:18). The book then notes that this was currently the land of several other peoples but, the book assures Abraham (Genesis 17:6–8), "I will make you exceedingly fruitful, and I will make nations of you, and kings shall come out of you ... And I will give you and your descendants the land wherein you are a stranger, all the land of Canaan, as an everlasting possession, and I will be their God." Many generations later, as Moses leads the Israelites toward the land that had been promised, God instructs them to take the land by force:

> When you draw near to a town to fight against it, offer it terms of peace. If it accepts your terms of peace and surrenders to you, then all the people in it shall serve you in forced labor. If it does not submit to you peacefully, but makes war against you, then you shall besiege it; and when the Lord your God gives it into your hand, you shall put all its males to the sword. You may, however, take as your booty the women, the children, livestock, and everything else in the town, all its spoil. You may enjoy the spoil of your enemies, which the Lord your God has given you. Thus you shall treat all the towns that are very far from you which are not towns of the nations here. But as for the towns of these peoples that the Lord your God is giving you as an inheritance, you must not let anything that breathes remain alive. (Deuteronomy 20:10–16, NRSV)

As Robert Eisen (2011) has shown, over the centuries Jewish authorities have interpreted the command to conquer by force in diverse ways. Some, in an "attempt to come to terms with the moral difficulties inherent in the Canaanite conquest," stress the need to try to avoid killing the innocent by first offering peace. Some assert that those who did vacate the land peacefully "were rewarded by being given another land" (Eisen, 2011:91, from *Numbers Rabbah* 19:27; *Tanhuma Tsav* 3; *Deuteronomy Rabbah* 13–14). Only those who chose to fight were annihilated. In any case, traditional rabbinic interpretation consistently backed away from the broad command to wipe out all native inhabitants of the land of Canaan, and some rabbinic sources stress that the command to conquer was strictly limited to the time and place in which it was given. The Israelites had no future obligation (or right) to kill anyone living peacefully in the land.

In the modern world, the divine promise of the land has been made more complex by the lack of archeological evidence for an Israelite conquest of the land. In fact, the majority of contemporary archaeologists believe the

Israelites, rather than conquering the land as outsiders, were among the native inhabitants of Canaan. As they embraced a unique religious identity, however, they came to see themselves as distinct from other residents of Canaan. Stories in which the Israelites had been told to wipe out the Canaanites were developed, in part, according to this theory, to discourage early Jews from marrying the polytheistic peoples among whom they lived.

Nevertheless, the stories of violent conquest of the land by the Israelites have been widely used to support Zionism, the movement developed among modern European Jews to escape the scourge of anti-Semitism by establishing a state in which they would be independent and able to protect themselves. It was this need for protection from the threat of extinction posed by Europe's anti-Semitism that resulted in the creation of the state of Israel in 1948. The displacement of non-Jewish Palestinian inhabitants of the land that would become the state of Israel, was thus not a result of blindly following biblical commands to annihilate those who resisted the Jews; it was and continues to be a tragic effect of anti-Semitism.

Interestingly, according to a 2013 report by the Pew Research Center, only 40% of American Jews now believe that God gave Israel to the Jews (2013: 86), while 75% of religious Jews feel emotionally attached to Israel, and 61% believe that Israel and an independent Palestinian state can coexist peacefully in the land (2013: 87).

Reference

Eisen, R. (2011) *The Peace and Violence of Judaism: From the Bible to Modern Zionism*, Oxford University Press, Oxford and New York.

The Jewish Theological Seminary of America (1988) God's Covenant: The Election of Israel, in *Emet Ve-Emunah: Statement of Principles of Conservative Judaism* p 28, www.icsresources.org/content/primarysourcedocs/ConservativeJudaismPrinciples.pdf (accessed January 7, 2014).

Pew Research Center (2013) *A Portrait of Jewish Americans: Findings from a Pew Research Center Survey of US Jews*, Pew Research Center, Washington DC.

Further Reading

Silberman, N.A. and Finkelstein, I. (2011) *The Bible Unearthed: Archaeology's New Vision of Ancient Israel and the Origin of Its Sacred Texts*. Touchstone, New York.

5. The Jews Killed Jesus

The Jews killed Jesus. That fact will never change. They have never repented.
(www.jewskilledjesus.com)

This claim is deeply rooted in the history of Christian theology, and has been used since the second century as a rationale for anti-Semitism. After the church councils of the fourth to sixth centuries declared that Jesus was God, the claim that the Jews killed him took on cosmic proportions. The Jews killed Jesus, and Jesus was God, so the Jews killed God. That "deicide" was the greatest crime imaginable. In Greek Orthodox and Byzantine Catholic churches, the Holy Thursday liturgy speaks of "the murderers of God, the lawless nation of the Jews." Until 1959, the traditional Roman Catholic liturgy for Good Friday (the day commemorating the death of Jesus by crucifixion) included a prayer "for the perfidious [or faithless] Jews: that Almighty God may remove the veil from their hearts; so that they too may acknowledge Jesus Christ our Lord."

These prayers reflect teachings derived from Christian scripture. In the Gospels we see Jewish authorities accusing Jesus of committing blasphemy by claiming to be the Son of God. That was a capital offense, so the authorities wanted Jesus executed (Matthew 26:63–65; Luke 22:70–71; John 19:7). When Jesus was brought to the Roman governor Pontius Pilate, however, Pilate found no grounds for convicting Jesus. The Jewish authorities had to put political pressure on Pilate by stirring up the local people to cry, "Crucify him!" According to Matthew 27:24–26, the crowd even assumed responsibility for the death of Jesus.

So when Pilate saw that he could do nothing, but rather that a riot was beginning, he took some water and washed his hands before the crowd, saying, "I am innocent of this man's blood; see to it yourselves." Then the people as a whole answered, "His blood be upon us and upon our children!" So he released Barabbas [another prisoner] for them; and after flogging Jesus, he handed him over to be crucified.

The first written source for the idea that Jews are "Christ-killers" is Paul's Letter to the Thessalonians, written in the 50s. In it, Paul refers to "the Jews, who killed both the Lord Jesus and the prophets, and drove us out" (Thessalonians 2:14–15).

In the second century, the theologian Justin Martyr wrote a fictional discussion with a Jew, *Dialogue with Trypho* (Brown, 2010). In Chapter 16 he explains to Trypho why the Jews have had their Temple destroyed and have been exiled from their homeland: these "tribulations were justly imposed on you since you have murdered the Just One [Jesus]."

Rhetorical attacks on Jews increased in the following centuries, especially after Christianity became the state religion of the Roman Empire in the late fourth century. Anti-Jewish diatribes became a standard genre in Christian writing called *Adversus Judaeos* (Against the Jews). John Chrysostom (1979) wrote the most, and the most vicious, of these documents. In eight sermons he rails against Christians who take part in Jewish festivals and other rituals. The Jews, he says, are "godless, idolaters, pedicides [killers of children], stoning the prophets and committing ten thousand horrors." He continues,

> The Jews are the most worthless of all men. They are lecherous, rapacious, greedy. They are perfidious murderers of Christ. They worship the Devil. Their religion is a sickness. The Jews are the odious assassins of Christ and for killing God there is no expiation possible, no indulgence or pardon. Christians may never cease vengeance, and the Jew must live in servitude forever. God always hated the Jews. It is essential that all Christians hate them.

And in case deicide weren't enough to get his congregation to shun all things Jewish, Chrysostom adds:

> The Jews sacrifice their children to Satan. They are worse than wild beasts. The synagogue is a brothel, a den of scoundrels, the temple of demons devoted to idolatrous cults, a criminal assembly of Jews, a place of meeting for the assassins of Christ, a house of ill fame, a dwelling of iniquity, a gulf and abyss of perdition. The Jews have fallen into a condition lower than the vilest animal. Debauchery and drunkenness have brought them to a level of the lusty goat and the pig. They know only one thing: to satisfy their stomachs, to get drunk, to kill, and beat each other up like stage villains and coachmen.

In the late Middle Ages, plays about Jesus' crucifixion became popular religious rituals in Europe. The most famous is the Oberammergau Passion Play, which has been performed since 1634 in Bavaria, Germany. These dramatic reenactments of the trial and death of Jesus, usually performed during the Christian season of repentance called Lent, often present an ethnically stereotyped Judas betraying Jesus for 30 pieces of silver, and then a mob of Jews crying, "Crucify him!" to Pontius Pilate as a Jewish leader says, "May his blood be upon our heads." For centuries, Jews living in areas where passion plays were performed had to be wary of Christians wanting to vent their fury on "Christ-killers."

The Protestant Reformation, begun by Martin Luther in the early 1500s, challenged many things about the Catholic Church, but its anti-Judaism was not one of them. While as a young man Luther expressed optimism about the possibility of converting Jews to Christianity, in his later writings he turned hateful toward them. In works like *On the Jews and Their Lies* (1543), he writes that the Jews are a "base, whoring people, that is, no people of God, and their boast of lineage, circumcision, and law must be accounted as filth." They are full of the "devil's feces ... which they wallow in like swine". Quoted in Michael (2006: 111–113), Luther proposes that their synagogues and schools be burned, their rabbis forbidden to preach and prayer books destroyed, their homes razed and property seized. Further, he writes that these "poisonous envenomed worms" should be forced into slavery or expelled permanently. Luther even implies a Christian obligation to kill Jews when he writes, "We are at fault in not slaying them."

The idea that the Jews killed Jesus even worked its way into Jewish religious literature. The Babylonian Talmud, Tractate *Sanhedrin*, folio 43a, has a *beraita*, a teaching from before 200 CE, that Jesus was executed by a Jewish court for the crimes of sorcery and sedition. In many standard texts of that Talmud, this has been removed, leaving a blank space on the page. In Jewish folk literature, too, such as *Toledot Yeshu*, a Jewish biography of Jesus, the death of Jesus is attributed to the Jews. Martin Lockshin of the Centre for Jewish Studies at York University suggests that "[i]t is likely that until at least the nineteenth century, Jews in Christian Europe believed that their ancestors had killed Jesus." (Lockshin, online).

It's not surprising that, as Germany adopted its anti-Semitic policies before World War II, the Nazis appealed to Luther's condemnation of the Jews. What was Hitler's Final Solution, after all, but a logical extension of Luther's idea that "[w]e are at fault in not slaying them"? In 1923 Hitler praised Luther as a great German genius, who "saw the Jew as we today are starting to see him." (Süss, 2006). Shortly after Kristallnacht – the coordinated attacks on Jews and their property of November 10, 1938 – the Bishop of Thüringen noted that Luther was born on the same day in 1483, and described the burning of synagogues as a fitting memorial (Goldhagen, 1997: 111). During the Holocaust, Catholics in Slovakia were taught by their priests that the Nazis were doing God's will in exterminating the Jews. In Slovakia in 1942, Rabbi Michael Dov-Ber Weissmandel begged Archbishop Kametko to intervene with President Tisso, to stop the expulsion of Jews from Slovakia to the Nazi death camps. The archbishop replied:

This is no mere expulsion. There you will not die of hunger and pestilence; there they will slaughter you all, young and old, women and children, in one day. This is your punishment for the death of our Redeemer. There is only one hope for you, to convert to our religion. Then I shall effect the annulling of this decree. (Berkovits, 1973: 16–17)

The horrors of the Holocaust shook the world to its core, and prompted Christian authorities to review their teachings. In 1959, Pope John XXIII ordered that the word "perfidious" be deleted from the Good Friday prayer. In 1962, the Second Vatican Council was called by Pope John to renew understandings of scripture in light of modern experience. A few years later, Pope Paul VI issued the encyclical *Nostra Aetate* (In Our Time) (1965), which resulted from the Church's deliberations on religious pluralism. *Nostra Aetate* repudiated the traditional blaming of all Jews over all time for the death of Jesus. "The Jews should not be presented as rejected or accursed by God," it said, "as if this followed from Sacred Scripture." In 1970 the Good Friday prayer was completely rewritten, removing negative references to Jews and instead recognizing them as the first to hear the word of God.

Pope John Paul II (r. 1978–2005) continued efforts to correct Christian attitudes toward Jews. In his first official trip through Germany in 1980, he met with the Jewish Central Council and the German Rabbinical Conference, where he called for more dialogue and said that God's covenant with the Jews had never been revoked. Pope Benedict XVI expressed his doubts about the historical accuracy of the line "His blood be upon us and upon our children," in his book *Jesus of Nazareth* (2011). Many scholars point out that these words were written 50 years after Jesus' death, by people trying to gain acceptance in the Roman Empire by distinguishing themselves from the Jews who had rebelled against the Roman government, leading them to attack Jerusalem in 70 CE. Some argue that by saying that Pilate found Jesus innocent, while "the Jews" accepted responsibility for the execution of Jesus, the writer of Matthew let the Romans off the hook for Jesus' crucifixion, perhaps in order not to offend the Romans himself (see *Anchor Bible Dictionary*, 1995: 399–400).

The Roman Catholic Church has also issued new guidelines for passion plays during Lent. The anti-Semitism of the traditional scripts has been greatly reduced. Pilate appears more powerful and autocratic. The role of the Temple traders has been reduced. Jesus' supporters have been added to the screaming crowd outside Pilate's palace. The line, "His blood be upon us and upon our children" has been deleted. And Jesus' Jewishness is stressed by having him speak several lines in Hebrew and be addressed as "Rabbi Yeshua." In 1998, the Evangelical Lutheran Church in America adopted a resolution urging any Lutheran church presenting a passion play to abide by the *Guidelines for Lutheran–Jewish Relations*. That document says that the New Testament "must not be used as justification for hostility towards present-day Jews," and that "blame for the death of Jesus should not be attributed to Judaism or the Jewish people." Unfortunately, however, as jewskilledjesus.com and other web sites make clear, Christians have a great deal more work to do before this root of anti-Semitism is destroyed.

References

Anchor Bible Dictionary (1995) Volume 5, Bantam, New York.

Benedict XVI (2011) *Jesus of Nazareth*, Doubleday, New York.

Berkovits, E. (1973) *Faith after the Holocaust*, KTAV, Jersey City NJ and Brooklyn NY.

Brown H. (ed) (2010) *Justin Martyr's Dialogue with Trypho the Jew*, Gale ECCO, Farmington Hills MI.

Chrysostom, J. (1979) Discourses against Judaizing Christians, translated by Paul Harkins *The Fathers of the Church* Volume 68, Catholic University of America Press, Washington.

Goldhagen, D. (1997) *Hitler's Willing Executioners*, Vintage, New York.

Lockshin, M.I. (online) *Who Killed Jesus? A History of the Idea that the Jews Killed Jesus*, www.myjewishlearning.com/beliefs/Issues/Jews_and_Non-Jews/Attitudes_Toward_Non-Jews/Christianity/who-killed-jesus.shtml (accessed January 7, 2014)

Luther, M. (1543) On the Jews and Their Lies. Translated by Martin Bermann, in *Luther's Works* (1971), Fortress Press, Philadelphia.

Michael, R. (2006) *Holy Hatred: Christianity, Antisemitism, and the Holocaust*, Palgrave Macmillan, New York.

Paul VI (1965) *Declaration on the Relation of the Church to Non-Christian Religions: Nostra Aetate (In Our Time)*, October 28, www.vatican.va/archive/hist_councils/ii_vatican_council/documents/vat-ii_decl_19651028_nostra-aetate_en.html (accessed January 2014).

Süss, R. (2006) *Luthers Theologisch Testament*, VU University Press, Amsterdam.

6. Blood Libel: Jews Use Christian Blood in Their Rituals

The Jews of Lincoln stole a boy of eight years of age, whose name was Hugh …
and they sent to almost all the cities of England where the Jews lived, and
summoned some of their sect from each city to be present at a sacrifice to take
place at Lincoln, for they had, as they stated, a boy hidden for the purpose of
being crucified. (A version of the murder of Little St Hugh, by Matthew Paris,
as quoted in Hyamson, 1908: 81)

Besides the death of Jesus, Jews have been blamed for countless other
crimes. Among the most preposterous of them is the claim – popular in the
Middle Ages in Europe – that Jews murdered Christian children and used
their blood for religious rituals. According to scholar David Biale (2007: 2),
this so-called "blood libel" "goes back in European history to the thirteenth
century … and it has continued in remarkably similar forms to the present
day." But an earlier case is identified by Douglas Raymund Webster (1913),
that of William of Norwich, a 12-year-old boy whose mutilated corpse was
supposedly found in the woods near Norwich, England, on the evening of
Passover in 1144. A local Benedictine monk, Thomas of Monmouth, wrote
a book about the child in which he claims that the nature of the wounds on
the corpse indicated that William had been ritually murdered by Jews.
William, says Thomas, was the choice for 1144. William's "martyrdom" was
so widely accepted that it was artistically depicted on an altar screen in
Holy Trinity Church in Loddon, Norfolk, built in 1490. The image of Jews
crucifying a Christian child and draining his blood can still be seen today.

Perhaps the most famous case of blood libel involves a 9-year-old English
child called Hugh, who was supposedly found dead in England in 1255.
Hugh went missing and several weeks later his body was found in a well.
Hugh's friends reportedly claimed that he had been abducted, tortured, and
then crucified – in an effort to mock Jesus – by a local Jew. The individual
was arrested by local authorities and, apparently under torture, admitted
killing the child for the benefit of the entire Jewish community. Ninety Jews
were accused of participating in torturing Hugh, draining his blood, and
crucifying him – to mock Jesus. Eighteen were hanged, and King Henry III
confiscated their property. Miracles were attributed to the child. He was
called Little Saint Hugh, and a shrine was put up in Lincoln Cathedral. His
"martyrdom" then was retold in English and Scottish ballads such as "Sir
Hugh or the Jew's Daughter (who lures the boy into her garden)." In Geoffrey

Chaucer's *Canterbury Tales*, the Prioress's Tale tells how the Jews hired a murderer to "cut his throat and cast him into a pit … into an outhouse, where these Jews purged their bowels." It took 700 years for the Anglican Church to disavow this fictitious story.

According to historian Walter Laqueur (2006: 55–66), there have been around 150 documented cases of blood libel that resulted in the arrest or, more commonly, the murder of Jews. Most, Laqueur says, were in the Middle Ages, although allegations of Jews using human blood for religious ritual persist to this day.

Why would Jews kill Christian children? Thomas of Monmouth claimed that a local Jew had informed him of an ancient prophecy according to which Jews could return to their ancient homeland if they made an annual sacrifice of a Christian child. But claims of blood libel were actually part of the virulent anti-Judaism that spread across England, and indeed throughout much of Christian Europe. As we saw, studies of the roots of anti-Judaism trace its numerous roots, including allegations that Jews claim they alone were selected by God for salvation and that Jews killed Jesus. A more mundane cause of anti-Jewish sentiment can be found in medieval laws regarding money-lending. Christians were not allowed to charge interest for lending money. Nor, according to the Hebrew Bible, were Jews allowed to charge interest to Jews (Exodus 22:24; Leviticus 25:36–37; Deuteronomy 23:20–21). But Jews were allowed to charge interest to non-Jews. Many Christians therefore had recourse to Jewish money-lenders, resulting in predictable resentment. In England, anti-Jewish sentiment reached such a crescendo that all Jews were expelled from the country in 1290, an exile that lasted over 350 years.

Similar stories of Jews' treachery emerged across Europe, particularly in times of crisis, such as during the fourteenth-century Black Death when the plague devastated populations around the Mediterranean. In lieu of more scientific explanations, claims that Jews had poisoned the wells of Christian communities gained popularity. We have seen already that the leader of the Protestant Reformation, Martin Luther (1543), published an entire book *On the Jews and their Lies*.

As discussed, it was only in the mid-twentieth century that Christian authorities seriously addressed the roots of anti-Semitism in their teachings. Public apologies were not forthcoming until the end of the twentieth century. Lutheran groups issued a series of apologies beginning in 1994, and Catholics followed suit in 1998. Unfortunately, however, anti-Semitism persists, including allegations that Jews use Christian blood.

References

Biale, D. (2007) *Blood and Belief: The Circulation of a Symbol between Jews and Christians*, University of California Press, Berkeley.

Hyamson, A. (1908) *History of the Jews in England*, Jewish Historical Society of England, London.

Laqueur, W. (2006) *The Changing Face of Antisemitism: From Ancient Times to the Present Day*, Oxford University Press, Oxford.

Luther, M. (1543) *On the Jews and Their Lies*. Translated by Martin Bermann, in *Luther's Works* (1971), Fortress Press, Philadelphia.

Webster, D.R. (1913) William of Norwich, in *Catholic Encyclopedia*, Volume 15, http://en.wikisource.org/wiki/Catholic_Encyclopedia_(1913)/St._William_of_Norwich (accessed January 7, 2014).

Further Reading

Dundes, A. (ed) (1991) *The Blood Libel Legend: A Casebook in Anti-Semitic Folklore*, University of Wisconsin Press, Madison.

Glassman, D. (1975) *Anti-Semitic Stereotypes without Jews: Images of the Jews in England 1290–1700*, Wayne State University Press, Detroit.

Rubenstein, W.D. (1996) *A History of the Jews in the English-Speaking World: Great Britain*, Macmillan, New York.

7. Benjamin Franklin Advised the US Government to Expel Jews

I fully agree with General Washington, that we must protect this young nation from an insidious influence and impenetration. The menace, gentlemen, is the Jews. In whatever country Jews have settled in any great number, they have lowered its moral tone; depreciated its commercial integrity; have segregated themselves and have not been assimilated; have sneered at and tried to undermine the Christian religion upon which that nation is founded, by objecting to its restrictions; have built up a state within the state; and when opposed have tried to strangle that country to death financially, as in the case of Spain and Portugal.

For over 1700 years, the Jews have been bewailing their sad fate in that they have been exiled from their homeland, as they call Palestine. But gentlemen, did the world give it to them in fee simple, they would at once find some reason for not returning. Why? Because they are vampires, and vampires do not live on vampires. They cannot live only among themselves. They must subsist on Christians and other people not of their race.

If you do not exclude them from these United States, in their Constitution, in less than 200 years they will have swarmed here in such great numbers that they will dominate and devour the land and change our form of government, for which we Americans have shed our blood, given our lives our substance and jeopardized our liberty.

If you do not exclude them, in less than 200 years our descendants will be working in the fields to furnish them substance, while they will be in the counting houses rubbing their hands. I warn you, gentlemen, if you do not exclude Jews for all time, your children will curse you in your graves.

Jews, gentlemen, are Asiatics, let them be born where they will nor how many generations they are away from Asia, they will never be otherwise. Their ideas do not conform to an American's, and will not even though they live among us ten generations. A leopard cannot change its spots. Jews are Asiatics, are a menace to this country if permitted entrance, and should be excluded by this Constitutional Convention.

A more modern example of anti-Jewish myths is the claim that US Founding Father Benjamin Franklin gave the above speech in 1787 at the Philadelphia Constitutional Convention. It was supposedly recorded by Charles Cotesworth Pinkney, a delegate to the convention from South Carolina. In a letter to John Quincy Adams of December 30, 1818, Pinckney claimed that he had kept a journal from the Convention. The first time the Franklin Prophecy appeared in public, however, was in 1934 in an (unattributed) article in the magazine *Liberation*. The magazine's editor, William Dudley Pelley, was an admirer of Germany's new Chancellor, Adolf Hitler, and had founded the Silver Legion, an anti-Semitic organization whose members wore Nazi-like silver uniforms. Most American states had chapters of the Silver Legion, and Pelley ran for President as the candidate of the Christian Party in 1936.

According to Pelley, Franklin's speech had been written down in Pinckney's diary, which was printed privately. A copy of the diary, he said, was held by the Franklin Institute in Philadelphia. The director of the Franklin Institute at the time, Henry Butler Allen (1938: 1–2), however, said that "historians and librarians have not been able to find [the diary] or any record of it having existed."

Since 1934 the Franklin Prophecy has appeared many times in anti-Semitic print media and can now be found on the Internet. Osama bin Laden referred to it in his "Letter to the American People" of October 2002:

> You are the nation that permits Usury, which has been forbidden by all the religions. Yet you build your economy and investments on Usury. As a result of this, in all its different forms and guises, the Jews have taken control of your economy, through which they have then taken control of your media, and now control all aspects of your life, making you their servants and achieving their aims at your expense; precisely what Benjamin Franklin warned you against.

But the Franklin speech is a forgery. An early article debunking it was published by the Anti-Defamation League (1954). The article includes this comment from noted historian Charles A. Beard:

> I cannot find a single original source that gives the slightest justification for believing that the Prophecy is anything more than a barefaced forgery. Not a word have I discovered in Franklin's letters and papers expressing any such sentiments against the Jews as are ascribed to him by the Nazis – American and German. His well-known liberality in matters of religious opinion would, in fact, have precluded the kind of utterances put in his mouth by this palpable forgery … In his writings on immigration, Franklin made no mention of discrimination against Jews.

Beard also pointed out that the Franklin Prophecy includes phrases unlike the language of Benjamin Franklin but similar to that in twentieth-century political discussions. In Franklin's time, for instance, no one talked about a "homeland" for the Jews; that term arose much later in discussions of Zionism and the need for a refuge from Europe's anti-Semitism (see Beard, 1935).

Interestingly, the first line of the Franklin Prophecy tries to give it extra authority by having Franklin "fully agree with" George Washington.

In reality, both Franklin and Washington were friendly to the Jews of America, and showed no anti-Semitism in their speeches and writings. When the Hebrew Congregation of Philadelphia sought to build their first permanent synagogue, Franklin signed the petition appealing for contributions from "citizens of every religious denomination" and donated five pounds himself.

When, as President, Washington visited Newport, Rhode Island in 1790 and was warmly received by the Hebrew Congregation there, he replied by writing them a letter that closed with these words:

> May the Children of the Stock of Abraham, who dwell in this land, continue to merit and enjoy the good will of the other Inhabitants; while everyone shall sit under his own vine and fig tree, and there shall be none to make him afraid (Hirschfeld 2005: 15).

References

Allen, H.B. (1938) Franklin and the Jews. *The Franklin Institute News* 3 (4) August, 1–2.

Anti-Defamation League (1954) "The Franklin Prophecy": Modern Anti-Semitic Myth Making. *Facts*, April–May.

Beard, C. (1935) Exposing the anti-Semitic forgery about Franklin, *Jewish Frontier*, March, 1–13.

bin Laden, O. (2002) Letter to the American People, *The Observer*, November 24, www.theguardian.com/world/2002/nov/24/theobserver (accessed January 7, 2014).

Hirschfeld, F. (2005) *George Washington and the Jews*, University of Delaware Press, Newark DE.

Liberation (1934) Did Benjamin Franklin Say This about the Hebrews? *Liberation* 5 (24) February 3.

Pinckney, P. (1818) Letter to John Quincy Adams, December 30, www.consource. org/document/charles-pinckney-to-john-quincy-adams-1818-12-30 (accessed January 10, 2014).

8. *The Protocols of the Learned Elders of Zion*: Jewish Leaders Plot Global Takeover

Whether a State exhausts itself in its own convulsions, whether its internal discord brings it under the power of external foes – in any case it can be accounted irretrievably lost: IT IS IN OUR POWER. The despotism of Capital, which is entirely in our hands, reaches out to it a straw that the State, willy-nilly, must take hold of. (*Protocol* No. 1, section 8)

Another modern example of anti-Semitic libel was produced by the Russian government, under the impressive title *The Protocols of the Learned Elders of Zion*. It was composed in around 1900 by the Russian Okhrana, the Czarist secret police, who claimed it was the minutes of a meeting of Jewish leaders conspiring to subvert the morals of society, control the world's economies, and ultimately dominate the world.

Sergyei Nilus, a Czarist official in Moscow, edited several editions of *The Protocols of the Learned Elders of Zion*. In different editions, he told various stories of how he had come by the document. In the 1911 edition he said that he had received it from someone who had stolen it from a Zionist organization in France. In the 1917 edition he attributed the document to

Theodor Herzl (1860–1904), the founder of modern Zionism. By 1933, 33 editions of *The Protocols* had been published. As *The Protocols* was more widely circulated, various "editors" made up more details about its origins. Some said that it was presented at the First Zionist Congress in Basel, Switzerland in 1897.

The Protocols is still widely circulated around the world, often by anti-Semitic religious groups. A group called Bible Believers, for example, posts it on their website (www.biblebelievers.org.au), and even adds notes of their own linking Jews with Roman Catholics. *The Protocols* claims that at least six popes were Jews, including Pius XI (1922–1939). The Bible Believers add that Ignatius Loyola, the founder of the Jesuits, was a Jew. After a passage in which *The Protocols* claims that "Roman Catholicism – the very origin and executor of Christianity – was merely a front for a hidden agenda operated from behind the scenes by a hidden hand," so that "Christianity was essentially a stepping-stone to the greater Judification of the world," the Bible Believers add this note: "Unfortunately our author is not a Spiritual man and fails to realize that Roman Catholicism was never at any time anything but the antithesis of Christianity."

The Introduction to a standard English translation of *The Protocols* explains the title of the document:

> The word "Protocol" signifies a precis gummed on to the front of a document, a draft of a document, minutes of proceedings. In this instance, "Protocol" means minutes of the proceedings of the Meetings of the Learned Elders of Zion. These *Protocols* give the substance of addresses delivered to the innermost circle of the Rulers of Zion. They reveal the converted plan of action of the Jewish Nation developed through the ages and edited by the Elders themselves up to date. Parts and summaries of the plan have been published from time to time during the centuries as the secrets of the Elders have leaked out.

There are 24 Protocols:

I   The Basic Doctrine
II   Economic Wars
III Methods of Conquest
IV   Materialism Replaces Religion
V   Despotism and Modern Progress
VI   Take-Over Technique
VII World-Wide Wars

VIII   Provisional Government
IX   Re-education
X   Preparing for Power
XI   The Totalitarian State
XII   Control of the Press
XIII   Distractions
XIV   Assault on Religion
XV   Ruthless Suppression
XVI   Brainwashing
XVII   Abuse of Authority
XVIII   Arrest of Opponents
XIX   Rulers and People
XX   Financial Programme
XXI   Loans and Credit
XXII   Power of Gold
XXIII   Instilling Obedience
XXIV   Qualities of the Ruler

After the Communist takeover of Russia, many attacks on the Jews linked them to the Communists. In 1919, anti-Communist Russians gave copies of *The Protocols* to American judges and members of the President's cabinet.

The Protocols gained considerable credibility in the United States when in 1920 Henry Ford, founder of the Ford Motor Company, published an Americanized version, first as a series of newspaper articles and then as *The International Jew: The World's Foremost Problem, Being a Reprint of a Series of Articles Appearing in The Dearborn Independent from May 22, 1920 [to January 14, 1922]*.

Henry Ford's theory of a Jewish plot to dominate the world resonated with many people in the US and Europe, including Adolf Hitler. In December 1922, the *New York Times* reported that Hitler's office was decorated with a large portrait of Ford and contained a large table covered with books, "nearly all of which are a translation of a book written and published by Henry Ford."

At the Nuremberg Trials following World War II, Baldur von Schirach, a high-ranking Nazi on trial for sending 66 000 Viennese Jews to Nazi concentration camps, said that as a young man he had been inspired by Henry Ford's set of pamphlets *The International Jew*. "We saw in Henry Ford the representative of success, also the exponent of a progressive social policy. In the poverty-stricken and wretched Germany of the time, youth looked toward America, and apart from the great benefactor, Herbert Hoover, it was Henry Ford who to us represented America" (*Nuremberg Trial Proceedings*, 1946).

Yet in 1921, a series of articles by Philip Graves in *The Times* of London had revealed that *The Protocols* was undeniably a forgery. He demonstrated that parts of the document came from earlier writings that were not about the Jews. There were two main sources, Graves said. One was *Dialogue between Machiavelli and Montesquieu in Hell*, an 1864 satire about the French Emperor Napoleon III, by Maurice Joly. Many of the ideas about world domination came directly from the speeches of Machiavelli in this book, some word-for-word. The other source was *Biarritz*, an 1868 novel by Hermann Goedsche, who is thought to have come up with the idea that the Jews planned to take over the world. In Goedsche's book, the princes of the 12 tribes of Israel gather at a Jewish cemetery to report on the progress of their plans for world domination.

After Graves debunked *The Protocols*, others did more research to add to his evidence. Some early promoters then changed their minds, including Henry Ford, who in 1927 publicly apologized for circulating the document, saying that his assistants had duped him. Yet the document continues to be published and, unfortunately, influence its ignorant readers.

References

Ford, H. (1920–1922) *The International Jew. The World's Foremost Problem. Being a Reprint of a Series of Articles Appearing in The Dearborn Independent from May 22, 1920 [to January 14, 1922]*, Dearborn Publishing Co., Dearborn, Michigan.

Graves, P. (1921) "Jewish World Plot." An Exposure. The Source of the Protocols. Truth at Last, *The Times of London*, 16–18 August.

New York Times (1922) Berlin hears Ford is backing Hitler, December 20, page 2, column 8.

Nuremberg Trial Proceedings, Vol. 14, 137, May 23, 1946.

Further Reading

Cohn, N. (1996) *Warrant for Genocide*, 2nd edition, Serif, London.

Segel, B. (1996) *A Lie and a Libel: The History of the Protocols of the Elders of Zion*, translated and edited by Richard Levy, University of Nebraska Pres,. Lincoln, NE.

9.   Hanukkah Is for Jews What Christmas Is for Christians

HAPPYHANUKKAHMERRYCHRISTMAS.

Holiday shoppers undoubtedly have noticed that Hanukkah cards and decorations are now being marketed alongside Christmas cards and decorations in North America. One card shows two conjoined snowmen, one wearing a yarmulke and holding a menorah and the other wearing a red stocking cap and holding a small evergreen tree. The greeting is "HAPPYHANUKKAHMERRYCHRISTMAS." Other fused words are "Hanuchristmas" and "Christmukkah." Some stores sell hybrid Hanukkah and Christmas paraphernalia, featuring both a menorah (a candelabra used in the celebration of Hanukkah) and a Christmas tree. Also available are decorations with Jewish themes for Christmas trees, such as a "Hanukkah Tree Topper" (a star of David with coiled wire to fit the top of a Christmas tree), Christmas stockings with a Star of David on them, and tiny models of menorahs made to be Christmas tree ornaments.

These items give the impression that the two holidays are somehow equivalent, as if Hanukkah is the Jewish Christmas and Christmas the Christian Hanukkah. After all, they fall in roughly the same time frame. Hanukkah runs for eight days beginning on the 25th day of the month of Kislev in the Jewish calendar. Christmas is on the 25th day of December. In some years, such as 2005, those dates coincide. And like other religious celebrations during the darkest part of the year, these holidays involve light. Hanukkah is called the Festival of Lights and on each of the eight evenings, candles are lit on the menorah. Christians light candles, too, and put lights on Christmas trees. Hanukkah and Christmas are also highly social holidays, with special foods and songs. In North America, Jews exchange gifts, as Christians around the world do. Both groups emphasize gifts for children.

But the assimilation of Christmas with the Jewish festival of Hanukkah is a recent and mostly North American phenomenon. According to Jonathan Sarna, professor of American Jewish history at Brandeis University, Jews used to exchange gifts only on Purim, but in the late nineteenth century, as Christmas became a national holiday in the United States, gift-giving shifted from Purim to Hanukkah. In twentieth century America, especially after the Holocaust, Jews tended to model Hanukkah on Christmas. These changes have not occurred in other countries, including Israel, to anything like the degree seen in North America (Rosenstock, 2010).

Dianne Ashton, Director of American Studies at Rowan University and author of *Hanukkah in America: A History* (2013), says that the custom of Hanukkah gifts really grew in the 1950s as a response to Jewish children's "Christmas envy." Jewish child psychologists and rabbis started promoting gift-giving as a way to make Jewish kids happy about being Jewish, instead of sad about not getting Christmas presents. Especially influential were two rabbis from Cincinnati who wrote in national Jewish newspapers, Ashton thinks. "[One] rabbi said Jewish children shall have a grand and glorious Hanukkah, a festival as nice as any Christmas, with songs, dramatics, candle lighting, ice cream and candy. This really shifted Hanukkah from primarily an observance of Jewish adults to a festival seen as particularly important for Jewish children, a way to keep them interested in Judaism" (Rowan Today, 2009).

The tendency to assimilate Hanukkah and Christmas may be laudable from the standpoint of social relations, particularly in view of the hideous legacy and lingering existence of anti-Semitism. However, it may cover up some important distinctions between the two traditions that deserve to be respected, each in its own right. Beyond the superficial similarities between Hanukkah and Christmas, the two holidays are quite different in at least three ways.

First, Christmas is the celebration of the birth of Jesus, whom Christians believe to be God. As such, it is one of the two most important days in the Christian calendar, the other being Easter. Hanukkah, on the other hand, is a minor Jewish holiday, not one of the seven Biblical holidays that God gave to Israel through Moses, as recorded in Leviticus, chapter 23. Hanukkah commemorates the victory of the Maccabees, Jewish fighters, over the oppressive Greco-Syrian Empire of Antiochus IV in 167 BCE, and the rededication of the Temple in Jerusalem after that victory.

Secondly, the birth of Jesus is recorded in Christian Scripture, but the revolt of the Maccabees and the rededication of the Temple are not recorded in the Hebrew Bible, which had been completed two centuries before the events valorized by Hanukkah.

Thirdly, and most importantly, there is an ideological clash between what Christmas and Hanukkah are about. Christmas celebrates the founder of a religious tradition that started out Jewish but then, when it became the state religion of the Roman Empire, persecuted Jews. Hanukkah celebrates the refusal of Jews in the second century BCE to assimilate into the Greek – Syrian Empire, the predecessor of the Roman Empire, even at the cost of their own lives. The candles on the menorah represent the eight days that the lamp stayed lit during the rededication of the Temple after the Jews recaptured it from the Greco-Syrian forces who had defiled it and killed Jews for refusing to worship Greek gods. So Hanukkah represents the struggle of Jews to remain faithful to their God and their traditions, rather than practice another religion. Mixing the celebration of Hanukkah with the celebration of another religion, then, makes little sense. That problem was brought out well in a 2011 essay by Jordana Horn in *Kveller*, a magazine for Jewish parents. Her central argument was this:

> The Maccabees would rather die than observe any religion other than their own – they recognized that they would and could not be anything other than who they were, Jews. And it is that determination to be who we are and no one else that is what we are celebrating when we celebrate Hanukkah. It's not presents, not the endless Jewish song YouTube videos, and not the "holiday spirit." What we are celebrating, I'd argue, is bravery and defiance in the name of protecting our Judaism and who we truly are. THAT is the true miracle. The miracles are those lights of people's Jewish identities, fighting against the darkness of the rest of the world that threatens to consume them.

> When we light the *hanukkiah*, we do it in our windows, to show the world that we are proud to be Jewish *and nothing else*. We celebrate who we are. We celebrate that despite thousands of years of persecution and hatred, we are still here. We are going to teach our children who we are and they will in turn teach it to theirs. We are heirs to a priceless legacy of history.

References

Ashton, D. (2013) *Hanukkah in America: A History*, New York University Press, New York.

Horn, J. (2011) Actually, You Can't Celebrate Hanukkah AND Christmas, *Kveller*, December 14, www.kveller.com/blog/parenting/actually-you-cant-celebrate-hanukkah-and-christmas (accessed January 7, 2014).

Rosenstock (2010) Chanuka Gift-giving, *San Diego Jewish Journal, December*. http://sdjewishjournal.com/site/1448/chanukah-gift-giving (accessed January 7, 2013).

Rowan Today (2009) Spin that dreidel: For American children, Hanukkah has become a festival of fun, December 9, www.rowan.edu/today/news/index/PR/2592 (accessed January 10, 2014).

Further Reading

Olitzky, K. and Judson, D. (2006) *Jewish Holidays: A Brief Introduction for Christians*, Jewish Lights Publishing, Woodstock, VT.

4
Myths About Christianity, Christians, and Christian Scripture

1. The Four Gospels Are Eyewitnesses' Accounts of the Life of Jesus
2. The Bible Says that When We Die, Our Souls Go to Heaven or Hell
3. Jesus Was Born on December 25 in a Stable in Bethlehem
4. Jesus Was a Christian
5. Jesus Preached Family Values
6. The Image of the Crucified Jesus Has Always Been Sacred to Christians
7. The Church Suppressed Science in the Middle Ages
8. Catholics Are Not Christians
9. The United States Was Founded as a Christian Country

Introduction

Most of the misperceptions described in this chapter, such as the date and place of Jesus' birth, fit the description of myth as misconceptions of historical events. Many such misconceptions have been clarified through careful scholarship without significantly affecting fundamental beliefs. On the other hand, some misperceptions, such as the claims that Jesus preached family values, and the United States was founded as a Christian country, have important implications for everyday life. The claim that Christianity suppressed science is an example of allegations used against Christianity. Like the rest of the myths in this book, all of them show the staying power of a good story.

50 Great Myths About Religions, First Edition. John Morreall and Tamara Sonn.
© 2014 John Wiley & Sons, Ltd. Published 2014 by John Wiley & Sons, Ltd.

1. The Four Gospels Are Eyewitnesses' Accounts of the Life of Jesus

Matthew, Mark, Luke and John
Guard the bed that I lie on:
Four corners to my bed
Four angels round my head,
One to watch and one to pray
And two to bear my soul away.
(Medieval nursery rhyme,
Roud Folk Song Index #1704)

This nursery rhyme reflects the common respect for the four gospels in Christian scripture, the New Testament. The acceptance of these four "canonical" gospels – those attributed to Matthew, Mark, Luke, and John – is so widespread that Religious Studies scholar Stephen Prothero expressed shock that only half of American adults could name "even one of the four gospels" in his popular *Religious Literacy: What Every American Needs to Know – And Doesn't* (2008). In fact, many more gospels circulated among Christians for the first several centuries of Christianity, and many of them survive today. It was only in the fourth century that Roman Christian authorities officially limited the gospels to four, suppressing the others. Many of the suppressed gospels were discovered buried in sealed containers in Nag Hammadi, Egypt in 1945. The collection contained a number of texts called Gnostic Gospels, stories of the life and teachings of Jesus told from a perspective that today seems odd, to say the least (see Pagels, 1979).

Even if people can't name the four canonical gospels, however, there is widespread belief that they convey factual accounts of events in the life of Jesus by people who witnessed them. This understanding of the gospels has been emphasized in recent years, for example, by Cambridge New Testament scholar Richard Bauckham in *Jesus and the Eyewitnesses: The Gospels as Eyewitness Testimony* (2006). The majority of Biblical scholars, however, disagree.

In the first and second centuries, the Gospels helped spread the new movement that would become Christianity. "Gospel" is from the Old English word for "good news." The Gospel of Mark opens: "The beginning of the good news of Jesus Christ, the Son of God." According to the gospels, Jesus is "the Messiah," a term referring to a king who would liberate the people of Israel from their oppressors; the Greek term for it was *Christos*, "anointed one," from which we get the word *Christ*. Though the essential messages of the four canonical gospels are similar, they differ significantly in detail.

Consider the four gospel stories of the women at the empty tomb after Jesus' death. The Gospel of Mark says that Mary Magdalene, Mary the mother of James, and Salome went to the tomb to anoint the body of Jesus. Wondering who would roll back the stone from the entry for them, they found that it had already been moved. "As they entered the tomb, they saw a young man dressed in a white robe, sitting on the right side." He assured them that Jesus had risen and told them to "go, tell his disciples and Peter that he is going ahead of you to Galilee. There you will see him, just as he told you" (Mark 16:5–7). The Gospel of Matthew says that there were two women that morning, not three, and when they arrived at the tomb there was an earthquake, and an angel came and rolled back the stone to open the tomb (Matthew 28:1–40). In the Gospel of Luke, the number of women grows to at least five: "Mary Magdalene, Joanna, Mary the mother of James, and the other women with them" (Luke 24: 10). And the number of men/angels doubles: "Suddenly two men in dazzling clothes stood beside them" (Luke 24:4). There is no mention of Galilee in either of these versions of the story. The Gospel of John says that Mary Magdalene went alone to the tomb and when she saw the stone rolled back, she did not go in but instead ran to the apostles Simon Peter and John and told them, "They have taken the Lord out of the tomb, and we do not know where they have laid him" (John 20:1–2). Simon Peter and John ran to the tomb and there they found the linen wrappings that had been removed from the corpse. They then went home and Mary stayed and began to cry. Then she saw two angels and someone she thought was a gardener, who asked her why she was crying. When the gardener spoke her name she realized it was actually Jesus, risen from the dead (John 20: 10–16).

What can account for the differences between these stories? The most obvious answer is that the evangelists (the assumed authors of the gospels) were not eyewitnesses of the accounts they describe.

The four canonical gospels often sound like eyewitness accounts. They describe Jesus up close, as a real person walking among all kinds of people, eating and drinking with them, preaching, and healing the sick. Indeed, the last part of the Gospel of John identifies the author as "the disciple whom Jesus loved … the one who had reclined next to Jesus at the [last] supper … This is the disciple who is testifying to these things and has written them" (John 21:20, 24). So it's not surprising that over the centuries, people have tended to think of the four Gospels as written by friends of Jesus. As well, today many people think of Matthew, Mark, Luke and John as being his apostles, the 12 men closest to Jesus, or at least his disciples [followers]. However, we know of no apostles or disciples named Mark or Luke. And while two of the apostles were named Matthew and John, scholars generally agree that those men did not write the Gospels of Matthew and John. Furthermore, in view of the inconsistencies in detail, scholars generally agree that none of the assumed authors of the four gospels actually witnessed the events they recorded or even knew Jesus personally.

In fact, scholars believe that all the gospels were written decades after Jesus was gone. Mark appeared around the year 70, Matthew and Luke probably in the 80s, and John between 90 and 100. The stories in the gospels developed over decades. Scholars identify three stages in this process. First was the oral stage: people passed on by word of mouth stories of what Jesus had said and done. Those included accounts of his preaching, miracles, crucifixion, and resurrection. In the second stage, people wrote down stories about Jesus' sayings and actions. In the third stage, the Gospel writers selected materials from the written and oral stories and shaped them into the Gospels. Scholars also agree that the Gospel of Mark was the first of the four Gospels to be written. They note that the Gospels of Luke and Matthew borrow heavily from it. Of the 661 verses in Mark, 360 appear in Luke and 606 appear in Matthew (Helms 1988: 35, 142). The identity of this Mark is unknown, though scholars agree that he was not an eyewitness to the events he describes. An ancient tradition says that someone named John Mark (mentioned in Acts 12:12 and 15:37) composed this gospel while in Rome, recording the preaching of Peter. Some of the author's word choices suggest that the intended audience were non-Jews living in Italy.

According to an early Christian tradition, the author of the Gospel of Luke was a physician, a non-Jew who converted, and a friend of Paul, the famous writer of letters (epistles) to various Christian communities around the Mediterranean (see Colossians 4:14; 2 Timothy 4:11; Philemon 24). (If this is true, the author of Luke may have received information from Paul, but Paul, like Luke, never met Jesus.) Both had joined the new movement years after Jesus had died, so scholars assume neither witnessed the events they describe.

The Gospel of Matthew, scholars say, was probably written in a Jewish-Christian community in Syria between 80 and 90. They believe that its author, like the author of Luke, drew material from a collection of Jesus' sayings that is now lost. Scholars call this collection Q, which is short for *Quelle*, a German word for "Source." As in the case of Luke, it is unlikely that someone who travelled with Jesus and heard his preaching would have needed to rely on a secondary source like Q.

But what about the Gospel of John, the one that indicates that the author is the apostle John? Through most of history, Christians have accepted that claim. But could the apostle John have actually written this gospel? The Gospel of John is quite different from the other three. They are called the Synoptic Gospels, from the Greek words for "together" and "appearance," because of their strong similarities. Books about the New Testament some-times have three parallel columns for the same parable, sermon, or story about Jesus as it appears in Matthew, Mark, and Luke. Those gospels generally agree on the order of events in Jesus public ministry, too. Unlike the Synoptic Gospels, however, 90% of the Gospel of John is unique to it. While the other Gospels have many parables, John has none. John's chronology of Jesus' ministry differs from those Gospels, too. He writes of several Passover feasts, making the ministry of Jesus appear to be three years, while the Synoptic Gospels speak of just one Passover feast, covering only a single year of Jesus' ministry. John tells the story of Jesus driving the moneychangers out of the temple (in Chapter 2:13–16) at the beginning of Jesus' ministry. Mark, Matthew, and Luke all say that this event took place in the last week of Jesus' life (Mark 11:15–17; Matthew 21:12–13; Luke 19:45–46).

Perhaps most importantly, in the Gospel of John, the portrayal of Jesus differs profoundly from that found in the other three gospels. They refer to Jesus as Son of God, but they say that he was born as a human being. In the Gospel of John, Jesus is fully divine and so has always existed. Jesus is *Logos*, the Word, a concept from Greek philosophy similar to Plato's Forms – the mental blueprints used by the creator Demiurge to make things in the world:

> In the beginning was the Word, and the Word was with God, and the Word was God. He was in the beginning with God. All things came into being through him, and without him not one thing came into being (John 1:1–3).

In light of this unique description of Jesus, modern scholars conclude that the Gospel of John presents a Christology (understanding of Jesus Christ) influenced by Greek philosophy that emerged after the death of Jesus and in an environment very different from that of Jesus' intimate associates.

The claim that the gospels were not written by witnesses to the events they describe should not be of concern to believers, however, since that is not their purpose. "[The gospels] don't claim to be eyewitness accounts" of Jesus' life, says Harvard Divinity School New Testament scholar

Allen D. Callahan (1998). Instead, their purpose is to convey messages about Jesus' teachings in ways that inspire, convince, and encourage their listeners. But the audiences of the evangelists were different from one another, and the authors seemed to address the specific circumstances of these diverse communities. The Gospel of Matthew, for instance, was intended mostly for Jews, and so it describes Jesus as fulfilling scriptural prophecies, such as that the Messiah would be descended from King David. David's hometown was Bethlehem, so in this Gospel Jesus is born in Bethlehem. The Gospel also says that Mary was a virgin, "to fulfill what had been spoken by the Lord through the prophet: 'Look, the virgin shall conceive and bear a son, and they shall name him Emmanuel,' which means 'God is with us'" (Matthew 1:22–25). In Jesus' public ministry in this Gospel, people call him "Rabbi," the Hebrew word for teacher. The Gospel of Luke, by contrast, was intended mostly for Greek-speaking non-Jews, who were not familiar with the Hebrew Bible and its prophecies. So this gospel includes few quotations from the Hebrew Bible and seldom argues that Jesus fulfills prophecies. Instead of having people call Jesus "Rabbi," the author of Luke describes them using the Greek word for "Master."

Again, the variations in the details of the stories of Jesus contained in the four canonical gospels and the questions scholars raise about the identity of their authors do not undermine the authenticity of the messages of these accounts. In the view of modern scholars, they simply indicate that the stories were not intended as literal histories. Otherwise, it is unlikely that the church authorities who selected these four accounts out of the many that were available would have chosen four divergent versions. The truths they convey transcend such details as the precise time and place of Jesus' birth and the number of women at his tomb.

References

Bauckham, R. (2006) *Jesus and the Eyewitnesses: The Gospels as Eyewitness Testimony*, Wm. B. Eerdmans, Grand Rapids, MI.

Callahan, A.D. (1998) What Are the Gospels? *PBS Frontline*, www.pbs.org/wgbh/pages/frontline/shows/religion/story/gospels.html (accessed January 8, 2014).

Helms, R. (1988) *Gospel Fictions*, Prometheus Books, Amherst NY.

Pagels, E. (1979) *The Gnostic Gospels*, Vintage Books, New York.

Prothero, S. (2008) *Religious Literacy: What Every American Needs to Know – And Doesn't*, HarperOne, New York.

2.　The Bible Says that When We Die, Our Souls Go to Heaven or Hell

> Now I lay me down to sleep.
> I pray the Lord my soul to keep.
> If I should die before I wake.
> I pray the Lord my soul to take.
>
> (Child's prayer)

When a family member dies and a young child asks what happened, it's common to say something like "Grandma went to heaven." If the child is confused at the funeral home because Grandma's body is right there in the casket, we may add something like this:

> That's Grandma's *body* in the casket. It's her *soul* that went to heaven. Her body died, but her soul can't die. Her soul will live forever with God.

Billy Graham (Meacham, 2006), the most successful evangelist of modern times, is a good example of this understanding of death. In an interview with *Newsweek* magazine, he said, "I do not fear death. I may fear a little bit about the process, but not death itself, because I think the moment that my spirit leaves this body, I will be in the presence of the Lord."

Many people have heard this description of death as the soul going to heaven so often that they assume it's in the Bible. It isn't. No writer of either the Hebrew Bible or the New Testament even mentions the soul in describing death. And none of them thought of the soul as naturally immortal, that is, unable to die.

As we saw in the second myth in Chapter 2, the Biblical words translated as "soul" – *ruah* and *nefesh* in Hebrew, and *spiré* and *pneuma* in Greek – are the words for air, wind, breath. That's true of the words for "soul" in most languages. Today we often think of "soul" or "spirit" as something nonphysical, but the writers of the Bible didn't. In the Bible, spirit is a fine, very light grade of matter, like what we now call a gas. A person's spirit or soul is what makes them be alive. As in other ancient cultures, the Hebrews probably thought this way because they observed that the difference between a living person and a corpse is that the living person breathes. So breath, spirit, soul, is what makes you be alive. There is nothing immortal about the breath, of course; at death it comes to an end just as everything else about the person does. As dead people are described in both the Hebrew Bible and the New

Testament, they have not gone anywhere, certainly not to heaven to be with God. Rather, as some Biblical writers put it euphemistically, they are "asleep in the dust." The author of Ecclesiastes 9:2–6 is blunter:

> The same fate comes to all, to the righteous and the wicked, to the good and the evil ... This is an evil in all that happens under the sun, that the same fate comes to everyone. ... whoever is joined with all the living has hope, for a living dog is better than a dead lion. The living know they will die, but the dead know nothing; they have no more reward, and even the memory of them is lost. Their love and their hate and their envy have already perished; never again will they have any share in all that happens under the sun.

The Psalms, the Book of Job, and most other books of the Hebrew Bible also understand death as the permanent destruction of the person. God himself says nothing about life after death in the Bible. On the contrary, he says to Adam, "You are dust, and to dust you shall return" (Genesis 3:19).

Only late in the Hebrew Bible do two prophetic visions offer some hope that the destruction of death can be reversed. One is in Isaiah 26:14–15, where the first line seems to refer to the people who have oppressed the Israelites:

> The dead do not live; shades [shadowy remains of the dead] do not rise – Because you have punished and destroyed them, and wiped out all memory of them.

Then, a few lines down in verse 19, there is a prophecy of something better – for the Israelites:

> Your dead shall live, their corpses shall rise.
> O dwellers in the dust, awake and sing for joy!
> For your dew is a radiant dew,
> and the earth will give birth to those long dead.

The other passage about a future resurrection – of some Israelites – is at the beginning of Chapter 12 of the Book of Daniel, in a vision about the end of the world:

> At that time Michael [an angel], the great prince, the protector of your people, shall arise. There shall be a time of anguish, such as has never occurred since nations first came into existence. But at that time your people shall be delivered,

everyone who is found written in the book. Many of those who sleep in the dust of the earth shall awake, some to everlasting life, and some to shame and everlasting contempt.

In the first century CE, when Jesus lived, there was considerable debate among Jews about whether these prophetic visions justified belief in a resurrection of the dead. One group, the Sadducees, stuck to the traditional view that death is permanent destruction. Another group, the Pharisees, had a more optimistic view that at the end of the world, God will bring the dead back to life, judge them, and reward or punish them. This idea about a Resurrection and Last Judgment, followed by reward and punishment, was shared by Jesus. Yet in all his references to the resurrection, Jesus never says that souls are what will be in heaven or hell. His teaching is that persons will be resurrected, judged, and rewarded or punished. For Jesus, as for other first century Jews, a human being is an integrated unit, a body animated by a life-force, a soul. He never says that the soul can exist apart from the body or that the soul is naturally immortal, much less that a soul could travel to heaven where it would count as a person's being in heaven – all of which later Christians would claim.

If the idea of immortal souls going to heaven isn't from the Hebrew Bible or the New Testament, how did it become accepted by Christians later on? The answer is that it crept into Christianity as the new movement gained more members who had been influenced by Greek philosophers, especially Plato. As we've seen, Plato thought of a human being as made up of two parts, one essential and the other non-essential. That is called *dualism*. The essential part is the soul or mind, which is naturally immortal – all by itself, it lives forever. The non-essential part, the body, is destroyed at death. But the human being lives on because the soul lives on. Regarding what happens to the soul at death, the Greeks had several speculations. As in Indian thought, many said that it is reincarnated into a new body on earth.

Over the first four centuries CE, Christian thinkers gradually switched from Biblical ideas about life after death to dualistic, Platonic ideas. The most influential of them was Augustine of Hippo (354–430), who said things that would have astounded Jesus, such as that a human being is a "rational soul using a mortal and earthly body." By the Middle Ages, Christians were talking about immortal souls going to heaven at death. Around 1000 some Christians were celebrating All Souls Day on November 2, to follow All Saints Day on November 1. Both holy days involve thinking of souls as if they are equivalent to persons. Both also involve the idea that before God has resurrected the dead, the dead are somehow alive in heaven and purgatory [according to Roman Catholic doctrine, a place of punishment where the souls of those who die in God's grace may make satisfaction for past sins and so become fit for heaven]. The writers of both the Hebrew Bible and the New Testament would have been surprised by these ideas. They thought of the dead as "asleep in the dust," not as souls that had traveled to heaven or hell.

Reference

Meacham, J. (2006) Pilgrim's Progress, *Newsweek*, August 13.

Further Reading

Cullman, O. (1965) *Immortality and Resurrection: Death in the Western World: Two Conflicting Currents of Thought*, Macmillan, London.

3. Jesus Was Born on December 25 in a Stable in Bethlehem

Away in a manger, no crib for his bed, the little Lord Jesus laid down his sweet head. The stars in the bright sky looked down where he lay, the little Lord Jesus asleep in the hay. (Nineteenth-Century Christmas Carol)

At the end of December thousands of churches and millions of households set up crèches – tableaus of a stable in which Mary and Joseph attend to the baby Jesus in a manger. Around them are farm animals along with the Three Wise Men, who had been guided to the stable by a star. This is a charming image, but scholars of religion and thoughtful Christians, both liberal and conservative, say it is full of fictional details not found in Scripture.

Most people realize that Jesus knew nothing of Christmas trees, mistletoe, and Santa Claus. Far fewer are aware that he did not know the Christmas story represented by the crèche either. Christmas stories began with the Gospels of Luke and Matthew, which were written at least 80 years after the birth of Jesus. The authors of Luke and Matthew never met Jesus, so they didn't get their information from him, but both present their stories as straightforward history, which is how many Christians today still understand them.

If we try to read the Gospels of Matthew and Luke as history, however, we run into problems. One is the way they trace the lineage of Jesus back to King David. Matthew lists 28 generations between David and Jesus, but Luke has 41 generations for the same period of a thousand years. Each gospel starts its genealogy with Joseph as the father of Jesus, but Matthew claims that Joseph's father was Jacob, while Luke says that Joseph's father was Heli. From Jacob, Matthew continues his lineage with Matthan, Eleazar, Eliud, Achim, Zadok, Azor, Eliakim, Abiud, and so on. From Heli, Luke continues his lineage with Matthat, Levi, Melchi, Jannai, Joseph, Mattathiah, Amos, Nahum, and so on. At the other end of the genealogy, Matthew lists King David, then Solomon, Rehoboam, Abijah, Asa, Jehosophat, and so on. For the same generations, Luke lists King David, then Nathan, Mattatha, Menna, Melea, Eliakim, and so on.

With such huge discrepancies, these genealogies cannot both be right, though, of course, both could be wrong. Since we have no good reason to prefer one to the other, we have no good reason to accept either of them as history. Why, then, would we accept as history other details about the birth of Jesus in the Gospels of Matthew and Luke?

The earliest record of the celebration of Jesus' birth on December 25 is from around 336, as Christians were gaining power in the Roman Empire. Those in Rome began celebrating the Feast of the Nativity on December 25. Historians tell us that the Romans had other religious holidays in late December, so this was a good time to put a Christian holiday into the calendar.

Since the eighteenth century, scholars of Christianity have noted parallels between Roman festivals and Christmas. Sir Isaac Newton (d. 1727) said that early Christians chose December 25 to coincide with the winter solstice, the shortest day of the year, after which the sun gradually rises higher in the sky and the days grow longer. In 1743 Paul Ernst Jablonski suggested that Christians aligned their feast with the Roman holiday *Dies Natalis Solis Invicti*, The Birthday of the Unconquered Sun. The scholar of mythology James Frazer (2005: xxxvii) extended that explanation in the early 1900s, commenting, "Thus it appears that the Christian Church chose to celebrate the birthday of its Founder on the twenty-fifth of December in order to transfer the devotion of the heathen from the Sun to him who was called the Sun of Righteousness."

The Birthday of the Unconquered Sun on December 25 coincided with a festival dedicated to Mithra, who was worshipped in India beginning about

600 BCE. Worship of Mithra spread to Persia and then southwest Asia (today's Turkey). In 200 CE Mithraism was popular among Roman soldiers in Germanic lands who had been recruited from southwest Asia. Mithra is sometimes represented in an evergreen tree, and our Christmas tree, which originated in Germany, may trace back to the tree of Mithra (Vermaseren, 1963: 75).

In the week leading up to December 25, Romans celebrated a third festival, Saturnalia, dedicated to the god Saturn. The Roman poet Catullus described Saturnalia as the best time of the year, with feasting, visiting friends, and giving gifts. So the merry mood we associate with Christmas has ancient Roman parallels. Christians who were opposed to this spirit, such as the Puritans, have condemned the celebration of Christmas. The Reverend Increase Mather of Boston (1687: 35) wrote that "the early Christians who first observed the Nativity on December 25 did not do so thinking that Christ was born in that Month, but because the Heathens' Saturnalia was at that time kept in Rome, and they were willing to have those Pagan Holidays metamorphosed into Christian ones" (see Nissenbaum, 1997: 4). Because of its pagan origins, the Puritans banned Christmas; celebrating it was illegal in Massachusetts from 1659 to 1681.

While celebrating the Nativity on December 25 fits well into the Roman calendar, it doesn't fit with Luke 2:8, which says that when Jesus was born "there were shepherds living in the fields, keeping watch over their flock by night." Shepherds don't live in the fields and graze their flocks in the winter, because the grass and vegetation have dried up then. Instead, they rely on hay cut earlier in the season.

Furthermore, none of the canonical gospels that discuss the birth of Jesus mentions a stable, though Luke 2:7 says that his mother "wrapped him in bands of cloth, and laid him in a manger." That could have been in a stable, though in much Christian art it is in a cave. The Church of the Nativity in Bethlehem was built in 330 by Constantine over the exact spot believed to be where Jesus was born. That spot is in a cave beneath the church.

Perhaps more significantly, scholars question the claim that Jesus was born in Bethlehem, a town six miles south of Jerusalem. This is mentioned in the Gospels of Matthew and Luke. But the two Gospels disagree on what Mary and Joseph were doing in Bethlehem. Matthew says that King Herod wanted to kill the infant Jesus, and ordered the slaughter of all children younger than two years old around Bethlehem. Joseph, being warned by an angel in a dream, escaped with the baby and Mary to Egypt. After Herod had died, another dream told Joseph they could return

(Matthew 2:6–23). But Luke says that Joseph and Mary were actually from Nazareth, 90 miles north. He says they only went to Bethlehem on the orders of the Roman emperor, Augustus, who wanted to take a census of people in the town of their ancestors. There is no historical record of a census across the Roman Empire conducted under Caesar Augustus. Nor is there historical evidence that the Romans conducted a census in the way Luke describes – by making people travel to their ancestral homeland to register. The purpose of a census is to count people where they live and work so that they may be taxed.

Further challenging the claim that Jesus was born in Bethlehem of Judea is archaeological work there that has turned up a great deal of material from 1200 to 550 BCE and from the sixth century CE, but nothing from the first century BCE or the first century CE. Aviram Oshri (2005), senior archaeologist with the Israel Antiquities Authority, researched the site of Bethlehem for more than 10 years and reported that it was not a functioning town for centuries before and after the birth of Jesus. He wrote in *Archaeology*, a publication of the Archaeological Institute of America, "there is a complete absence of information for antiquities from the Herodian period – that is, from the time around the birth of Jesus" (Oshri, 2005: 42). However, it is clearly important to the evangelists that Jesus be born in Bethlehem, regardless of where his parents were from, because Bethlehem was the hometown of King David. According to Matthew and Luke, Jesus was the Messiah and the Messiah was expected to come from the royal line of David. Matthew adds a prophecy from Micah 5:2: "And you, Bethlehem, in the land of Judah, are by no means least among the rulers of Judah; for from you shall come a ruler who is to shepherd my people Israel" (Matthew 2:2–6). Thus, Luke tells us,

> Joseph also went from the town of Nazareth in Galilee to Judea, to the city of David called Bethlehem, because he was descended from the house and family of David. He went to be registered with Mary, to whom he was engaged and who was expecting a child (Luke 2:1–5).

Such quibbling over historical details is unlikely to affect the cherished tradition of celebrating Jesus' birth in a stable in winter in Bethlehem. For Christians, the important thing is that he was born, with a sacred mission, providing a perfect example of the scholarly notion of "myth" – a belief of questionable historic accuracy but conveying profound truth.

References

Frazer, J. (2005) *The Golden Bough: A Study in Magic and Religion*, Cosimo, New York.

Mather, I. (1687) *A Testimony against Several Prophane and Superstitious Customs, Now Practiced by Some in New England*, London.

Nissenbaum, S. (1997) *The Battle for Christmas: A Cultural History of America's Most Cherished Holiday*, Vintage Books, New York.

Oshri, A. (2005) Where was Jesus Born? Archaeology 58 (6), 42–45.

Vermaseren, M.J. (1963) *Mithras the Secret God*, Barnes & Noble, New York.

Further Reading

Crossan, J.D. (2004) *Jesus: A Revolutionary Biography*, HarperSanFrancisco, San Francisco.

4. Jesus Was a Christian

Jesus Christ was born circa 6 BC in Bethlehem. Little is known about his early life, but as a young man, he founded Christianity, one of the world's most influential religions. (biography.com (online))

A few years ago, Anglican Archbishop Desmond Tutu, winner of the 1984 Nobel Peace Prize, published a book called *God Is Not a Christian* (2011). To that book, he could have added a chapter, "Jesus Is Not a Christian, Either." Many Christians think of Jesus as the founder of a new religion called "Christianity." But he never used the words "Christianity" or "Christian" because they didn't exist until after he was gone.

Our word "Christ" comes from the Greek *Christos*, which means "the Anointed One." That's a translation of the Hebrew *Messiah*, which means the king descended from King David who was prophesied to save the people of Israel from their oppressors. Calling Jesus "the Christ" is saying that he is the Messiah.

In the New Testament, "Christian" occurs just three times, in accounts of events that took place after Jesus was gone. Acts 11:26 says that, "it was in Antioch [Syria] that the disciples were first called 'Christians.'" Then in Acts 26:28–31, when Paul is being interrogated by the Jewish King Agrippa, the king says to Paul, "Are you so quickly persuading me to become a Christian?"

The third Biblical use of the term is in 1 Peter 4:16: "Yet if any of you suffers as a Christian, do not consider it a disgrace, but glorify God because you bear this name."

Another name for the followers of Jesus was "Nazarenes" – after Jesus' hometown of Nazareth. In Acts 24:5, when Paul is tried before the Roman governor, the prosecutor Tertullus says, "We have, in fact, found this man a pestilent fellow, an agitator among all the Jews throughout the world, and a ringleader of the sect of the Nazarenes."

The way that Tertullus spoke of Paul shows that he thought of him not as part of a new religion, but as part of a Jewish sect. And that's how Paul thought of himself, as is clear when he defended himself against Tertullus' charges:

> As you can find out, it is not more than twelve days since I went up to worship in Jerusalem. They did not find me disputing with anyone in the temple or stirring up a crowd either in the synagogues or throughout the city ... But this I admit to you, that according to the Way, which they call a sect, I worship the God of our ancestors, believing everything laid down according to the law or written in the prophets. (Acts 24:11–14)

Both before and after he began to follow Jesus, Paul worshipped in the Temple in Jerusalem, visited synagogues, and believed in the Mosaic law and the Prophets. When he defended himself before King Agrippa, he pointed out that he had always been a Jew and before following Jesus had "belonged to the strictest sect of our religion and lived as a Pharisee" (Acts 26:5). If he had been part of another religion, he would not have worshipped in the Temple and followed Jewish customs, and the Jewish authorities would have convicted him of heresy or apostasy. But King Agrippa and the other authorities interrogating him "said to one another, 'This man is doing nothing to deserve death or imprisonment'" (Acts 26: 31).

Even more than with Paul, it's obvious that Jesus was born, lived, and died a Jew. His mother and family were Jewish, as were his 12 Apostles. He worshipped and taught in the Temple and often discussed the Law of Moses and other parts of Hebrew scripture. Like the Pharisees with whom he frequently talked, he believed in the Resurrection of the Dead and the Last Judgment at the end of the world. He said that his mission was "not to abolish but to fulfill" the law and the prophets – that is, the Jewish religion in which he grew up. His followers said that he was the Messiah, and to show that he was the Jewish king prophesied in the scriptures, the Gospels of Matthew and Luke trace Jesus' ancestors back to King David. In Matthew 15:23–24, when the Canaanite woman asks for help with her troubled daughter, at first Jesus says, "I was sent only to the lost sheep of the house of Israel." And all four Gospels say that when he was crucified, the inscription above his head read "King of the Jews."

After Jesus was gone, his followers continued to worship as Jews, in the Temple. The Acts of the Apostles says that Paul, Peter, and John preached in the Temple and in synagogues, and addressed people there as "Men of Israel." There were diverse schools of thought among Jews at the time. Some of these are designated by the names Pharisees, Sadducees, and Zealots. Jesus and his followers agreed with some of these groups and disagreed with others. Along with the Pharisees, they believed in the resurrection and life after death, for example, which the Sadducees did not. They were pacifists, too, and so rejected the Zealots' desire to overthrow the Romans violently. The biggest difference between the followers of Jesus and other Jewish groups was their belief that Jesus was the Messiah; but belief in a Messiah, after all, was and remained a Jewish belief. None of these disagreements between Jews made the followers of Jesus, or any other Jewish group, into a new religion.

If Jesus had wanted to start a new religion, furthermore, it seems reasonable that he would have written, or had someone write, instructions for how it should be organized and be kept going. But, as far as we know, Jesus didn't write anything or ask anyone to write anything. Forty to seventy years after he was gone, people who had never met him wrote the Gospels, but they contained only vague instructions for organizing the group.

If, then, Jesus was a Jew, and his first followers were Jews, how did there come to be a new religion called "Christianity"? As many scholars have pointed out, this was a gradual process taking place in the second half of the first century, and perhaps beyond. One thing that caused it was Paul's missionary work beyond Palestine in places like south-west Asia (now Turkey) and Greece. There he preached to both Jews and gentiles (non-Jews). In converting gentiles, he did not require men to become Jews first by being circumcised. Over time, as more and more gentiles joined the group, the movement became less and less Jewish.

Another cause of the split between the followers of Jesus and other Jews was the destruction of the Temple in Jerusalem in 70 CE. Jesus died around 30 CE. At the time, many Jews disliked being ruled by the Romans. Before that, they had been ruled by the Greeks, and before that by the Persians, going back six centuries. Some Jews, most notably the Zealots, wanted to fight to free themselves from foreign domination. Hatred of the Romans grew, until in 66 CE there was an open revolt. The Romans responded by destroying the Temple in Jerusalem and much of the rest of the city. After that, being Jewish could no longer consist of sacrificing and worshipping in the Temple – there was no Temple. So, new ways of being Jewish evolved. For the Pharisees, those included prayer and study of the Law and its application to everyday life. That tradition gradually developed into the Judaism led by rabbis (teachers) that is today called simply Judaism. The followers of Jesus, for whom the Law was less important, developed in different ways, eventually becoming the traditions called Christianity. The other two major Jewish groups, the Zealots and the Sadducees, disappeared after the Temple was destroyed.

It was after the destruction of the Temple that the four Gospels were written, and in them we read of tension between Jesus and people called "the Jews." It's unlikely that Jesus would have distinguished himself from "the Jews," since he was one, but the Gospel writers of the 70s, 80s, and 90s had partially or completely split from Jews, and so could portray them unfavorably. John's Gospel, the last to be written, shows the most hostility to "the Jews."

Traditional histories often claimed that after the Temple was destroyed in 70 CE, Christianity "emerged" from Judaism, but today many scholars say that both Christianity *and* rabbinic Judaism grew out of what Jews had been doing before 70 CE. That's how Robert and Mary Coote explain things in their book *Power, Politics and the Making of the Bible* (1990). Alan Segal (1986: 1) says that rabbinic Judaism and Christianity were born together: "One can speak of a 'twin birth' of two new Judaisms, both markedly different from the religious systems that preceded them."

However we think of events following the destruction of the Temple in 70 CE, it's clear that four decades earlier, Jesus, along with his family and friends, were Jews, not Christians.

References

biography.com (online) Jesus Christ Biography, www.biography.com/people/jesus-christ-9354382 (accessed January 8, 2014).

Coote, R. and Coote, M. (1990) *Power, Politics and the Making of the Bible*, Fortress Press, Minneapolis.

Segal, A.F. (1986) *Rebecca's Children: Judaism and Christianity in the Roman World*, Harvard University Press, Cambridge MA.

Tutu, D. (2011) *God Is Not a Christian*, Harper Collins, New York.

Further Reading

Crossan, J.D. (2010) *The Historical Jesus: The Life of a Mediterranean Jewish Peasant*, HarperCollins, New York.

Galambush, J. (2005) *The Reluctant Parting: How the New Testament's Jewish Writers Created a Christian Book*, HarperSanFrancisco, San Francisco.

Sheehan, T. (1986) *The First Coming: How the Kingdom of God Became Christianity*, Random House, New York.

5. Jesus Preached Family Values

A global Christian ministry dedicated to helping families thrive: We provide help and resources for couples to build healthy marriages that reflect God's design, and for parents to raise their children according to morals and values grounded in biblical principles. (Dr. James C. Dobson (online), founder of "Focus on the Family")

Begun in 1977, "Focus on the Family" radio shows are now broadcast on 2000 radio outlets. The web site christian-life-advisor.com promotes: "Christian Family Values. The heartbeat of the Christian family!" Similar programming, along with Christian music, can be found on the Family Life Radio Network. The idea that "family values" are the central message of Jesus, in rather stark contrast to the focus on Jesus' anguished crucifixion, is a rather modern phenomenon.

The American Family Association (AFA) was also founded in 1977, by Donald E. Wildmon, pastor of First United Methodist Church in Southaven, Mississippi. Originally called the National Federation for Decency, AFA now owns and operates nearly 200 radio stations under the American Family Radio banner. Its news program onenewsnow.com is syndicated around the world. Through web sites such as onemillionmoms.com and onemilliondads.com, it rallies its two million online supporters to complain to sponsors of television shows it finds objectionable:

AFA believes that a culture based on biblical truth best serves the well-being of our nation and our families, in accordance with the vision of our founding documents; and that personal transformation through the Gospel of Jesus Christ is the greatest agent of biblical change in any culture. ... It is AFA's goal to be a champion of Christian activism. If you are alarmed by the increasing ungodliness and depravity assaulting our nation, tired of cursing the darkness, and ready to light a bonfire, please join us. Do it for your children and grand-children. (AFA, online)

"Family values" activism quickly became associated with anti-lesbian, gay, bisexual and transgender (LGBT) issues. After Home Depot, the largest home improvement chain in the US, supported several gay rights parades, AFA organized a boycott of their stores. When a Christian employee of Macy's was fired for refusing to let a cross-dressing man use a women's dressing room, AFA organized a boycott of Macy's stores. The headline in the web site trustchristorgotohell.org was: "BOYCOTT SODOMITE MACY'S! Christian woman fired for refusing cross-dressing queer back into women's dressing rooms."

The Family Research Council is another activist Christian movement. It calls itself "the leading voice for the family in our nation's halls of power," and claims that, "Since 1983, Family Research Council (FRC) has advanced faith, family and freedom in public policy and public opinion."

As the term "family values" is used by these Christians, it typically includes opposition not only to homosexuality, but to polygamy, premarital sex, and abortion. For them, these values are grounded in the teaching and example of Jesus. What they fail to take into account is how little Jesus said about any of these matters – or indeed about the nuclear family, which is the "family" in "family values."

Life in ancient Palestine was very different from life today in industrial-ized Western societies. The nuclear family – one father, one mother, and one or more children – is a modern institution. In the Bible, many heroes and religious leaders had not only several wives but also "concubines" – a general term for secondary wives, mistresses, and slaves to have sex with. Abraham, the patriarch of the monotheistic tradition, married Sarah; but when she was unable to get pregnant, he took her slave Hagar as his concubine, and she gave birth to Ishmael. King David had eleven children by seven wives (1 Chronicles 3). His youngest son, Solomon, succeeded him as king and built the Temple in Jerusalem. The Bible tells us that King Solomon had 700 wives and 300 concubines (1 Kings 11:1–3). From before 1000 BCE to well after the time of Jesus – that is, all the centuries during which the Old Testament and New Testament were written – polygamy was legal among the people of Israel, though it was uncommon in the lower classes because few men had enough money to support multiple families.

If we consider how Jesus lived and what he said, too, we can see that he did not valorize the nuclear family. In first century Palestine, a person's descendants and their ancestors determined their identity, so every adult was expected to marry and reproduce. An unmarried 30-year-old man was rare. Jesus, however, did not marry or have children, as far as the historical record shows.

The ideal way of life that Jesus preached was also very different from the modern nuclear family. Today, one or both parents work at full-time jobs, but there is no indication that Jesus ever had any job at all. The family life valorized by Christians today is in a stable home, ideally a house they own. But the Gospels don't indicate that as an adult, Jesus had any stable home.

The Gospels, furthermore, don't describe Jesus' lack of a job and lack of a home as merely his personal choice of lifestyle. They say that he advocated poverty for his followers, too. When Jesus preached, "Blessed are you who are poor, for yours is the kingdom of God" (Luke 6:20), the word he used was not *penēs*, the Greek word for poor peasants, but *ptōchoi*, the term for destitute beggars. That fits with the next line: "Blessed are you who are hungry now, for you will be filled" (Luke 6:21). Many Christians skip these lines in Luke to focus instead on Matthew 5:3: "Blessed are the poor in spirit," which is usually interpreted as praising humility rather than destitution. But, as the *New Oxford Annotated Bible* (Coogan *et al.*, 2010: 1840) comments on Luke 6:20, "The focus is on economic and social conditions, not spiritual states."

At no point does Jesus advocate getting a job, making a living, or saving to support a family. In fact, not only did Jesus not promote stable family life, he seems to have argued against it:

> Do not think that I have come to bring peace to the earth; I have not come to bring peace, but a sword. For I have come to set a man against his father, and a daughter against her mother, and a daughter-in-law against her mother-in-law, and one's foes will be members of one's own household. Whoever loves father or mother more than me is not worthy of me; and whoever loves son or daughter more than me is not worthy of me. (Matthew 10:34–37 NRSV)

More explicit is Jesus' preaching in Luke 14:26: "Whoever comes to me and does not hate father and mother, wife and children, brothers and sisters, yes, even life itself, cannot be my disciple" (NRSV). In Luke 9:59–62, when he tells two men to follow him, he expects them to break immediately with their families, not even saying goodbye:

To another he said, "Follow me." But he said, "Lord, first let me go and bury my father." But Jesus said to him, 'Let the dead bury their own dead; but as for you, go and proclaim the kingdom of God." Another said, "I will follow you, Lord, but let me first say farewell to those at my home." Jesus said to him, "No one who puts a hand to the plow and looks back is fit for the kingdom of God." (NRSV)

Jesus' life and preaching, then, show what John Dominic Crossan (1994: 58) calls "an almost savage attack on family values, and it happens very, very often." But if Jesus wasn't preaching the "family" in family values, what about the "values" part? If the way of life he advocated is quite unlike the nuclear family of today's evangelical Christians, would he not at least agree with their moral judgments about such things as homosexuality, premarital sex, and abortion?

On the issue of homosexuality, Jesus said nothing. Many Christians rely on the teaching of the Hebrew Bible, especially Leviticus 20:13: "If a man lies with a male as with a women, both of them have committed an abomination; they shall be put to death; their blood is upon them"(NRSV). But Jesus challenged many of the teachings from the Hebrew scriptures. The Gospels tell how he was criticized for healing people on the Sabbath (Mark 3:1–5), for instance, and for picking grain to eat on the Sabbath (Mark 2:23–28). These were not petty issues at the time; the penalty was death. (Exodus 31:14, 35:2; Numbers 15:32–36) But Jesus' response was that "The Sabbath was made for humankind, not humankind for the Sabbath" (Mark 2:27 NSRV). Lacking any statements by Jesus on homosexuality, there is no way to be certain he would not have rejected the Leviticus condemnation and its harsh punishments, as well.

It is worth noting that Leviticus also prohibits eating pork and shellfish, for example, but most Christians do not feel bound by those rules. Nor do they impose the death sentence on those who work on the Sabbath, as Exodus 35:2 mandates. Why is it the prohibition of homosexual acts that is considered binding? More to the point, in Jesus' time, gays and lesbians were not widely accepted in Jewish society, but neither were Samaritans, lepers, Roman soldiers, or independent women. Jesus freely associated with members of all these groups, and did what he could to help them. For doing so, he was criticized by the religious authorities. If, as the Gospels indicate, he treated each person as inherently valuable and worthy of love, there is little reason to think that Jesus would support the "family values" movement in condemning people based on their sexuality.

References

AFA (online) *Who Is AFA?* www.afa.net/Detail.aspx?id=31 (accessed January 8, 2014).

Coogan, M.D., Brettler, M.Z., Newsom, C.A. and Perkins, P. (eds) (2010) *The New Oxford Annotated Bible with Apocrypha: New Revised Standard Version.* Oxford University Press, Oxford.

Crossan, J.D. (1994). *Jesus: A Revolutionary Biography*, HarperSanFrancisco, San Francisco.

Dobson, J.C. (online) Focus on the Family, www.focusonthefamily.com/about_us.aspx (accessed January 8, 2014).

6. The Image of the Crucified Jesus Has Always Been Sacred to Christians

> O sacred head, surrounded
> by crown of piercing thorn!
> O bleeding head, so wounded,
> reviled and put to scorn!
> Our sins have marred the glory
> of thy most holy face,
> yet angel hosts adore thee
> and tremble as they gaze.
> (Hymn with words by Henry Williams Baker (1821–1877),
> after Bernard of Clairvaux (1091–1153)
> and Paul Gerhardt (1607–1676))

The most universal symbol of Western Christianity is the cross. Throughout the West, crosses identify churches and other Christian buildings. Since the Middle Ages, the floor plans of most churches have been cross-shaped. Many Roman Catholic churches are named "Holy Cross," and "Cross" and "Calvary" are in the name of many Protestant churches. A standard marker for a Christian grave is a cross. There are thousands of works of art depicting the crucifixion of Jesus – the nailing of Jesus to a cross. Many Christian religious orders incorporate crosses into the design of their clothing, and hundreds of millions of Christians wear crosses as necklaces and other jewelry.

Western Christians are taught that by dying on the cross Jesus saved the human race from eternal punishment. That's why he was born, many would say, and why he lived on earth. Many add that his dying on the cross paid the debt owed to God for human sins, making it possible for people to go to heaven after they die. That atoning death was the most important event in history, according to believers, so it's fitting that the cross symbolize Western Christianity.

In the spring, Christians observe the season of Lent, a time devoted to repentance and reflection on Jesus' crucifixion. The Passionists, an order of Roman Catholic priests, devote their lives to preaching about how Jesus was crucified. They give sermons on how the nails were not pounded through the palms of his hands – if they had been, his weight would have made the nails tear through the flesh of his hands and he would have fallen off the cross. Instead, the nails were pounded between the bones in his wrists, so that they would remain, in excruciating pain, on the cross. Actor/director Mel Gibson in 2004 made the movie *The Passion of the Christ* to dramatize just how much Jesus suffered in being crucified.

But as scholars Rita Nakashima Brock and Rebecca Ann Parker have demonstrated, the emphasis on the crucifixion as the central part of Jesus' mission is a rather late development. In their *Saving Paradise: How Christianity Traded Love of This World for Crucifixion and Empire* (2008: xi), they argue that Christian artwork depicting the crucifixion meant for public display in churches appears only after the ninth century. In Italy, Turkey, and other places where early Christians had lived, they visited churches, monasteries, catacombs, shrines, and museums, where they found dozens of images of Jesus from before the tenth century, but in none of them was he dead on a cross.

Instead, the images of Jesus from the first half of Christian history show him healthy and happy – as a shepherd, a healer, a miracle worker, or a teacher. In many, he is beardless with long hair. He often stands in a beautiful landscape with colorful plants, flowing rivers, and doves, swans, or deer. Brock and Parker summarize:

> As we looked at other early church interiors, we saw more clearly how each captured dimensions of paradise. The spaces placed Christians in a lush visual environment: a cosmos of stars in midnight skies, golden sunlight, sparkling water teeming with fish, exuberant fauna, and verdant meadows filled with flowers and fruit trees ... Paradise, we realized, was the dominant image of early Christian sanctuaries. (Brock and Parker, 2008: xiv).

But if for nine centuries Christians venerated a robust Jesus living in paradise, how did later Christians come to worship an emaciated Jesus being tortured to death? To understand that transformation in Christian imagery, Brock and Parker say, it's important to consider who made the first crucifixion artwork for churches. The oldest surviving such work is the Gero Cross (named for the archbishop who commissioned it) in Cologne Cathedral. It's a full-scale crucifix carved in oak around 965 by Saxons. The Saxons were a Germanic people who had been forcibly converted to Christianity by the armies of Charlemagne, the Frankish king, after he defeated them in a series of wars (772–804). Vanquished, they had to choose between baptism and death. Not only had Charlemagne waged war on the Saxons for more than 30 years, but after winning, he deported 10 000 of them and gave their land to the Abotrites, a group who had helped him defeat them. As Brock and Parker explain, the Gero Cross reflects the violence through which the Saxons had been converted to Christianity. They imposed their tragic vision of their own suffering onto their new religion, making Jesus into a victim like them. In the centuries that followed, crucifixion art became more and more bloody, bringing out the horrific details of Jesus' suffering so central to the vision of the Passionist Fathers and Mel Gibson.

The display of crucifixes in Western churches coincided with an influential shift in Christian theology. It was this period that saw the promulgation of the Atonement theory – the idea that Jesus' crucifixion paid the debt for human sin – in Anselm of Canterbury's (d. 1109) *Cur Deus Homo* (*Why the God-Man?*). Earlier generations of Christians had quite different explanations for what Jesus had accomplished by his life and death. Virtually all Christian theologians said that by sinning, Adam and Eve and all their descendants had fallen under the jurisdiction of Satan, and that the death of Jesus on the cross was part of the bargain God made with Satan to ransom or "save" them. Those thinkers included Origen, Irenaeus, Gregory of Nyssa, Ambrose, Augustine, John Chrysostom, and Gregory the Great. For all of them, Anselm had a simple question: How could Satan possibly have gotten jurisdiction over the human race from the infinite, all-powerful God? God can instantly and effortlessly achieve whatever he wants, so the idea that he had to make a deal with Satan to get the human race back, just couldn't be right.

In place of all redemption theories then current, Anselm proposed his own theory – the Atonement. As the King of the Universe, he said, God is owed complete obedience by his creatures. So when Adam and Eve disobeyed God in the Garden of Eden, they cheated him out of what he was owed. In sinning, they created a debt, and in order for God to forgive their sin, he had to be paid back. Making things worse for the human race, who inherited Original Sin from Adam, an offense against an infinite being – God – is an infinite offense, and so requires an infinite payment.

The human race could not make an infinite payment, of course. Only an infinite being – God – could. So what was needed was an infinite payment *to* God, made *by* God on behalf of humans. That, according to Anselm, is what the death of the God-man, Jesus, accomplished. In Anselm's words, since the payment is one that "none but God can make and none but man ought to make, it is necessary for the God-man to make it" (*Cur Deus Homo*, Ch. 6). Jesus made that payment by dying on the cross.

Anselm's theory of Atonement became popular with Western Christians, but not with Eastern Christians such as the Greek Orthodox, who had officially split from Roman Catholicism in the Great Schism of 1054, after centuries of drifting apart. And because they did not see the crucifixion as the essence of Jesus' life, Eastern Christians did not venerate the crucified Christ. Even in the West, not everyone went along with Anselm. One early critic, Peter Abelard (d. 1142), commented:

> How cruel and perverse it seems that [God] should require the blood of the inno-
> cent as the price of anything, or that it should in any way please him that an
> innocent person should be slain – still less that God should hold the death of his
> Son in such acceptance that by it he should be reconciled with the whole world.
> (*Commentary on Epistle to the Romans*, quoted in Brock and Parker, 2008: 293)

Nevertheless, in Western Christianity, the Atonement Theory prevailed.

Four centuries later, the reformers Martin Luther (c. 1546) and John Calvin (d. 1564) modified Anselm's Atonement Theory to focus on the crucifixion as a punishment for sin. Their ideas are now called the Penal-Substitutionary Theory of Atonement. According to that theory, although Jesus was sinless, God assigned the guilt for people's sins to him, and he, taking their place, bore the punishment they deserved. His death on the cross was a full payment for all human sins, so it satisfied both the wrath and the righteousness of God. Thus God was now free to forgive sinners.

However central the crucifixion has become to Christians in the last 900 years, it was not always so.

Reference

Anselm of Canterbury (2013) *Cur Deus Homo: To Which Is Added a Selection of His Letters*, Hard Press Editions, Stockbridge, MA.

Brock, R.N. and Parker, R.A. (2008) *Saving Paradise: How Christianity Traded Love of This World for Crucifixion and Empire*. Beacon Press, Boston.

7. The Church Suppressed Science in the Middle Ages

A Europe-wide phenomenon of scholarly amnesia … afflicted the continent from AD 300 to at least 1300. During those centuries Christian faith and dogma suppressed the useful image of the world that had been so slowly, so painfully, and so scrupulously drawn by ancient geographers – Daniel Boorstin (1983: x), Librarian of Congress

The quotation above reflects a common misperception about the fate of scientific inquiry at the hands of Christianity in the Middle Ages. Similarly, in *Cosmos*, the all-time best-selling science book in English, astronomer Carl Sagan (1980: 280) presents a timeline of people associated with astronomy that begins in ancient Greece with Thales of Miletus (d. around 546 BCE), and goes up to Hypatia of Alexandria (d. 415 CE), but then skips a thousand years to pick up with Christopher Columbus and Leonardo da Vinci. Sagan's comment on what he calls the "Dark Ages" is: "The millennium gap in the middle of the diagram represents a poignant lost opportunity for the human species." More recently, Charles Freeman (2003) argues that science declined catastrophically after Christianity became the state religion of the Roman Empire.

Even people who haven't read these books have heard that during the "Dark Ages" European Christians thought the earth was flat. It took Christopher Columbus and then modern scientists, so the story goes, to prove that it was round.

Many of us have heard such descriptions of the opposition between science and Christianity so often that we may think of it as an ancient conflict. In fact, it began less than 150 years ago. Only after 1800 did people who studied nature begin calling their work "science" and themselves "scientists." Before that they called what they did "natural philosophy" or "natural history." Over the centuries there had been discussions about "reason" and "faith," but there was no assumed conflict between what we now call "science" and Christianity. In the early 1800s, however, books started to appear with "science" in their titles that discussed how science and Christianity were, or were not, opposed. By 1860 several American colleges and seminaries were hiring professors whose job was to show the compatibility of science with Christianity (Numbers, 2009: 3).

In the late nineteenth century, two influential Americans championed the idea that the Catholic Church in particular has suppressed science: John

William Draper, a scientist, physician, and historian; and Andrew Dickson White, co-founder and first President of Cornell University. According to Draper (1874: 52), the early medieval Church:

> asserted that all knowledge is to be found in the Scriptures and in the traditions of the Church ... The Church thus set herself forth as the depository and arbiter of knowledge ... She thus took a course which determined her whole future career: she became a stumbling-block in the intellectual advancement of Europe for more than a thousand years.

Further, Draper said, "Roman Christianity and Science are recognized by their respective adherents as being absolutely incompatible; they cannot exist together" (1874: 363).

This attack on Catholicism was expanded by Andrew Dickson White in his two-volume *A History of the Warfare of Science with Theology in Christendom* (1896). White's thesis that Catholicism had suppressed science is clear in chapter titles such as "From Creation to Evolution," "From Genesis to Geology," "From Magic to Chemistry and Physics," "From Miracles to Medicine," and "From "Demoniacal Possession To Insanity.""

Despite the popularity of the "warfare" paradigm of the relation between science and Christianity – from Draper and White to Boorstin and Sagan – contemporary historians of science say that it's largely a myth. A useful correction to that myth are the 25 essays collected in Ronald Number's book, *Galileo Goes to Jail and Other Myths about Science and Religion* (2009).

In a chapter titled "That Medieval Christians Taught That the Earth Was Flat," for example, Lesley Cormack notes that the ancient Greeks had figured out that the earth was spherical. Aristotle argued that the changing positions of the constellations in the sky as one moved across the earth showed that the earth must be spherical. Eratosthenes calculated that its circumference was about 25 000 miles; modern estimates put it at 24 902 miles. Early Christian thinkers who mentioned the shape of the earth almost all agreed that it was spherical. They included Ambrose (d. 397), Jerome (d. 420), and Augustine (d. 430). The single dissenter was Lactantius (d. ca. 320), but he rejected all the philosophy and science of the Greeks. Among medieval Christian writers there was similar consensus, with the exception of Cosmas Indicopleustes, a sixth-century Nestorian Christian from Egypt. In the High Middle Ages, Christian writers like Thomas Aquinas cited with approval Aristotle's proof of the spherical shape of the earth.

Those who argue for the opposition between Catholicism and science often cite the early theologian Tertullian (d. ca. 240), who asked in his *Prescription against Heretics*, (2012, Chapter 7), "What indeed has Athens [Greek philosophy] to do with Jerusalem (Christianity]?" Nothing, he concluded. And "What concord is there between [Plato's] Academy and the Church?" None, he claimed. For Tertullian, the life of the Christian is based on faith, not philosophy. But even this fierce opponent of non-Christian sources made use of them when it suited his purposes, as David Lindberg shows (Numbers, 2009: 8–18). In his work *Ad Nationes* (2010, Chapter 3), Chapter 3, for example, when Tertullian wants to refute the idea that the universe could be a god, he argues, "It must needs have been formed either by some being, according to the enlightened view of Plato, or else by none, according to the harsh opinion of Epicurus; and since it was formed, by having a beginning, it must also have an end." But something that has a beginning and an end cannot be a god, he concludes. Here and elsewhere, Tertullian showed considerable knowledge of natural philosophy and philosophy generally. The same is true of other early Christian critics of Greek philosophy, such as Basil of Caesarea (d. ca. 379). But these individuals did not speak for the Church. Indeed, they lived before Christianity was the official religion of the Roman Empire.

When Christianity was named the empire's official ideology, its most influential spokesman was Augustine (d. 430). Indeed, many consider him the most influential Christian thinker in history. And he was in favor of the use of reason. Augustine's general approach is summarized in his slogan "Believe so that you may understand; understand that you may believe" (Letter 120, in Sparrow-Simpson, 2012). There are some things that God had to reveal, Augustine said, such as the nature of Jesus Christ, but there are also many things that humans can know through experience and reasoning, such as the movement of the stars and the nature of plants and animals. He believed that what people have learned about the natural world is not in conflict with what God has revealed, but actually supports it.

Using Aristotle's meaning of "sciences" as kinds of knowledge, in the Middle Ages theology was often called Queen of the Sciences, with "natural philosophy" as one of the theology's handmaidens. This paradigm is at work in Augustine's *Literal Meaning of Genesis* (1982). Explaining how God created the world, Augustine uses dozens of ideas from Greek and Roman science about the planets, the moon, light, sound, weather, seasons, time, tides, the four elements, plants, and animals. To understand the religious significance of God's creation, Augustine says, we have to know something about the things he created and how they operate. Such knowledge comes from natural philosophy – that is, science – which he strongly encouraged so that Christians would not be shunned by more knowledgeable non-Christians:

> Even a non-Christian knows something about the earth, the heavens, and the other elements of this world, about the motion and orbit of the stars and even their size and relative positions, about the predictable eclipses of the sun and moon, the cycles of the years and seasons, about the kinds of animals, shrubs, stones, and so forth, and this knowledge he holds to, as being certain from reason and experience. Now it is a disgraceful and dangerous thing for an infidel to hear a Christian … talking nonsense on these topics; and we should take all means to prevent such an embarrassing situation. (Augustine of Hippo, 1982: 42–43)

It was Augustine's assertion of the compatibility between science and theology that became church policy in the Middle Ages. In fact, church officials supported the development of European universities, many of which grew out of monastery schools and cathedral schools. By 1200, Bologna, Paris, and Oxford had universities, and by 1500 there were 60 across Europe. The University of Oxford began about 1115, with students gathered around Augustinian canons of the Priory of St Frideswide. They were granted the right to confer advanced degrees by Pope Innocent IV in 1254. The University of Cambridge was created around 1209 and recognized by Pope John XXII in 1318.

About 30% of the curriculum in medieval universities dealt with the natural world. By 1500, hundreds of thousands of students had been educated in disciplines like geometry, optics, physics, astronomy, logic, and biology (Grant, 1984). These subjects were part of the undergraduate curriculum and were taught without reference to church doctrine. Theology was taught by a separate faculty, usually at the Masters level, and most university students received no theological training (Shank, 2009). Among the subjects taught at the Masters level, theology was the least popular, trailing law and medicine.

Even in schools of theology, arguments from natural philosophy were often used. The most famous are the Five Ways of proving the existence of God discussed by Thomas Aquinas, an avid reader of Aristotle. The First Way, taken from Aristotle's *Physics*, argues that the motion and other change in the world requires an Unmoved Mover. The Second Way, also from

Aristotle, argues for a First Cause of the things in the universe. The Third Way, "from possibility and necessity," uses the common-sense principle that if the universe had ever been a void, nothing would have ever come from that void. The Fourth Way – for God as the most perfect thing, causing the perfections in other things – Thomas got from *The Book of Causes*, a book that was attributed to Aristotle but was actually derived from the Neoplatonic philosopher Proclus. Thomas' Fifth Way, from the order and design in nature, is much like today's intelligent design argument for God. It comes from many philosophical sources, originally from Plato's *Timaeus*.

These arguments, grounded in natural philosophy, are the most famous work of Thomas Aquinas, and within five decades of his death he was canonized by Pope John XXII. In 1567, he was declared a Doctor of the Church (meaning he was a trusted authority) by Pope Pius V, and in 1879 Pope Leo XIII declared that Thomistic thought was the definitive exposition of Catholic doctrine, and that it must be taught in all Catholic seminaries and universities. None of this recognition by popes could have occurred if the medieval church had been opposed to science.

The following comment about astronomy from John Heilbron can be applied to the sciences generally:

> The Roman Catholic Church gave more financial and social support to the study of astronomy for over six centuries, from the recovery of ancient learning during the late Middle Ages into the Enlightenment, than any other, and probably all, other institutions. (Heilbron, 1999: 3)

The great discoveries of Galileo, Newton, and the Enlightenment were in the future, of course, but the church-supported scientific work of the Middle Ages prepared the way. As Lawrence Principe, Professor of Chemistry and of the History of Science and Technology at Johns Hopkins University, says:

> Historians of science now recognize that the impressive developments of the period called the Scientific Revolution depended in large part on positive contributions and foundations dating from the High Middle Ages ... Medieval observations and theories of optics, kinematics, astronomy, matter, and other fields provided essential information and starting points for developments of the sixteenth and seventeenth centuries. The medieval establishment of universities, the development of a culture of disputation, and the logical rigor of Scholastic theology all helped to provide a climate and culture necessary for the Scientific Revolution. (Principe, 2009: 105)

References

Augustine of Hippo. (1982) The literal meaning of Genesis, translated by John Taylor, in *Ancient Christian Writers: The Works of the Fathers in Translation*, volumes 41–42 (eds Johannes Quaesten *et al.*), Newman, New York.

Boorstin, D. (1983) *The Discoverers: A History of Man's Search to Know His World and Himself*, Random House, New York.

Draper, J.W. (1874) *History of the Conflict between Religion and Science*, D. Appleton and Co, New York.

Freeman, C. (2003) *The Closing of the Western Mind: The Rise of Faith and the Fall of Reason*, Knopf, New York.

Grant, E. (1984) Science in the medieval university, in *Rebirth, Reform, and Resilience: Universities in Transition, 1300–1700* (eds J. Kittleson and P. Transue), pp. 68–102, Ohio State University Press, Columbus OH.

Heilbron, J. (1999) *The Sun in the Church: Cathedrals as Solar Observatories*, Harvard University Press, Cambridge MA.

Numbers, R.L. (ed) (2009) *Galileo Goes to Jail and Other Myths about Science and Religion*, Harvard University Press, Cambridge MA.

Lawrence Principe (2009) That Catholics did not contribute to the scientific revolution, in *Galileo Goes to Jail and Other Myths about Science and Religion* (ed R.L. Numbers), Harvard University Press, Cambridge MA.

Sagan, C. (1980) *Cosmos*, Ballantine, New York.

Shank, M. (2009) That the medieval Christian Church suppressed the growth of science, in *Galileo Goes to Jail and Other Myths about Science and Religion* (ed R.L. Numbers) pp. 19–27, Harvard University Press, Cambridge MA.

Sparrow-Simpson, W.J. (ed) (2012) *The Letters of St. Augustine*, Hard Press Editions, Stockbridge MA.

Tertullian (2010) *Ad Nationes Book II*, Kessinger, Whitefish MT.

Tertullian (2012) *On the Testimony of the Soul and on the "Prescription of Heretics"*, Hard Press Editions, Stockbridge MA.

White, A.D. (1896) *A History of the Warfare of Science with Theology in Christendom*, D. Appleton and Co., New York.

8.   Catholics Are Not Christians

Alert!!!! The Roman Catholic "Church" is Not Christian. Practically all precepts of the Roman Catholic religion contradict the Bible repeatedly … The Roman Catholic church is the largest cult in the world and most preachers will not openly say so because it is so large. (jesus-is-lord.com (online))

According to jesus-is-lord.com and jesus-is-savior.com, Catholics are not Christians. The web site faithdefenders.com provides 10 reasons for this claim. First is the fact that the Catholic Church holds that Mary, mother of Jesus, can intercede with God on behalf of those who pray to her. Second, the Catholic Church teaches that Mary was conceived without Original Sin and that, when she died, she was taken to heaven, body and soul. Also, the Church teaches that Mary was always a virgin. Fourth, the Church teaches that people will go to purgatory, where they will be cleansed of the stain of sin before entering heaven. Fifth, the Church sanctions images of Jesus, Mary, angels, and saints. Perhaps more egregiously, the Church requires people to confess their sins to a priest who is empowered to absolve them, and requires people to receive other sacraments (described by faithdefenders as "works") in order to achieve salvation. The Church also teaches that popes are successors of the original delegate or "vicar" empowered by Jesus to serve as supreme authority for the community. Ninth, Catholics baptize infants in order to remove the stain of Original Sin. And finally, the Church requires celibacy of its priests. For these reasons, the argument concludes, it should be obvious "that Biblical Christianity and Catholic teaching do not agree … One cannot be both a Bible-believing Christian and an observant Catholic at the same time" (faithdefenders.com, online).

This contemporary view reflects the traditional position of Baptists. Among Baptists' earliest official documents is the 1689 *Baptist Confession of Faith* (Baptist Church, online). This creed remains influential among Baptists, having been adopted in 1742 by the Philadelphia Association of Baptist Churches. It contains 32 chapters dealing with key issues of Baptist belief, including those that prompted the separation of Baptists from Anglican Christianity in the first place. Included among the basic beliefs are many of those shared by most Christians, such as belief in Triune God (the "Trinity," a single God with three "persons": Father, Son, and Holy Spirit), the divine origin of all that exists, Original Sin, God's agreement to save those people who do his will (the "covenant"), Jesus as mediator for human salvation, and free will, which is the ability to choose whether or not to believe in Jesus as the sole source of salvation. That is, people cannot earn salvation through doing good works; good works merely manifest that people are already saved by having chosen to believe in salvation through Jesus and undergo full-immersion baptism.

Chapter 26 of the *Baptist Confession of Faith* also discusses the nature of the universal ("catholic") Christian Church (Baptist Church, online). The Church comprises "the whole number of the elect" (those who have chosen to demonstrate their belief in salvation through full-immersion baptism) and it has but one leader, Jesus. "The Lord Jesus Christ is the Head of the church, in whom, by the appointment of the Father, all power for calling, institution, order or government of the church, is invested in a supreme and sovereign manner." The chapter continues: "[N]either can the Pope of Rome in any sense be head thereof, but is that antichrist, that man of sin, a son of perdition, that exalts himself in the church against Christ, and all that is called God; whom the Lord shall destroy with the brightness of his coming." The pope, being the antichrist, cannot be considered a Christian. It follows that those who submit to papal authority, calling themselves Catholics, also cannot be considered Christians.

Catholics, of course, consider themselves Christians. And technically, a Christian is anyone who considers Jesus to be Christ – "Messiah." Christians may disagree with one another, but in common parlance, they remain Christians so long as they choose to identify themselves as Christians.

Still, it is understandable that Baptists reject papal authority. Their historic origins are in English Christianity, which declared itself independent of the pope's authority in the First Act of Supremacy of 1534. King Henry VIII declared himself and his successors leaders of the Church of England. Anyone who disagreed was liable to be considered a traitor. Henry was succeeded by his nine-year-old son Edward VI, whose regents continued and extended Henry's religious policies. When Edward died at age 16, he was succeeded by his half-sister Mary, who repealed the Act of Supremacy and reinstated Catholicism. Anyone who disagreed with her was liable to be considered a heretic. Mary earned the nickname "Bloody Mary" by having hundreds of religious dissidents executed. A number of English clergy went into exile to avoid persecution. Mary's half-sister Elizabeth I succeeded her, and in 1558, the Second Act of Supremacy identified again the British monarch as head of the Church. In response, in 1570 Pope Pius V excommunicated those who obeyed the British monarch Elizabeth I, calling her a heretic. Yet there remained dissent and discontent among clergy for what appeared to be excessive worldliness and politicization of Christianity. It is to one of these early seventeenth-century dissenting clergy, John Smyth, that historians trace the origins of Baptist teaching.

Smyth and his followers stressed purity of Christian teaching, basing themselves solely on Scripture, rather than doctrines devised by Church authorities. Included in Biblical teachings is the notion of the antichrist (mentioned in the epistles of John). The reference is taken as a prediction that when Jesus returns at the end of time, he will confront and defeat this intensely evil person. The phrases used in the 1689 *Confession of Faith*, however – "man of sin," a "son of perdition" – come not from John but from an Epistle attributed to Paul, 2 Thessalonians. That letter argues against the opinion that Jesus had already come back to his community, and said the Second Coming will occur only after terrible things happen and that "man of sin...son of perdition" will be revealed. (2 Thessalonians 2:3).

The use of such explicit terminology clearly indicates that the Baptists at the time felt seriously threatened by the Roman Church. Perhaps that sense of threat has passed, yet the notion that Catholics are not Christians lingers, and not only among online pundits. Differences between Catholics and Baptists were significant enough to be addressed by religious authorities in the last century.

The Southern Baptist Convention of the United States issued a resolution in June 1994 called *Resolution on Southern Baptists and Roman Catholics*. That document reiterated the disagreements between the two:

> Baptists have historically differed from Roman Catholics on such matters as: the nature and means of salvation, the character and function of the church, the role and interpretation of baptism and the Lord's Supper, devotion to the Virgin Mary, the veneration of the Saints, papal infallibility, the structure of church government, and the relation of scripture and tradition as sources of spiritual and teaching authority for belief and practice. (Southern Baptist Convention, 1994)

The resolution conceded, however, that the two denominations shared concerns for the sanctity of human life and family values, opposition to pornography, and "securing the rights of all individuals without respect to difference of religion, race, gender, and class, and many other areas of moral concern." So all "Christian organizations" should work together on shared concerns. Nevertheless, the document concluded that it remains committed to the "historic Baptist doctrine" of justification "by grace alone through faith alone in Christ alone without any addition of good works or human efforts; and we affirm that justification by faith alone is an essential of the Christian message." Therefore, the Southern Baptist Convention "affirm[s] its commitment to evangelism and missionary witness among populations and individuals not characterized by genuine faith in Christ alone." In other words, the document affirms that Catholics still need to be converted so that they may become "part of Bible-teaching, Christ-honoring congregations."

Although slightly ambivalent, this statement may be read as meaning that Catholics still need to convert in order to become Christians. Yet progress has been made in communications between the two denominations. Catholic-Baptist dialogues have been ongoing since the 1980s. In 2007 Pope Benedict XVI convened a series of discussions between Baptists and Catholics. Upon the announcement of Pope Benedict's resignation in 2013, the president of the Baptist World Assembly, John Upton, expressed appreciation for the pope's gracious welcome and respect for the "insights and opinions of other Christian communities." The Assembly's General Secretary Neville Callam observed that Benedict XVI had "provided the Christian community with a rich storehouse of spiritual reflections worthy of detailed study," and that the dialogues have "furthered Christian witness" (Baptist World Alliance, 2013).

References

Baptist Church (online) *The Baptist Confession of Faith of 1689 with Scripture Proofs*, Center for Reformed Theology and Apologetics (CRTA), www.reformed.org/documents/index.html?mainframe=http://www.reformed.org/documents/baptist_1689.html (accessed January 8, 2014).

Baptist World Alliance (2013) *BWA Leaders Laud Pope Benedict XVI*, http://christianchurchestogether.org/baptist-world-alliance-leaders-laud-pope-benedict-xvi (accessed January 8, 2014).

faithdefenders.com (online) *Ten Reasons Why Christians and Catholics Do Not Agree*, www.faithdefenders.com/articles/worldreligions/Ten_reasons_why_Christ_Catho.html (accessed January 8, 2014).

jesus-is-lord (online) *Alert!!!! The Roman Catholic "Church" is Not Christian*, www.jesus-is-lord.com/cath.htm (accessed January 8, 2014).

Southern Baptist Convention (1994) *Resolution on Southern Baptists and Roman Catholics*, www.sbc.net/resolutions/amResolution.asp?ID=964 (accessed January 8, 2014).

Further Reading

Freeman, C.W. (2009) Baptists and Catholics together? Making up is hard to do, *Commonweal*, January 16.

9. The United States Was Founded as a Christian Country

The Constitution established the United States of America as a Christian nation. (US Senator John McCain, candidate for President in 2008, in a 2007 interview with beliefnet.com (Gilgoff, 2007))

In the United States, Christianity and politics are thoroughly intertwined. Church sanctuaries often feature American flags. The US Senate and House of Representatives appoint chaplains, all of whom have been Christian, to open each session with a prayer. Politicians often appeal to God in speeches; some, like Texas Governor Rick Perry, lead Christian prayer services. In 2004, Rev. Al Sharpton, a Baptist minister, campaigned for the Democratic presidential nomination. In 2008, Rev. Mike Huckabee, a Southern Baptist minister, finished second in the delegate count for the Republican nomination. Since 1953, there has been an annual National Prayer Breakfast in Washington, DC on the first Thursday of February. Hosted by members of Congress and organized by The Fellowship Foundation, a conservative Christian group, it is actually a series of meetings, breakfasts, lunches, and dinners, mixing religion, politics, and business.

American coins and currency feature the words "In God We Trust" and the Pledge of Allegiance is to "one nation under God." One verse of the National Anthem is:

> O, thus be it ever when freemen shall stand,
> Between their lov'd homes and the war's desolation;
> Blest with vict'ry and peace, may the heav'n-rescued land
> Praise the Pow'r that hath made and preserv'd us a nation!
> Then conquer we must, when our cause is just,
> And this be our motto: "In God is our trust"
> And the star-spangled banner in triumph shall wave
> O'er the land of the free and the home of the brave!

President Ronald Reagan often used Christian language in his speeches. Accepting the Republican nomination in 1984, he spoke of America as a "city on a hill," a phrase from the Sermon on the Mount (Matthew 5:14) that has resonated with Americans since the Puritan John Winthrop first used it in a sermon in 1630. Reagan's 1989 farewell speech referred to America as "a tall proud city built on rocks stronger than oceans, wind-swept, God-blessed, and teeming with people of all kinds living in harmony and peace."

When Americans celebrate events from their history, they often link them to Christianity. For the country's Bicentennial Anniversary, Jerry Falwell Ministries published a Bicentennial Bible featuring an image of the Liberty Bell on the front cover next to "1776 – 1976," over a quotation from 2 Corinthians 3:17: "... where the Spirit of the Lord is, there is liberty."

Given all this mingling of Christianity with American politics, it's not surprising that many people think that the United States was founded by Christians to be a Christian country. That claim has been made by dozens of politicians and media personalities, such as Senator John McCain in the opening quotation. In fact, however, the US Constitution makes no mention of Christianity, Jesus, God, or the Bible. The Constitution does mention religion, but only to assert that "[n]o religious test shall ever be required as a qualification to any public office or public trust under the United States" (Article 5, Section 3). And the First Amendment to the Constitution went further, insisting that the country would never have an official religion.

Most American colonies, like most European countries of the time, had official religions supported by the government, but the framers of the constitution rejected the idea of an official religion for the new nation. A national religion can become the pretext for supporting tyrants and persecuting minorities, both of which had happened in Europe. The US founders, therefore, insisted that religion be kept out of politics. A precedent for the separation of religion and politics in the Constitution was established in the Virginia Statute of Religious Freedom, written by Thomas Jefferson in 1777 and passed with revisions in 1786. According to James Madison, Jefferson's friend and his successor as President, that Statute "extinguished forever the ambitious hope of making laws for the human mind" (Madison, 1786) It read, in part:

> Be it enacted by General Assembly that no man shall be compelled to frequent or support any religious worship, place, or ministry whatsoever, nor shall be enforced, restrained, molested, or burthened in his body or goods, nor shall otherwise suffer on account of his religious opinions or belief, but that all men shall be free to profess, and by argument to maintain, their opinions in matters of Religion.

The fact that the United States was not founded as a Christian country was stated explicitly in a treaty written under the presidency of George Washington and signed under the presidency of John Adams. In 1796 the new nation completed a treaty with Tripoli (in what is now Libya). Article XI says that because nothing links the United States to Christianity, the American government looks forward to good relations with the largely Muslim state of Tripoli:

> The government of the United States of America is not in any sense founded on the Christian religion – as it has in itself no character of enmity against the laws, religion or tranquility of Musselmen [Muslims] – and as the said states never have entered into any war or act of hostility against any Mahometan [Muslim] nation, it is declared by the parties, that no pretext arising from religious opinions shall ever produce an interruption of the harmony existing between the two countries. (Avalon Project, online)

The fact that the United States was not founded as a Christian nation does not, of course, rule out the possibility that the founders were Christians. But a close look at what they said and wrote shows that most of them were not Christians but deists. Deism is a worldview that arose in the Enlightenment of the eighteenth century and became popular among scientists and intellectuals. Deists believe that God created the world and lets it operate according to the laws of nature, sometimes called scientific laws.

Unlike human laws, the laws of nature cannot be violated. Consider the laws of gravity. If someone is standing directly under a falling rock, it will hit them. Here is one difference between deists and Christians. Christians believe that God answers some prayers by violating the laws of nature. If someone walking through a canyon looked up to see a falling rock, and prayed to God, then God might make the rock change its course or even disappear. But deists say that having established the laws of nature, God would not violate them. Because deists believe that the world is governed by laws of nature, then, they don't believe in miracles or in prayers asking to God to intervene in the natural order of things.

Further, because deists do not believe that God intervenes in nature, they reject the idea that God has revealed Scriptures to human beings. For them, Scripture is a collection of human writings. If God does not intervene in the world, too, then God did not become a human being. Jesus is not God. Deists, therefore, also reject the doctrine of the Trinity.

As a representative sample of the Founding Fathers of the United States, let's consider Benjamin Franklin, Thomas Paine, George Washington, John Adams, Thomas Jefferson, and James Madison. According to most historians, none was a Christian.

Benjamin Franklin (d. 1790) was the oldest of the founders and the most famous American of his time. A scientist, political leader, and writer, he helped organize the revolution and write the Declaration of Independence and the Constitution. In matters of religion, Franklin started out as a Dissenter – a Christian who rejected the Church of England. But Franklin describes a transformative event in his teenage years:

> Some books against Deism fell into my hands... It happened that they wrought an effect on me quite contrary to what was intended by them; for the arguments of the Deists, which were quoted to be refuted, appeared to me much stronger than the refutations; in short, I soon became a thorough Deist. (Franklin, 1996: p. 27)

Because he saw God as the Creator who lets the world operate on its own, Franklin did not think that churches and worship were appropriate. "I cannot conceive otherwise than that He, the Infinite Father, expects or requires no worship or praise from us, but that He is even infinitely above it (Franklin, 1728).

Thomas Paine (d. 1809) is often credited with starting the American Revolution when in January 1776 he published *Common Sense* (Paine, 2005). At the time, most Americans hoped that their differences with Britain could be resolved peacefully, but Paine's incendiary pamphlet argued that Britain would never treat them fairly and so they should declare their independence. In religious matters, Paine was just as revolutionary. His best-selling book *The Age of Reason: Being an Investigation of True and Fabulous Theology* (1794, 1795, 1807) brought deism to the American masses, along with a rational critique of Christianity and all other sectarian religions.

Paine's deism is presented in Chapter 10 of Part I of *The Age of Reason*:

> The only idea man can affix to the name of God, is that of a *first cause*, the cause of all things ... Everything we behold carries in itself the internal evidence that it did not make itself ... and it is the conviction arising from this evidence, that carries us on, as it were, by necessity, to the belief of a first cause eternally existing, of a nature totally different to any material existence we know of, and by the power of which all things exist; and this first cause, man calls God.

If religious leaders had been content with this belief in a first cause, Paine says, they might have formed reasonable institutions. But instead they developed ideas that are incompatible with an eternal, infinite, all-good God:

Whenever we read the obscene stories, the voluptuous debaucheries, the cruel and torturous executions, the unrelenting vindictiveness, with which more than half of the Bible is filled, it would be more consistent that we call it the word of a demon than the word of God. It is a history of wickedness that has served to corrupt and brutalize mankind. (Paine, 1794, 1795, 1807, Part I, section 4)

What is it the New Testament teaches us? To believe that the Almighty committed debauchery with a woman engaged to be married; and the belief of this debauchery is called faith. (Paine, 1794, 1795, 1807, Part II, section 20)

George Washington (d. 1799), perhaps the most revered of the founders, and the country's first president, attended Anglican church services, yet most historians describe him as a deist (Boller 1963: 14–15). This is based on Thomas Jefferson's claim that "Gouverneur Morris had often told me that General Washington believed no more of that system (Christianity) than did he himself" (Thomas Jefferson, 1800). And while Washington seldom wrote about religious matters, he did occasionally express his disdain for the divisiveness of religion:

Religious controversies are always productive of more acrimony and irreconcilable hatreds than those which spring from any other cause. (George Washington, letter to Edward Newenham, October 20, 1792, in Seldes, 1983)

Like Washington, John Adams (d. 1826), the second president of the United States, had a negative attitude toward the many divisions within Christianity, which he thought were based on doctrines created by church leaders, rather than scripture. Indeed, he seemed to reject the authority of the church. "Where do we find a precept in the Gospel," he wrote in his diary, "requiring Ecclesiastical Synods? Convocations? Councils? Decrees? Creeds? Confessions? Oaths? Subscriptions? and whole cart-loads of other trumpery that we find religion incumbered with in these days?" Included in this "trumpery" was the divinity of Jesus, which Adams called "a convenient cover for absurdity" (Adams, 1850: 4).

Thomas Jefferson (d. 1826), the main author of the Declaration of Independence and the third president, believed in the Creator, and in Jesus as a moral teacher. But he rejected the teaching that Jesus is God, referring to the doctrine as "the hocus-pocus phantasm of a God like another

Cerberus, with one body and three heads" (letter to James Smith, December 8, 1822; Adams and Lester, 1983). Like the first two presidents, Jefferson thought that the division of Christians into thousands of denominations was a mistake. In his "Notes on Virginia," he wrote:

> Millions of innocent men, women and children, since the introduction of Christianity, have been burnt, tortured, fined, imprisoned; yet we have not advanced an inch towards uniformity. What has been the effect of coercion? To make one half the world fools, and the other half hypocrites. To support roguery and error all over the earth. (Peden, 1954)

More radical than Adams, Jefferson was very critical of the Gospels: "We discover in the gospels a groundwork of vulgar ignorance, of things impossible, of superstition, fanaticism and fabrications" (Ford, 1904–05: 325). To salvage what he thought were the valuable moral teachings of Jesus, Jefferson edited the New Testament by literally cutting out the supernatural parts and then pasting the remaining parts together. Today it is called *The Jefferson Bible*; he called it *The Life and Morals of Jesus of Nazareth* (Jefferson, 2009). It skips all the miracle stories and ends with a passage from John 19: "Now, in the place where He was crucified, there was a garden; and in the garden a new sepulchre, wherein was never man yet laid. There laid they Jesus. And rolled a great stone to the door of the sepulchre, and departed."

James Madison (d. 1836), often called the Father of the Constitution, was also critical of the various divided churches. In 1785, when the State of Virginia was considering a bill to levy a tax to support the teaching of Christianity, Madison wrote in section 7 of his *Memorial and Remonstrance Against Religious Assessments*:

> Experience witnesseth that ecclesiastical establishments, instead of main-taining the purity and efficacy of Religion, have had a contrary operation. During almost fifteen centuries has the legal establishment of Christianity been on trial. What have been its fruits? More or less in all places, pride and indolence in the Clergy, ignorance and servility in the laity, in both, superstition, bigotry and persecution. (Burkett, 2013)

If, then, the United States was not founded as a Christian nation, when and how did that idea get started? In the nineteenth century, the new country underwent several waves of Christian evangelism – preaching of the Gospel – as well as the birth of new religions like the Church of Jesus

Christ of Latter Day Saints (Mormons) and the Seventh-Day Adventists. Many preachers added to traditional Christian teachings the idea that the new nation had a special relationship to God; some called it "the New Israel." But this sentiment did not reflect the views of the country's founders. So critical of Christianity were they that in a sermon reported in newspapers in 1831, the Reverend Doctor Bird Wilson, an Episcopal minister in Albany, New York, complained that "the founders of our nation were nearly all Infidels," and that of the presidents who had "thus far been elected not a one had professed a belief in Christianity" (Remsberg, 1906: 120).

References

Adams, C. (1850) *The Works of John Adams, Second President of the United States: With a Life of the Author, Notes, and Illustrations*, Volume 2, p. 4, Charles C. Little and James Brown, Boston.

Adams, D.W. and Lester, R.W. (eds) (1983) *Jefferson's Extracts from the Gospels: "The Philosophy of Jesus" and "The Life and Morals of Jesus"*, Princeton University Press, Princeton, 408–410.

Avalon Project (online) The Barbary Treaties 1786–1816: Treaty of Peace and Friendship, Signed at Tripoli November 4, 1796, http://avalon.law.yale.edu/18th_century/bar1796t.asp (accessed January 11, 2014).

Boller, P. (1963). *George Washington and Religion*, Southern Methodist University Press, Dallas.

Burkett, C. (ed) (2013) *50 Core American Documents*, Ashbrook Press, Ashland OH, p. 9.

Ford, P. (ed) (1904–1905) *Works of Thomas Jefferson*, Volume 4. New York: G. P. Putnam's Sons.

Franklin, B. (1728). *Articles of Belief and Acts of Religion*.

Franklin, B. (1996) *Autobiography of Benjamin Franklin*, Dover, New York.

Gilgoff, D. (2007) *John McCain: Constitution Establised a "Christian Nation"*, www.beliefnet.com/News/Politics/2007/06/John-Mccain-Constitution-Established-A-Christian-Nation.aspx (accessed January 8, 2014).

Jefferson, T. (1800) private journal, February, in *The Works*, Vol. 4 (Thomas Jefferson, 1904–1905), G.P. Putnam's Sons, New York, p. 572.

Jefferson, T. (2009) *The Jefferson Bible: The Life and Morals of Jesus of Nazareth*, Wilder Publications, Radford VA.

Madison, J. (1786) *Madison Letter to Jefferson on the Bill Concerning Religious Freedom*, January 22, www.churchstatelaw.com/historicalmaterials/8_7_7.asp (accessed January 11, 2014).

Paine, T. (1794, 1795, 1807) The Age of Reason: Being an Investigation of True and Fabulous Theology. *Common Sense and Other Writings* (T. Thomas, 2005), Barnes and Noble Classics, New York.

Paine, T. (2005) *Common Sense and Other Writings*, Barnes and Noble Classics, New York.

Peden, W. (ed) (1954) *Notes on the State of Virginia*, Chapel Hill: University of North Carolina Press for the Institute of Early American History and Culture, Williamsburg, Virginia, Query 17.

Remsberg, J. (1906) *Six Historic Americans*, The Truth Seeker, New York.

Seldes, G. (ed) (1983) *The Great Quotations*, Citadel Press, Secaucus, New Jersey, p. 726.

5

Myths About Islam, Muslims, and the Qur'an

1. Most Muslims Are Arabs and All Arabs Are Muslim
2. Muslims Worship a Different God
3. The Qur'an Condemns Judaism and Christianity
4. "Jihad" Means Holy War
5. The Qur'an Encourages Violence
6. The Qur'an Condones Mistreatment of Women
7. The Qur'an Promises Suicide Bombers 72 Heavenly Virgins
8. Muslims Reject Democracy
9. Muslims Fail to Speak Out against Terrorism
10. American Muslims Want to Impose Islamic Law on the United States

Introduction

In Chapter 1 we mentioned several human characteristics that lead to myth-making. One is that we are social animals prone to xenophobia – fear of strangers that often leads to hatred. In Chapter 3 we saw examples of that tendency in anti-Semitic myths. In this chapter we see another example: fear and hatred of Muslims. Today it is called Islamophobia, a term first used in a biography of Islam's prophet Muhammad, written in French in 1918, during the French occupation of Algeria – Alphonse Étienne Dinet and Sliman ben Ibrahim's *La Vie de Mohammed, Prophète d'Allah* (1937). The phenomenon has roots going all the way back to Islam's first appearance as a threat to Roman dominance of the Middle East. But it has become a significant phenomenon in the United States and Europe since the atrocities committed by terrorists in the name of Islam over the past 20 years.

50 Great Myths About Religions, First Edition. John Morreall and Tamara Sonn.
© 2014 John Wiley & Sons, Ltd. Published 2014 by John Wiley & Sons, Ltd.

Reference

Dinet, A.É. and ben Ibrahim, S. (1937) *La Vie de Mohammed, Prophète d'Allah,* G.-P. Maisonneuve, Paris.

1.   Most Muslims Are Arabs and All Arabs Are Muslim

> No, Ma'am. [Barack Obama] is a decent family man, a citizen who I just happen to have serious differences with on fundamental questions. (John McCain at a campaign rally in Columbus, Ohio, October 10, 2008, in response to a comment that Mr. Obama was dangerous because he was an Arab (Shear, 2008))

The incident above reveals common myths about Muslims: that all Muslims are Arabs, and that they are to be feared. In fact, the vast majority of Muslims are not Arabs. Islam is the second largest religion in the world, with about 1.6 billion people, or 23% of the global population. There are 22 countries with Arabic-speaking majorities – Algeria, Bahrain, Comoros, Djibouti, Egypt, Iraq, Jordan, Kuwait, Lebanon, Libya, Malta, Mauritania, Morocco, Oman, Qatar, Saudi Arabia, Somalia, Sudan, Syria, Tunisia, United Arab Emirates, and Yemen – but they comprise less than 20% of the Muslims in the world. The vast majority of Muslims are not Arabs.

The country with the greatest number of Muslims is Indonesia, 4000 miles from the nearest Arab country. Indonesia is home to over 200 million Muslims, more than twice the number in Egypt, which is the most populous Arab country. After Indonesia, the countries with the greatest population of Muslims are Pakistan, with 11% of the total number; India, with 10.9%; and Bangladesh, with 9.2%. None of them is an Arab country. Other non-Arab countries with large Muslim populations are Nigeria, with 75.7 million; Uzbekistan, with 26.8 million; China, with 23.3 million; and Russia, with 16.4 million. China has more Muslims than Syria, and almost as many as Saudi Arabia.

Even in the Middle East, the countries with the largest Muslim populations are not Arab. There is no single definition for "Arab," but most commonly, the term refers to those who are native speakers of Arabic. Arabic is a Semitic language, like Hebrew. In fact, Arabic is the most widely spoken Semitic language, followed by Amharic (spoken in Ethiopia, a Christian majority country in East Africa), and then Hebrew (one of the two official languages of Israel; Arabic is the other one). Aramaic, the language Jesus spoke, is also a Semitic language and is still spoken by some people in Syria. The largest populations of Muslims in Middle Eastern countries are in Turkey and Iran. Turkish is part of a different language group, Turkic, with a structure, vocabulary, and script completely different from Arabic. The language of Iran is Persian; in fact, Iran was called Persia until 1935. Persian is an Indo-European language, related to English and German. It uses a modified Arabic script but its vocabulary and structure are also distinct from those of Arabic.

In addition, not all Arabs are Muslim. All Arab-majority countries except Saudi Arabia have significant non-Muslim populations, primarily Christian. Egypt's Christian population is the largest in the Middle East – estimates range from 10 to 18% of the population – although proportionately, Lebanon's is larger: nearly 40% of the population. Although most Middle Eastern Jews moved from Arab countries to Israel after it was founded in 1948, there are still Persian Jews, Turkish Jews, and Arab Jews. The ambassador from Bahrain to the United States, Houda Nonoo, is a Jewish woman.

In the United States, the majority of people identifying themselves as Arab-Americans – nearly two-thirds – are Christian, not Muslim. These include political figures such as Darrell Issa, John Sununu, Spencer Abraham, Donna Shalala, and George Mitchell, as well as sports figures Doug Flutie and Bobby Rahal, fashion designer Joseph Abboud, heart surgeon Michael DeBakey, astronaut Christa McAuliffe, and entertainers Frank Zappa, Paula Abdul, Wendie Malick, Tony Shalhoub, and Salma Hayek.

Confusion about Arabs and Muslims has had tragic repercussions in the arena of hate crimes. There is no doubt that the perpetrators of the terrorist attacks on September 11, 2001 were Arab men. That, of course, does not mean that all Arab men are terrorists but, predictably, hate crimes against Arabs spiked after those atrocious events. Unfortunately, however, hate crimes against Arab Americans and Muslim Americans had also followed the 1995 terrorist attack at the Federal Building in Oklahoma City, Oklahoma, where a truck laden with explosives killed 168 people and wounded over 500. Convicted for that bombing were Timothy McVeigh and Terry Nichols, both white, non-Arab Christians. Furthermore, many people who are neither Arab nor Muslim have been victimized by hate crimes directed at Arabs and/or Muslims. Sikh men, followers of a monotheistic tradition from South Asia and identifiable by their distinctive turbans, have been victimized repeatedly. Just four days after the 9/11 attacks, an Arizona gas station owner, Balbir Singh Sodhi, was murdered in apparent retaliation for the attacks. In November 2009, when a Greek Orthodox priest asked a man for directions, the man beat him with a tire iron, held him on the ground and called 911 reporting that he had captured a terrorist.

Reference

Shear, M.D. (2008) McCain Moves to Soften the Tone at Rallies, if Not in Ads, *Washington Post*, October 11.

2. Muslims Worship a Different God

> The entire world is being convulsed by a religious struggle … whether Hubal, the Moon God of Mecca, known as Allah, is supreme, or whether the Judeo-Christian Jehovah, God of the Bible, is Supreme. (Pat Robertson, chairman of the Christian Broadcasting Network, founder of Regent University, and contender for US Presidency in 1988, speech in Herzliya, Israel, December 2003 (Robertson, 2003))

As the above quote indicates, there is widespread belief that Allah, the God worshipped by Muslims, is different from the God worshipped by other monotheists. Another evangelical preacher who insists that Muslims worship a pagan god is Rod Parsley, television evangelist and pastor of the World Harvest Church in Columbus, Ohio. During the 2008 US presidential election, he campaigned with candidate John McCain. In his book *Silent No More: Bringing Moral Clarity to America … While Freedom Still Rings* (2006), Parsley presents Islam as an "anti-Christ religion" predicated on "deception." The prophet Muhammad "received revelations from demons and not from the true God," and, in fact, he says, "Allah was a demon spirit."

Evangelical Christians are not the only ones to say that Muslims worship a different god. The posting "Why Allah is not God?" on the popular website Islam Watch (online) argues two things. First, Allah could not be the God of the Bible, because he is not morally perfect, since he encourages racism, sexism, slavery, and the slaughter of unbelievers. Second, Muhammad invented Allah to justify his own immoral behavior.

A careful study of the Qur'an and Muhammad's life will reveal to any objective-minded person that Muhammad never talked to a supernatural deity or received revelation from such an entity. Muhammad invented Allah and turned him into a criminal god to give political power to himself and utilize his made-up teachings, allegedly received from a fictional Allah, as a religious and legal justification for his criminality. Allah existed only in Muhammad's imagination. Muhammad and Allah were the same – two in one. Sanctioned by Allah, Muhammad practiced deceit, torture, murder, assassination, massacre, genocide, pillage, robbery, enslavement and rape as halal (legal) acts, deserving of paradise, as long as they were perpetrated on the infidels. These evil, immoral teachings became the eternal laws of Allah (Islam Watch, online).

Despite such claims, "Allah" is just the Arabic word for "the (one) God." It's the word Christian Arabs and Jewish Arabs use to refer to God. Christian missionaries translating the Bible into Arabic used "Allah" for God, something they would not have done if they thought "Allah" meant a pagan god. In the description of the creation of the world on the first page of Genesis, we find "Allah" over a dozen times. In the Arabic translation of the Gospels, Jesus is called the "son of Allah."

Related languages also show the equivalence of "Allah" and "God." In Aramaic, the language Jesus spoke, the word for "God" is "Allaha." In the Maltese language, which is based on Arabic and spoken mostly by Catholics, the word for "God" is "Alla."

Saying that Muslims do not worship "God" because they worship "Allah," then, is like saying that Germans do not worship "God" because they worship "Gott," and Spanish-speakers do not worship "God" because they worship "Dios." By that twisted logic, Germans and Spaniards don't eat "bread" either, because they eat "Brot" and "pan."

Pat Robertson's claim that Allah is the pre-Islamic god Hubal is found in Robert Morey's (2011) book *The Islamic Invasion: Confronting the World's Fastest Growing Religion*. Morey contends that the Sabians were the dominant culture in Arabia before Muhammad, and they worshipped a moon god, calling him "allah." He seems to draw his conclusion that Muhammad worshipped the same moon god from the Qur'an's use of the word "Allah" for God.

Actually, Allah does have pre-Islamic heritage, but not as any single god. As a generic term, it is related to the Hebrew *el*, and could refer to any god. Historic evidence indicates that pre-Islamic Arabs recognized the existence of a powerful creator god, referred to as Allah, who existed along with other, lesser gods. Indeed, the Qur'an refers to three goddesses in the vicinity of Mecca, the birthplace of Muhammad, as daughters of Allah. The same term is mentioned in the ancient Babylonian (present-day Iraq) Epic of Atrahasis (around 1700 BCE), as well as in inscriptions from the Nabataean kingdom (second century BCE in present-day Jordan and parts of Arabia). On the eve of Islam, the Kaaba, a sanctuary in Mecca, was a pilgrimage site for followers of hundreds of tribal gods. Scholars believe it was also associated with this more powerful creator god Allah.

This accords with Islamic belief. According to the Qur'an, the Kaaba was originally built by the patriarch Abraham and his son Ishmael, and dedicated to the only God, Allah, but over the centuries, people had lost their way and reverted to devotion to tribal deities. Muhammad's mission was to remind people of the one true God, Allah. Ultimately, he cleansed the Kaaba of the relics of the false gods and rededicated it to Allah.

This commitment is reflected in the Islamic testimony, "There is no god but God/Allah, and Muhammad is the messenger of God/Allah." It is also reflected in the Qur'an:

> Your Lord is God/Allah, who created the heavens and earth in six days, then established Himself on the throne; He makes the night cover the day in swift pursuit; He created the sun, moon, and stars to be subservient to His command; all creation and command belong to Him. Exalted be God/Allah, Lord of all the worlds! (Qur'an 7:54)

The Qur'an also forbids worship of the moon or anything except the one God: "The night, the day, the sun, the moon, are only a few of His signs. Do not bow down in worship to the sun or the moon, but bow down to God who created them." (41:37)

The Qur'an specifically states to Jews and Christians, "We believe in what was revealed to us and in what was revealed to you; our God and your God are One [and the same]; we are devoted to Him" (Qur'an 29:46). Interestingly, US president George W. Bush accepted this claim. In an October 4, 2007 interview with Al-Arabiya television (Bisahara, 2007), he said, "I believe in an almighty God, and I believe that all the world, whether they be Muslim, Christian, or any other religion, prays to the same God." In the same interview he reiterated, "I believe there is a universal God. I believe the God that the Muslim prays to is the same God that I pray to. After all, we all came from Abraham. I believe in that universality." Yet within days, the Internet and media erupted with outrage over the then-president's claims. In a poll of Evangelical Christian leaders, 79% opposed his views. Several pastors suggested that he be expelled from the church he attends. In an article titled "The Same God?" syndicated columnist Cal Thomas wrote:

> The doctrines of what is called Christianity not only stand in stark contrast to Islam, they also teach something contrary to what the president says he believes ... If we all worship the same God, the president should answer the call of Iranian President Mahmoud Ahmadinejad and Osama bin Laden, convert to Islam and no longer be a target of their wrath. What difference would it make if we all worship the same God? (Thomas, 2007)

Unlike myths based on simple misinformation, this is an example of the tenacity of myths whose roots are in xenophobia. Despite the claims of the Qur'an, of professed Muslims, and of scholars, many people suffering from fear of Muslims simply refuse to accept that Muslims are mainstream monotheists.

References

Bisahara, F. (2007) *Interview with George Bush*, Al Arabiya Television, October 4, www.alarabiya.net/articles/2007/10/05/39989.html (accessed January 10, 2014).

Islam Watch (online) *Why Allah Is Not God*, www.islam-watch.org/Larry/Why-Allah-is-not-God.htm (accessed January 10, 2014).

Morey, R. (2011) *The Islamic Invasion: Confronting the World's Fastest Growing Religion*, Xulon, Maitland FL.

Parsley, R. (2006) *Silent No More: Bringing Moral Clarity to America ... While Freedom Still Rings*, Charisma House, Lake Mary, FL.

Robertson, P. (2003) *Why Evangelical Christians Support Israel*, www.patrobertson.com/Speeches/IsraelLauder.asp (accessed January 10, 2014)

Thomas, C. (2007) *The Same God?* October 8, www.calthomas.com/index.php?news=2062 (accessed January 8, 2014).

3. The Qur'an Condemns Judaism and Christianity

> The Muslim holy book...contends that Allah transformed disobedient Jews into 'apes, despised' (2:65; 7:166), and 'apes and pigs" (5:60). (Spencer 2013)

Preachers, academics, and media personalities who attack Islam often use terms like "Islamofascism" and associate it with a "Clash of Civilizations" to make Islam seem like a strange, foreign religion hostile to Judaism and Christianity. Muhammad, the prophet of Islam, is sometimes described as an enemy of "the Judeo-Christian tradition." In this view, the Qur'an, the scripture that Muslims believe was revealed by God through Muhammad, is to the Bible as the Antichrist is to Christ.

In the 2008 US Presidential election, as mentioned in the last myth, John McCain appeared with Rod Parsley, television evangelist and pastor of the World Harvest Church in Columbus, Ohio. In his book *Silent No More* (2006), Parsley has a chapter, "Islam: The Deception of Allah," that warns about the "war between Islam and Christian civilization."

> I do not believe our country can truly fulfill its divine purpose until we understand our historical conflict with Islam ... The fact is that America was founded, in part, with the intention of seeing this false religion destroyed, and I believe September 11, 2001, was a generational call to arms that we can no longer ignore. (2006: 90)

In the summer of 2010, Rev. Terry Jones, Pastor of the Dove World Outreach Center in Gainesville, Florida, declared that September 11, 2010 would be "International Burn a Qur'an Day." Publicly destroying copies of the Qur'an, he said, would show Christians' righteous contempt for "a religion of the Devil." After entreaties from President Barack Obama and many religious leaders, Rev. Jones cancelled the event. But six months later Jones held a trial called "International Judge the Qur'an Day," with himself serving as judge, wearing judicial robes. The charge was "inciting violence," and after six hours the jury found the Qu'ran guilty. The punishment – destruction by burning – was carried out by Pastor Wayne Sapp.

Attacks like this on the Qur'an and Muhammad go back a long way in Christian history. Just a century after Muhammad died in 632, John of Damascus, the last of the Greek Fathers of the Church, vilified him as a false prophet and heretic. John grew up in Damascus, Syria, under Muslim rule. Part Two of his monumental work *The Fountain of Knowledge*, is "Concerning Heresy" (Chase, 1958:153–159). He describes most heresies in a few lines, but Islam gets several pages. Referring to Muslims as "Ishmaelites," John calls Islam a superstition and a forerunner of the Antichrist. He traces the Muslims' ancient roots back to Abraham and his concubine Hagar. But instead of seeing that lineage as a historic connection confirming the authenticity of the tradition, as Muslims do, John says they were idol worshippers and that Muhammad was a false prophet. Describing the Qur'an as a set of "ridiculous compositions," John ridicules the Qur'an's permission for polygyny, concubinage, and divorce, along with some strange stories not actually found in the Qur'an, and dismisses the entire second chapter of the Qur'an as too full of "stupid and ridiculous things" to even bother enumerating. John then makes the utterly false claim that Islamic law requires female circumcision and expresses exasperation that Muslims don't undergo Baptism or keep the Christian Sabbath (Chase, 1958).

This first authoritative Christian writing about Islam thus describes Muhammad as an immoral heretic saying "stupid and ridiculous things," a rejecter of Christianity. Political competition between the European Christian and Middle Eastern Islamic empires mounted, eventually resulting in a series of European attacks in the Middle East beginning in 1096 – the Crusades. In the context of these wars, Muslims were demonized as heathens, and stories of Muhammad's rejection of Christianity became even more fanciful. According to one popular tale, Muhammad was a cardinal who was so disappointed at not being elected pope that he started the new movement of Islam.

Perhaps no better example of the conviction that Muhammad was an enemy of Christianity exists than Dante's *The Divine Comedy*, considered by some to be one of the greatest works of Western literature. The first volume, *Inferno*, describes nine circles of hell for progressively greater sins. In the ninth ditch of the eighth circle are "sowers of discord," people who tear apart the fabric of society. The prime examples here are Muhammad and his cousin and son-in-law, Ali. Punishments in the *Inferno* fit the crime, so Muhammad and Ali are torn apart by a demon with a sword, over and over for all eternity.

> No cask ever gapes so wide for loss of mid- or side-stave as the soul
> I saw cleft from the chin right down to where men fart.
> Between the legs the entrails dangled. I saw the innards
> and the loathsome sack that turns what one has swallowed into shit.
> While I was caught up in the sight of him, he looked at me and,
> with his hands, ripped apart his chest, saying: 'See how I rend myself,
> 'see how mangled is Muhammad! Ahead of me proceeds Ali, in tears,
> his face split open from his chin to forelock.
> 'And all the others whom you see sowed scandal and schism
> while they lived, and that is why they here are hacked asunder.

A devil's posted there behind us who dresses us so cruelly, putting each of this
crew again to the sword as soon as we have done our doleful round. For all
our wounds have closed when we appear again before him.

(Dante, 2002, Canto 28, 22–42)

Over the centuries, the range of Muhammad's enemies was extended to
include not only Christians but Jews as well. And images of Muhammad
suffering in hell as a result have proliferated. One random contemporary
example:

And who is the greatest sower of discord in Dante's Hell? It is none other than
Muhammad ... who, as I have often observed, was the greatest hater and gen-
erator of hatred in history, the "successful Hitler," teaching Moslems for the
last 1,400 years that all non-Moslems are perverse enemies of Allah who
deserve to be killed for the crime of not believing in Allah and his Prophet;
the man who launched a war of Moslems against all of non-Moslem humanity
that cannot end so long as Islam exists. (View from the Right, online)

In fact, however, Muhammad was rejected neither by Christian nor Jewish
teaching. In seventh-century Arabia where he lived, there was a great deal
of religious diversity. Some were polytheists, some were Jews, some were
Christians, some were Sabians (an ancient monotheistic tradition), and
some were non-sectarian monotheists. These "Hanifs" worshipped one
God – the God of Abraham – but did not identify themselves as Jewish or
Christian or Sabian. The Qur'an mentions all these groups and their
prophets, and presents Muhammad as a prophet calling upon people to
remember and follow the teachings of the Torah and Gospels. The word
"Islam" means "submission"; it is to God that the Qur'an teaches everyone
should submit. Far from rejecting Jews and Christians, then, the Qur'an
embraces them as "People of the Book" who received revelation from the
one and only God.

The Qur'an presents Muhammad as carrying on and purifying the
tradition started by the Biblical patriarch Abraham. That's why Judaism,
Christianity, and Islam are called the "Abrahamic" traditions. Just as Jesus
began his preaching as a reformer within the Abrahamic tradition later
called "Judaism," and started the new Abrahamic tradition later called
"Christianity," so Muhammad was not starting a new religion distinct
from the other Abrahamic traditions. Rather, he was trying to get people
to live in accordance with those traditions. What he preached was the
basic message of the Bible – there is only one God, and he created human

beings to do his will by creating just societies. In the Qur'an, Muslims are told to protect not just mosques but synagogues and churches because "God is worshipped therein."

As Muhammad began preaching in Mecca, his hometown, he saw Jews and Christians as natural allies. After moving to Medina in 622 CE, he established the Constitution of Medina, an agreement between groups there that included several Jewish tribes. It guaranteed equal rights, including religious freedom, as long as everyone upheld the constitution. The Constitution of Medina's guarantees of religious freedom were used as the model for religious freedom wherever Islamic law prevailed.

While the Qur'an reaffirms the Hebrew Bible and the New Testament as God's revelation, it has disagreements with some Jewish and Christian interpretations of those scriptures. The Qur'an rejects the claim that Jews have an exclusive relationship with God, insisting that all people have equal access to God. It also rejects the belief that Jesus is God and that God is a Trinity of three persons. In the Qur'an's view, these claims compromise monotheism. The Qur'an reaffirms the truth and authenticity of the earlier scriptures and simply calls upon people to understand them properly and to live in accordance with their teachings.

All the prophets are presented with profound respect in the Qur'an, especially Jesus, whom the Qur'an describes as one of the greatest prophets, a miracle worker, and the Messiah. The Qur'an says that Jesus was born of a virgin, healed the blind and sick, and brought dead people back to life. It even tells of a miracle not found in the Gospels – shaping a bird out of clay and then breathing life into it (Qur'an 3:39; 5:110). The Qur'an has a chapter named after Mary, Jesus' mother. She is the only woman mentioned by name in the Qur'an, and her name is found more often in the Qur'an than in the Gospels.

The Qur'an calls upon all people to recognize the one God and carry out God's will to establish a just society, to recreate in society the equality all people share in the eyes of the Creator. And it claims that all believers, whether Jews, Christians, or Sabians – "whoever believe in God and the [Last Judgment] and does good deeds, they shall have their reward from their Lord and there is no fear for them nor shall they grieve" (Qur'an 2:62; 5:69). So what is important in the Qur'an's view is not one's religious identity but whether or not one believes the truth and acts with justice. The Qur'an says specifically that not all Jews and Christians are alike. Some of them believe and act righteously, and some don't (3:109–10). So Muslims are told not to argue with them. Tell them, it continues, "Our God and your God are one, and to him we surrender" (29:46).

So widespread is the belief that the Qur'an condemns Christianity and Judaism that some Muslims even believe it. This could result from reading certain passages of the Qur'an out of context. For example, there was a point in the early days of Islam when some Christians and Jews were ridiculing Islam. Despite that, some members of the Muslim community wanted to forge alliances with them. In that context, the Qur'an advised the Muslims not to take these Jews and Christians as allies (5:51). There is also a passage about some members of the communities who had received revelation in the past but turned away from it, and as a "punishment" and "lesson" to others, God turned them into apes (or apes and swine, in one reference) (5:59–60; 2:63–65; 7:166).

But other verses make clear that the Qur'an does not condemn all Jews and all Christians. In fact, the Qur'an insists that Jews and Christians "are not all alike." Some of them are righteous so there is nothing to prevent friendship with them (3:113–114; 3:199). The Qur'an is very clear in its acceptance of religious diversity. It concludes, in fact, that religious diversity is part of the divine plan:

> For each of you [religious communities], We have appointed a law and a method [of practice]. If God had so willed, He would have made you one community. But [in order] to test you through that which he has given you [the three scriptures], compete in good works. You will all return to God and He will make clear to you the matters on which you differed. (Qur'an 5:48; cf. 11:118)

References

Chase, F.H. (ed) (1958) *The Fathers of the Church: St. John of Damascus, Writings.* Catholic University of America Press, Washington.
Dante (2002) *Inferno*, translated by Robert Hollander, and Jean Hollander, Anchor, New York.
Parsley, R. (2006) *Silent No More: Bringing Moral Clarity to America … While Freedom Still Rings*, Charisma House, Lake Mary, FL.
Spencer, R. (2013) *Does the Qur'an Teach Hate?* www.jihadwatch.org/2013/09/robert-spencer-in-frontpage-magazine-does-the-quran-teach-hate.html (accessed January 8, 2014).
View from the Right (online) *Muhammad in Hell*, www.amnation.com/vfr/archives/018507.html (accessed January 8, 2014).

Further Reading

Reeves, M. (2003) *Muhammad in Europe: A Thousand Years of Western Myth-Making*, New York University Press, New York.

Sonn, T. (2010) *Islam: A Brief History*, second edition, John Wiley & Sons, Ltd, Chichester.

Tolan, J. (2002) *The Saracens: Islam in the Medieval European Imagination*, Columbia University Press, New York.

4. "Jihad" Means Holy War

What does the Arabic word *jihad* mean? One answer came last week, when Saddam Hussein had his Islamic leaders appeal to Muslims worldwide to join his jihad to defeat the "wicked Americans" should they attack Iraq; then he himself threatened the United States with jihad. As this suggests, jihad is "holy war." Or, more precisely: It means the legal, compulsory, communal effort to expand the territories ruled by Muslims at the expense of territories ruled by non-Muslims. (Daniel Pipes (2002))

In spring 2013 Pamela Geller, described by the New York Times as "executive director of the pro-Israel group American Freedom Defense Initiative" (Yaccino and Teng, 2007) and avid blogger (her blog, Atlas Shrugs, can be found at http://atlasshrugs2000.typepad.com) began a campaign to educate the public about the true dangers of jihad. It involved posting pictures and quotations from terrorists advocating killing Jews, and was a response to a campaign that American Muslims were running. The Muslims' campaign featured ads in an effort to counter the stereotypes of Muslims as terrorists (Yaccino and Teng, 2007).

Despite the efforts of non-Muslims such as Geller, Muslims remain convinced that their understanding of the meaning of jihad is accurate. Yet so common is the assumption that "jihad" means "war" or "holy war" or "war against infidels" that those are the most common definitions given of the term on online dictionaries.

In fact, the term "jihad" is used by Muslims exactly the way "crusade" is used by Christians. It is a generic term for concerted effort or struggle against major obstacles, such as injustice, disease, or poverty. Unfortunately, its misuse by terrorists to rationalize their actions has led to confusion about its meaning. "Jihad" does not mean "holy war." Its meaning is much broader than that, and can only be understood within the context of Islamic teachings.

Islam sees itself as mainstream monotheism. It shares history and values with Judaism and Christianity, its siblings in the religious tradition that began with the covenant between God and Abraham (and therefore called the Abrahamic tradition). Jews and Christians are called "People of the Book" in Islam because they, too, received true revelation from the prophets. The Qur'an often refers approvingly to the Torah and the Gospels, calling upon people to remember their teachings. According to Islamic teaching, all prophets have called upon humanity to do the same thing. They must obey the command to recreate in society the equality all people share in the eyes of God. God created all human beings equal – not in wealth or power or talent but in moral responsibility, basic rights, and dependence upon God. The Qur'an says that God designated human beings as his stewards, to protect and maintain that equality, paying special attention to society's weakest members: the poor, orphans and slaves. It recognizes that this is a difficult task. Human beings tend to be weak and sometimes lose their courage in the face of adversity. But the Qur'an promises guidance, and forgiveness when we go astray. What is important is that we continue to make the effort. God promises great reward to those who continue the struggle sincerely, and grueling punishment for those who do not. The basis of judgment is our effort. God will judge us not on the basis of great achievements but on the basis of our intentions. All those who struggle in the way of God, as the Qur'an puts it, those who believe and do good works – whether Jewish, Christian, Muslim or otherwise – have nothing to fear. "Believers, bow down and prostrate yourselves in prayer and worship your Lord and do good deeds, and you will prosper. And struggle for God as you should struggle" (Qur'an 22:78–79). That struggle is *jihad* in Arabic, the language of the Qur'an.

There are two levels of jihad. All efforts to control one's baser instincts – greed, laziness, self-concern – are aspects of "greater jihad." But there are times when the struggle for justice entails fighting. The Qur'an says that in some cases, suffering in patience is recommended. In Chapter 16, Muslims are told that "those who emigrated in God's cause after they were wronged, [God] shall surely lodge them in this world in a goodly lodging, and the wage of the world to come is better…" (16:42). But in other cases, those who have suffered oppression are told to "call [the oppressors] to the way of your Lord with wisdom and good advice, and dispute with them in the better way … And if you punish, do so as you have been punished; and yet surely if you are patient, it is better for those who are patient" (16:126–127). In Chapter 22:40 the Qur'an declares, "Permission is given to those [who fight] because they were wronged; surely God is able to help them." Similarly, just as God commanded the Israelites to fight their oppressors, and kill them if necessary (Deuteronomy 20:10–14), the Qur'an says, "Fight in the way of God those who fight you, but do not commit aggression; God does not love aggressors" (2:191). The chapter continues:

> And kill [those who fight against you] wherever you find them
> and drive them out from where they drove you out;
> persecution is worse than killing.
> But do not fight them at the Holy Mosque
> unless they fight you there.
> Then, if they fight you, fight them.
> That is the recompense of unbelievers.
> But if they stop, surely God is
> forgiving and merciful.
> Fight them until there is no persecution
> and religion is God's. Then if they
> stop, there [shall be] no aggression
> except against the oppressors.
>
> (Qur'an 2:191–94)

When the struggle for justice requires fighting, it is called "lesser jihad."

Islamic law cannot control the "greater jihad," of course, since it involves virtually every effort to "do good and prevent evil," as the Qur'an puts it. But it does prescribe extensive legislation to control military jihad. Military jihad can only be declared by a duly constituted government, it must be preceded by due warning and efforts to reach a peaceful settlement (the "call to Islam"), civilians – particularly women, children, the elderly, and clergy – must be protected, property must not be destroyed unnecessarily, and requests for ceasefire must be honored.

These legal requirements for jihad clearly exclude terrorism. For that reason, Islamic authorities around the world have condemned the attacks of 9/11, as well as other terrorist attacks, as violations of Islamic law. In fact, there is a category in classical Islamic law that covers terrorism: *hirabah*. Hirabah is a term used to cover highway robbery, piracy, and all unprovoked attacks in which innocent people lose their lives. It is the only crime in Islamic law with a mandatory death sentence. Classical Islamic law prescribes various punishments for theft, adultery, false accusation of adultery, apostasy, and drunkenness, all with strict rules of evidence and allowance for extenuating circumstances. But hirabah is considered such a heinous crime because it violates the very purpose of Islam. The term *islam*, meaning "submission to the will of God," is related to the term *salaam*, which means "peace." An Islamic society is considered to be one in which basic human rights (life, religion, family, property, and mind/dignity) are protected and all members therefore live in peace. Hirabah is related to the term *harb*, which means "war." But it is not the kind of war allowed by Islamic law and known as "lesser jihad." *Harb* is illegal warfare, and often is associated with areas that are hostile to Islam, where human rights and dignity are not protected. Hirabah and terrorism are thus the opposite of Islam. Just as in other mainstream monotheisms, while it may sometimes be justified as a last resort, in Islamic teaching there is nothing holy about war.

References

Pipes, D. (2002) What is jihad? *New York Post*, December 31, 2002, www.daniel pipes.org/990/what-is-jihad (accessed January 8, 2014).

Yaccino, S. and Teng, P.S (2013) Using billboards to stake claim over jihad. *International New York Times*, March 6, www.nytimes.com/2013/03/07/us/ad-campaigns-fight-it-out-over-meaning-of-jihad.html?pagewanted=all&_r=0 (accessed January 8, 2014).

Further Reading

Afsaruddin, A. (2013) *Striving in the Path of God: Jihad and Martyrdom in Islamic Thought*, Oxford University Press, New York.

Esposito, J. (2003) *Unholy War: Terror in the Name of Islam*, Oxford University Press, New York.

Lawrence, B. (1998) *Shattering the Myth: Islam Beyond Violence*, Princeton University Press, Princeton NJ.

5. The Qur'an Encourages Violence

Question: "Does the Qur'an really contain dozens of verses promoting violence?"

Summary Answer: The Qur'an contains at least 109 verses that call Muslims to war with nonbelievers for the sake of Islamic rule. Some are quite graphic, with commands to chop off heads and fingers and kill infidels wherever they may be hiding. Muslims who do not join the fight are called "hypocrites" and warned that Allah will send them to Hell if they do not join the slaughter. Unlike nearly all of the Old Testament verses of violence, the verses of violence in the Qur'an are mostly open-ended, meaning that they are not restrained by the historical context of the surrounding text. (*What does the Religion of Peace Teach About Violence?* [sic] (TheReligionofPeace.com, online))

Thanks to the atrocities committed by terrorists in the name of Islam, many people have become convinced that the Qur'an really does teach that Muslims should continually engage in violence as a means to ensure that all people become Muslims. Since Muslims currently make up about 23% of the world's population, this claim might well give non-Muslims reason to fear. Fortunately, however, very few Muslims view their religion the way it is depicted in the above quotation from the sarcastically-titled web site "The Religion of Peace." In fact, the vast majority of Muslims live in accordance with their perception of Islam as a religion of peace, and believe that the Qur'an's calls for violence are indeed historically contextualized, just like the Hebrew Bible's command to kill all the men, women, children, and animals in Jericho and Ai (Joshua 6:20–21; 8:1–29).

We have noted above that Islam condemns suicide as well as terrorism. Muslims understand jihad as concerted effort to be good people and do the will of God. When that effort involves military conflict, it must be conducted in accordance with strict rules that require that it be declared only as a last resort, by a duly acknowledged head of state, and that non-combatants be protected. Since terrorist attacks violate all of those requirements, they are condemned. Instead of qualifying as jihad, terrorism is classified in Islamic law as *hirabah*, unlawful warfare. As the Qur'an says, "If anyone kills a person – unless in retribution for murder or for spreading corruption in the land – it is as if he kills all mankind, while if any saves a life, it is as if he saves the lives of all mankind." (5:32)

There are, however, verses in the Qur'an that do call for fighting. They are traditionally known as the "Sword Verses" and are found in Chapter 9 (Surat al-Taubah) of the Qur'an. The main one is:

And when the sacred months have passed, then slay the polytheists wherever you find them and capture them and besiege them and sit in wait for them at every place of ambush. (Qur'an 9:5, the "Sword Verse"; cf 9:29, included by some commentators as a Sword Verse)

Those unacquainted with the Qur'an's overall teaching and mainstream interpretation of this verse may well read this as an open-ended command to kill people who worship more than one god, provided it is not done during a truce. That is, after all, how the verse begins. But there are two issues that must be taken into consideration in order to comprehend how the verse is understood by mainstream Muslims.

First, the Qur'an is read in terms of its historical context, and that context changed over the 22-year period during which the Qur'an was delivered to the community of believers in seventh-century Arabia. The Qur'an describes itself as "guidance for the people." It includes general moral principles that are considered eternally valid, such as the demand that people be honest, sincere, generous with those in need, and patient during times of strife. It also includes advice that is geared to the specific challenges the community was facing. And when the circumstances changed, sometimes the specific advice changed.

For example, when Muhammad first began preaching his message of social justice, criticizing those who hoarded wealth and oppressed the poor, he attracted a popular following among the poor, and hostility from many of the rich. The wealthy people of Mecca began to persecute Muhammad's followers, and caused them a great deal of suffering. Weak and defenseless, they sought guidance about how to respond. In that context the Qur'an advised them to bear their suffering with patience and to avoid acts of vengeance. The Qur'an says:

> Revenge against evil is an evil, too; whoever pardons and makes peace, his reward is with God. As for those who defend themselves when they have been wronged, there is not blame; only oppressors are blameworthy ... But if one is patient in adversity and forgives, this is indeed the best resolution of affairs. (42:40–43)

Elsewhere, it says, "As for those who fled their homes after persecution and struggled actively and were patient to the last, your Lord will be forgiving and merciful." (16:110)

Eventually Muhammad and his followers moved from their home town in Mecca to Medina, north of Mecca, where they were welcomed by local tribes and were able to establish a strong and prosperous community. But the people from Mecca continued to attack them, and they sought guidance from Muhammad. As it happened, the conflict with the Meccans became most dire during a period in the calendar that was traditionally set aside as a truce. This was a tribal society living in the desert on very scarce resources. There was fierce competition for these resources, and tribes often waged raids on one another. The traditional "months of truce" had been established as a kind of time-out, when tribes could make their religious pilgrimages and carry out trade without fear of being accosted. So the Muslim community was conflicted. Unlike their situation in Mecca, they were now strong enough to defend themselves, but not only had they been told that enduring hardship patiently was preferable, now they were being attacked during the months of truce. What should they do?

In this changed context, the Qur'an gives the Muslims permission to fight:

> They ask you [Muhammad] about fighting during the months of truce. Tell them that to fight [during the months of truce] is a serious offense. But to keep people from serving God, to violate the sanctity of the mosque, to evict its people – these are worse than fighting during the months of truce. Discord and strife are worse than killing. (2:217; cf. 22:39–40)

This was the context for the Sword Verses.

There was another challenge facing the beleaguered Muslim community: some of the people attacking them were actually members of their own tribes. This is a classic conundrum for tribal peoples, one that forms a key element in Hinduism's beloved *Bhagavad Gita*. In that epic story, there was a tribal war and the hero did not want to do battle with his kinsmen. But Lord Krishna counseled him to fight anyway because it was his duty. Similarly, the Qur'an acknowledges that people are hesitant to fight. So it tells them they should not put tribe and the properties they left behind in Mecca ahead of the survival of the Muslim community (9:24). Instead, they must fight until the persecution stops and the attackers are willing to acknowledge the sovereignty of the Muslim community.

Yet even with the permission to fight in self-defense, and the command to engage in battle when they are being attacked, Muslims are reminded: "But if they should repent, establish prayer, and give charity, let them go their way. Indeed, God is forgiving and merciful." This is the second half of the Sword Verse quoted above (9:5). The very next verse continues: "And if any of the polytheists seeks your protection, then grant it to him so they he may hear the words of God. Then deliver him to his place of security. That is because [the polytheists] are people without knowledge. So long as they behave honorably toward you, behave honorably toward them. Surely God loves those who are honorable" (9:6–7). In a similar passage, the Qur'an repeats the call for the Muslims to fight those who are attacking them but not to be the ones who start it. "Expel them from where they have expelled you, for [causing] strife is worse than killing. And do not fight them in the sacred mosque unless they fight you there … Then if they stop, then indeed God is forgiving and merciful." (2:190–92)

So, no, non-Muslims need not fear that Muslims will lie in wait for them and wage continuous warfare until they all become Muslims. Just as the Hebrew Bible's instruction to fight those who "refuse to make peace," and "put to the sword all the men in it," and take the women, children, livestock and "everything else in the city…as plunder" (Deuteronomy 20:10–14, NIV) is not read as an eternal command, so too are the Qur'an's Sword Verses read in historical context. And while the Sword Verses are directed toward the specific circumstances of battle, other verses provide more general guidelines. Key among them is: "Fight in the way of God those who fight you, but do not commit aggression" (2:190). Furthermore, when hostilities have ended, "God does not forbid you from showing kindness and dealing justly with those who have not fought you about religion and have not driven you out of your homes. God loves the just" (60:8).

References

TheReligionofPeace.com (online) "What does the Religion of Peace Teach About Violence? www.thereligionofpeace.com/quran/023-violence.htm (accessed January 8, 2014).

Further Reading

Afsaruddin, A. (2013) *Striving in the Path of God: Jihad and Martyrdom in Islamic Thought*, Oxford University Press, New York.
Esposito, J.L. (2003) *Unholy War: Terror in the Name of Islam*, Oxford University Press, New York.
Lawrence, B. (1998) *Shattering the Myth: Islam Beyond Violence*, Princeton University Press, Princeton NJ.

6.   The Qur'an Condones Mistreatment of Women

The Qur'an mandates these punishments. It gives a legitimate basis for abuse, so that the perpetrators feel no shame and are not hounded by their conscience or their community." (Ayaan Hirsi Ali (2013: 307), *Infidel*, discussing abuse of women among Muslims)

In the last several decades, the mistreatment of women and girls has been prominent in world news, with hundreds of stories about rape, the abortion of female fetuses, girls being denied health care or education, "honor killings," "dowry deaths," and female genital mutilation. These stories come from diverse countries around the world, but those that come from Muslim communities have come in for special attention. They are the stories most likely to mention the religion of the perpetrators and to associate the mistreatment with the religion. Some news programs and many anti-Islamic web sites directly blame the abuse of females on Islam itself, saying that its scripture, the Qur'an, authorizes men to abuse women.

The quotation cited above is a case in point. Ayaan Hirsi Ali recounts the hideous treatment she underwent as a child in Somalia, at the hands of people who believed they were religiously justified in their abuse. Her experiences were so terrible that they caused her to reject Islam and become an atheist.

In another example of the myth that Islam condones violence against women, the home page of a website called "Infidel Task Force," (www.infideltaskforce.com) declares, "We are against Radical Islam and the terror it brings." Infidel Task Force features centrally the work of Wafa Sultan, a Syrian-born psychiatrist who emigrated to the United States in 1989. Her book *A God Who Hates: The Courageous Woman Who Inflamed the Muslim World Speaks Out Against the Evils of Islam* (2009) is based on her bitter memories of growing up in Syria, where, she says, Islam encourages men to treat women as little better than dogs. She describes a wide range of abuses, including an incest rape where the man murdered the woman when he learned that she was pregnant. After years of thinking about such cases, Dr Sultan concludes that the abuse of females in Muslim countries, along with other kinds of violence by Muslim men, come from a single source – Islam. The God of the Qur'an, she says, is a god of hate.

Wafa Sultan and Ayaan Hirsi Ali are examples of former Muslims who have undergone terrible abuse and identified its source as Islam. But other Muslims see abuse of women as a violation of Islam. The Pakistani (Pashtun) teenager Malala Yousafzai, for example, who was shot in the face as she rode the bus to school, said in a speech to the United Nations, "The terrorists are misusing the name of Islam and Pashtun society for their own personal benefits ... Islam is a religion of peace, humanity, and brotherhood" (Yousafzai, 2013).

There are numerous Muslim scholars who recognize that abuse of women does indeed take place in Muslim communities and that some Muslims believe it is sanctioned by the Qur'an. These scholars therefore focus their energies on demonstrating that the Qur'an is actually a document whose treatment of women is not only more extensive than that of any other religion but is devoted to protecting the rights of all people, women included.

The Qur'an is unique among monotheistic scriptures in explicitly addressing both females and males. In an iconic verse:

> Whoever does good deed, male or female, shall enter Paradise. Those who have surrendered to God, male and female, believing men and women, sincere men and women, truthful men and women, patient men and women, humble men and women, charitable men and women, men and women who keep the fast, modest men and women, men and women who remember God often – for them God has prepared forgiveness and a rich reward. (33:35)

The world in which Muhammad lived had enormous disparity between the rich and poor, and widespread disrespect for women. It was not uncommon for impoverished people to kill infant girls, since they were less economically productive and the families couldn't support them. The Qur'an forbids this practice, saying that at the Final Judgment, victims of female infanticide will be asked, "For what sins were [you] slain?" (81:8). The Qur'an further criticizes those who don't value the birth of a girl. When such a parent becomes embarrassed that his offspring is female and wonders "whether he shall keep her in disgrace or push her into the ground," the Qur'an says, this is pure evil (16:57–58). It insists further that daughters as well as sons must inherit from their parents. This is a right that was denied European women until the end of the sixteenth century (Kofsky, 1988: 317, 342).

On the assumption that women will marry, and mandating that husbands support their wives and children, the Qur'an stipulates that their inheritance share is half that of their brothers (if they have brothers; 4:7–12). Nevertheless, women are allowed to earn and control their own wealth. The Qur'an says, "Men shall have a share of what they have earned and women a share of what they have earned" (4:33). Furthermore, the Qur'an prohibits the traditional "bride price," whereby the groom gives a gift to the parents of the bride, which appears as a payment for a purchase. The Qur'an stipulates that the dowry must be given to the bride herself to do with as she chooses (4:4). Similarly, the Qur'an forbids the inheriting of women as if they were property, as was common before Islam (4:19).

The Qur'an also intervenes in a number of pre-Islamic marriage practices in ways that protect women from abuse. In pre-Islamic Arabia, women were indeed treated as property and men could marry as many as they could afford, and discard them at will. The Qur'an limits polygyny (multiple wives). When discussing orphans and their need for protection, it states, "If you fear that you will not treat orphan girls justly, then marry them as you please, two or three or four. But if you fear that you will not be just, then [marry] just one [orphan] or your slave" (4:3). As well, the Qur'an describes marriage as a relationship sustained by bonds of "love and mercy" (30:21). It says that spouses should be like protective garments for one another (2:187). It also prohibits capricious divorce, requiring two temporary separations and arbitration by honorable community members. If, after that, the couple cannot get along, then they can divorce (65:1–2).

The Qur'an is indeed a document of its time. As noted above, it acknowledges slavery. As in other traditions at the time, slavery was integral to the socioeconomic fabric. And as in Judaism, a child born to a man's slave had the same rights as children of his wives. But the Qur'an advocates for human dignity and encourages people to free slaves. Today, slavery is illegal in all countries, including Muslim ones. Discussion of perhaps the Qur'an's most controversial verse pivots upon this issue: the historic context of many verses.

The controversial verse is Chapter 4:34:

> Men are responsible for women, by means of what God has favored some with, and with what they spend out of their own money. Righteous wives are devout and guard what God would have them guard in [their husbands'] absence. If you fear high-handedness from them, remind them [of the teachings of God], then leave them alone in their beds, then *idribuhunna*. If they obey you, you have no right to act against them: God is most high and great.

The verse is controversial not because of the idea that men are heads of households. This is common in religious traditions, including Christianity. Paul's letter to the Ephesians teaches, "Wives, be subject to your husbands as to the Lord. For the man is the head of the woman just as Christ also is the head of the church … just as the Church is subject to Christ, so must women be to their husbands in everything" (5:22–24, New English Bible). Progressive Muslims, like progressives in other traditions, may dispute that traditional view, but Qur'an 4:34 is particularly controversial for two other reasons. First, it appears to mean that men are responsible for – or, in some translations, even "in charge of" women – because they support them. But we know, for example, that Muhammad's first wife, Khadija, was wealthy and probably 15 years older than Muhammad, and that he worked for her. Since Muhammad's example is normative for Muslims, it's difficult to argue that the Qur'an means that men must always be the breadwinners and thus lawmakers within a family. More controversial, however, is the meaning of the term left untranslated in the verse. Traditionally, *idribuhunna* was interpreted as "hit" or "strike," and many translations today still use that translation, adding the traditional caveat that the blows must be light and never on the face.

On the other hand, a number of contemporary interpreters translate the verb as "go away from" or "depart from" them. The verb has several meanings in Arabic and examples outside of the Qur'an can be found to show that it had a number of meanings, including those mentioned in diverse translations (perhaps similar to the way "strike" can mean "hit" or "set out" or "dawned on" in English). But more importantly, the translation "beat them" or even "strike them" violates both the letter of the Qur'an and the normative example established by Muhammad. Elsewhere in the Qur'an, husbands are told that they must never "harm" or "oppress" wives, even those with whom they cannot get along (65:6).

There is no denying that many Muslims continue to believe that it is acceptable for husbands to discipline their wives physically. This has given rise to widespread reform movements within Islam over the past century and a half. Since the late nineteenth century, they have been calling upon Muslims to properly understand their own scriptures in order to elevate the status of all members of society, with special focus on women. Yet there is also no denying that religious norms are often confused with cultural norms. The case of the Taliban in Afghanistan and Pakistan is the most salient. "Taliban" means "students" in the Pashtun language, and these "students" are primarily from the massive Pashtun tribal confederation. Pashtuns have a profound commitment to their ancient tribal honor, traditionally based on generosity, bravery, and women's chastity. The mere suggestion that a female has engaged in unsanctioned sexual activity may be considered sufficient provocation for her relatives to kill her as a sign that their tribal honor is intact. That is why women are kept segregated from men and within the confines of the home. Presumably, it is why Pakistani teenager Malala Yousafzai – a Pashtun – was shot by a tribesman when she insisted on leading other girls to school. But Malala knows that Islam does not sanction such behavior, even though her assailants may believe otherwise. That is why, when she addressed the United Nations following her release from hospital in July 2013, she proclaimed: "The terrorists are misusing the name of Islam and Pashtun society … Pashtuns want education for their daughters and sons" (Yousafzai, 2013).

So while there are undoubtedly Muslim women who have suffered griev-ously at the hands of Muslims who believe their abuse is religiously sanc-tioned, the argument that the Qur'an sanctions abuse of women is impossible to maintain in view of the Qur'an's overall teaching and the example set by Muhammad.

References

Ali, A.H. (2013) *Infidel*, Atria, New York.

Kofsky, A.S. (1988) Narrative analysis of women's property rights in Jewish and Anglo-American law, *Journal of Law and Religion* 6: 317, 342.

Sultan, W. (2009) *A God Who Hates: The Courageous Woman Who Inflamed the Muslim World Speaks Out Against the Evils of Islam*, St. Martin's, New York.

Yousafzai, M. (2013) Text of Speech at the United Nations, July 12, https://secure.aworldatschool.org/page/content/the-text-of-malala-yousafzais-speech-at-the-united-nations

Further Reading

Ahmed, Leila. (1993). *Women and Gender in Islam: Historical Roots of a Modern Debate*.: Yale University Press. New Haven, CT.

Wadud, Amina. (1999). *Qur'an and Woman: Rereading the Sacred Text from a Woman's Perspective*.: Oxford University Press. New York.

7.   The Qur'an Promises Suicide Bombers 72 Heavenly Virgins

Don't die a virgin. Terrorists are up there waiting for you. (Sign on a gas station in Milwaukee (Hausmann, 2013))

The idea that Muslim men are welcomed to heaven by 72 virgins has caught the fancy of Western popular opinion. It is cited in dozens of books and websites, and has become fodder for comedians and Islamophobes alike. For example, in December 2011, comedian Denis Leary's production company posted on whosay (www.whosay.com/DenisLeary) a six-year-old parody of cartoon character Charlie Brown converting to Islam and becoming a terrorist, with hopes of 72 virgins.

The claim is well known among Muslims, as well, and undoubtedly some take it literally. Conservative commentator Pamela Geller's (2009) web site went to the trouble of recording several Muslims' claims that the belief is based on the Qur'an. The 72 virgins claim is most widely associated with terrorists, however, who allegedly believe their earthly suffering will be offset by the pleasures offered in heaven.

In reality, however, Islam does not promise any reward to those who commit suicide, or to those who engage in acts of terrorism. As discussed above, both suicide and terrorism – the indiscriminate killing of innocent people – are condemned as grave sins in Islam.

The Qur'an specifically condemns suicide: "Do not kill (or destroy) your-selves: for God has surely been to you Most Merciful! If any do that in aggression and injustice, soon shall We cast them into the Fire: And easy it is for God" (4:29–30). The prohibition of suicide is repeated throughout Islamic teachings, reflecting despair, or loss of hope in God. It is forbidden in Islamic law.

Terrorism is also condemned in Islamic law. There are hundreds of con-demnations of terrorist acts made by Muslim authorities available online at http://kurzman.unc.edu/islamic-statements-against-terrorism. Many of the condemnations point out that terrorist acts cannot be counted as jihad. Again, as noted above, jihad refers to struggling to do the will of God. It can include self-restraint (traditionally called "greater jihad") and any kind of effort to further the Islamic goal of social justice. When the struggle for justice must take military form, it is subject to extensive legislation, including the require-ment that it be declared only as a last resort, by a duly acknowledged head of state, and that non-combatants be protected. Terrorist attacks meet none of those requirements and are therefore condemned. Instead of qualifying as jihad, terrorism is classified in Islamic law as *hirabah*, unlawful warfare.

Hirabah is forbidden for two major reasons. First, innocent people are killed. The Qur'an says that "if anyone kills a person – unless in retribution for murder or for spreading corruption in the land – it is as if he kills all mankind, while if any saves a life, it is as if he saves the lives of all mankind" (5:32). Secondly, random violence causes everyone to become fearful, and that causes social disharmony, "disorder in the land." This kind of fear is considered the opposite of the sense of peace and security that Islam is meant to bring. "Peace" is part of the standard Islamic greeting: *Salam alaykum*, "Peace be with you." The terms *salam* and Islam have the same Arabic root. Because of the enormity of the damage done, then, Islamic law mandates capital punishment for terrorism.

But what about people who do live righteously and earn eternal reward in heaven? Does the Qur'an teach that they will be greeted in heaven by dozens of virgins?

Like the Bible, the Qur'an describes the afterlife in graphic detail, comparing the suffering in hell to burning in fire, and the pleasures of heaven to a garden full of physical delights. People will sit on comfortable couches upholstered with beautiful fabric, there will be abundant water and fruit and meats and even wine that produces neither intoxication nor hangovers. And there will be chaste and ageless companions for everyone. It is these "chaste companions" or "partners" that have been interpreted by some traditional commentators as females who have never had sex.

In four passages, the term "houri" is mentioned, twice as partners for those in heaven (44:54, 52:20), and once as a reward (56:22–24). The references are brief and elliptical, however, and the term "houri" is not from an Arabic root, so its meaning is a matter of speculation. Language scholars assume it referred to lustrous white color, and indeed the adjective "pearly" is also used in the same context. The Qur'anic references modify the word "eye" so the phrase comes out as "white-eyed" or "with eyes lustrous as pearls." But what could "white-eyed" or "pearly-eyed" partners refer to?

Historians of religion see a parallel between the Qur'an's brief references to lustrous partners and the ancient Zoroastrian teaching about angelic figures who guide the souls of the righteous to heaven. Zoroastrianism, the ancient religion of Persia, teaches that people will be judged at the end of time. Those who have been honest and just will be rewarded; those who have not will be punished. In some descriptions, judgment will be in the form of a challenge. People will have to walk across a narrow bridge suspended high over smoldering pools of molten rock. On the other side of the bridge is Paradise. The souls of the pure will glow with a light that is reflected on the other side, in the form of a pure (or "virginal") figure, a kind of soul twin or partner who will guide the righteous safely across the chasm and into Paradise where they will be united.

The belief in such guides for the soul is found in some African traditions as well as in folk traditions in Judaism and Christianity, where they often take the form of angels. Scholars call such figures "psychopomps," and many interpret the Qur'anic houris as just such figures. The traditional commentators who interpreted them in sexual terms were doubtless unaware of the psychopomp phenomenon. They probably knew that the number 72 is mentioned nowhere in the Qur'an, but in a stunning coincidence, the number 72 is a special number in Zoroastrianism, representing the 72 chapters of Zoroastrian scripture. Zoroastrian men wear a special belt during prayer made up of 72 perfectly white wool threads. It is probably not a coincidence that the name for this belt – kushti (or kusti) – means "pathfinder" or "guide for the soul."

References

Geller, P. (2009) 72 Virgins… Myth or Truth? Atlas Shrugs, January 19, http://atlasshrugs2000.typepad.com/atlas_shrugs/2009/01/72-virgins-myth-or-truth.html (accessed January 8, 2013).

Hausmann, J. (2013) "Don't Die a Virgin" Gas Station Sign Stops Traffic, www.heavy.com/news/2013/03/dont-die-a-virgin-gas-station-sign (accessed January 8, 2014).

8.   Muslims Reject Democracy

We must adhere to Islam and Islam alone. We should not be conned or succumb to the disingenuous and flawed narrative that the only way to engage politically is through the secular democratic process. It is prohibited and haram [forbidden]. (Leader of conservative Muslim group, Hizb ut-Tahrir, at a rally in New South Wales, Australia, July 4, 2010 (R.E.A.L Organisation, 2010)).

In view of comments such as that of the outspoken Hizb ut-Tahrir group cited above, it is perhaps not surprising that many people believe Muslims reject democracy. Indeed, many non-Muslim scholars have voiced this opinion. Most famous among them was American political scientist Samuel Huntington. He looked around Muslim-majority countries and found that they were "overwhelmingly nondemocratic: monarchies, one-party systems, military regimes, personal dictatorships, or some combination of these, usually resting on a limited family, clan, or tribal base and in some cases highly dependent on foreign support" (Huntington 1996: 113). Huntington gained notoriety for predicting a "clash of civilizations" between the "Islamic civilization" and the democratic West. So entrenched was the perception that Muslims were at least content without democracy that the wave of democratic uprisings that began in Tunisia in 2010 – the "Arab Spring" – shocked many observers. As then-Secretary of State, Hillary Clinton, put it, "We're facing an Arab awakening that nobody could have imagined and few predicted just a few years ago. And it's sweeping aside a lot of old preconceptions." (Myers, 2011) The preconception she was talking about is that Muslims reject democracy.

In fact, neither Hizb ut-Tahrir nor others who reject democracy speak for the majority of Muslims. Recent polls have demonstrated that Muslims worldwide overwhelmingly favor democracy. The results of the first ever Gallup global poll of Muslims' opinions were published in Esposito and Mogahed (2008). Covering views from 1.3 billion people in some 40 Muslim-majority countries, the poll found that "when asked what they admire most about the West, Muslims frequently mention political freedom, liberty, fair judicial systems, and freedom of speech." When the pollsters probed more deeply regarding specific components of democratic governance, they found that "substantial majorities in nearly all nations surveyed (95% in Burkina Faso, 94% in Egypt, 93% in Iran, and 90% in Indonesia) said that if drafting a constitution for a new country, they would guarantee freedom of speech, defined as "allowing all citizens to express their opinion on the political, social, and economic issues of the day" (Esposito and Mogahed, 2008).

The data presented in the Gallup polls clearly demonstrate that twenty-first century Muslims, on the whole, support democracy. Conducting vast opinion polls among Muslim communities across the globe is a recent phenomenon, but had the same questions been asked in the twentieth century, the results may have been different. There was, in fact, a distinct hesitancy among Muslim political reformers to use the term "democracy." That's because some early reformers rejected its use, saying it was alien to Islam. Allowing human beings unfettered freedom would allow people to give legal sanction to immoral actions, so the reasoning went, such as prostitution and theft. These concerns stemmed from the experience of Muslims during the period when European countries controlled most Muslim countries. Syria, Morocco, Algeria, and Tunisia, for example, got independence from France only in the 1940s to the 1960s. Egypt and Iraq got independence from Britain in the 1950s, and Libya got independence from Italy in the same period. The European countries were all democracies but behaved extremely immorally, in the view of the people they colonized.

Despite the rejection of the term "democracy," however, these early reformers still called for representative, consultative governments, with a balance of power between legislative and executive branches, and human rights, including religious freedom. And by the late twentieth century, mainstream reformers overcame their distaste for the "d" word and began to use it widely. Rachid Ghannouchi (1994), for example, the leader of the Islamist al-Nahda party that won the majority of votes in Tunisia's first democratic elections, explained that Islamic governance is inherently democratic and there is no sense in refusing that term since that only confuses non-Muslims. Mohamed Khatami, elected president of Iran in 1997, similarly insisted that the best form of government for Muslims in the modern world is democracy (1997).

In 2013, two of the governments brought to power in the elections demanded by Arab Spring activities, have encountered opposition. Egypt's Muslim Brotherhood-led government was unseated in a popularly supported military coup, and Tunisia's al-Nahda-led government continues to face popular displeasure. But as in Western democracies, opposition to people elected through democracy is quite different from opposition to democracy itself.

Following the Arab Spring uprisings, the Pew Research Center (2012) conducted a poll of six Muslim-majority countries about attitudes toward democracy. The results: "More than a year after the first stirrings of the Arab Spring, there continues to be a strong desire for democracy in Arab and other predominantly Muslim nations. Solid majorities in Lebanon, Turkey, Egypt, Tunisia and Jordan believe democracy is the best form of government, as do a plurality of Pakistanis." Regarding more specific aspects of democratic governance, solid majorities support equal rights for women, although, of course, there were more women than men who expressed this view. Not surprisingly, some Arabs registered disenchantment with democracy in light of the turmoil that has accompanied the democratic transitions. Egyptian support for democracy was down 4 points in 2012 from the 71% support in 2011, for example. Nevertheless, the numbers reveal consistent support for democracy and democratic principles.

References

Esposito J. and Mogahed, D. (2008). *Who Speaks for Islam? What A Billion Muslims Really Think*, Gallup Press, New York.

Ghannouchi, R. (1994) *Islam and Civil Society in Tunisia*. Presented at "Islam and Civil Society in South Africa: Prospects for Tolerance and Conflict Resolution" conference at University of South Africa, Johannesburg, August 6.

R.E.A.L. Organisation (2010) *Hizb ut-Tahrir Attacks Democracy, Freedom in Australia*, July 6, www.realcourage.org/2010/07/hizb-ut-tahrir-attacks-democracy-in-australia (accessed January 10, 2014).

Huntington, S. (1996) *Clash of Civilizations*, Simon and Schuster, New York.

Khatami, M. (1997) *Hope and Challenge: The Iranian President Speaks*, Institute of Global Cultural Studies, Binghamton University, Binghamton, NY.

Myers, S.L. (2011) Tumult of Arab Spring Prompts Worries in Washington, *New York Times*, September 17.

Pew Research Center (2012) Most Muslims Want Democracy, Personal Freedoms and Islam in Political Life, July 10, www.pewglobal.org/2012/07/10/most-muslims-want-democracy-personal-freedoms-and-islam-in-political-life (accessed January 9, 2014).

ut-Tahrir, H. (2010) *Hizb ut-Tahrir Attacks Democracy, Freedom in Australia*. http://www.realcourage.org/2010/07/hizb-ut-tahrir-attacks-democracy-in-australia/ (accessed January 10, 2014).

Further Reading

Esposito J. and Voll, J. (2012) *Islam and Democracy*, Oxford University Press, New York.

9. Muslims Fail to Speak Out against Terrorism

Why do Muslims fail to speak out against terrorism? (Dr Alvin Augustus Jones, radio host, during interview of Kamran Pasha about his novel *Mother of the Believers* (Pasha, 2009))

Author Kamran Pasha reported being asked the question above as an example of a perennial, but false claim: "It is a question that I get almost every single day, and it leaves me flabbergasted" (Pasha, 2009). With good reason. In fact, Muslim authorities have consistently and repeatedly condemned terrorism since terrorism emerged as a political tool among Muslims. The first joint statement against terrorism, "The Arab Convention on the Suppression of Terrorism," was issued by the Arab League in 1998.

Appealing to "humanitarian" principles and Islamic law, the document excluded actions by groups struggling to liberate their territories from foreign occupation and, beyond that, condemned attacks on individuals, sabotage, and the manufacture, selling, and possession of "weapons, munitions or explosives, or other items that may be used to commit terrorist offences."

The 1998 Arab League statement was in response to terrorism conducted in Arab countries. During the 1990s, the Jama'a Islamiyya, a radical group, conducted numerous terrorist attacks in its campaign to bring down the Egyptian government. The most egregious was the November 1997 attack at Luxor, which killed 62 people, mostly tourists, but overall the majority of their victims were Egyptians. Then as now, in fact, the majority of victims of terrorism conducted in the name of Islam are Muslims. In December 2009, the US Military Academy at West Point published a report on the victims of al-Qaeda's terrorism, which concluded that "the vast majority of al-Qa'ida's victims are Muslims ... From 2004 to 2008, only 15% of the 3,010 victims were Western" (Helfstein *et al.*, 2009: 1). The report includes the victims of the Madrid and London bombings. Since 2004, the US Department of State has issued annual reports on terrorism worldwide, Islamic and otherwise. Its 2012 report (National Counterterrorism Center, 2012) concluded: "Muslims continued to bear the brunt of terrorism. ... In cases where the religious affiliation of terrorism casualties could be determined, Muslims suffered between 82 and 97 percent of terrorism-related fatalities over the past five years."

Regardless of the identity of the victims, Islamic authorities condemn terrorism. While many Muslims could not believe that Muslims could actually perpetrate such atrocities, Muslim authorities worldwide spoke out with unqualified condemnations. This began on the day of the attacks, when the chairman of the American Muslim Alliance, Dr. Agha Saeed, said, "These attacks are against both divine and human laws and we condemn them in the strongest terms. The Muslim Americans join the nation in calling for swift apprehension and stiff punishment of the perpetrators, and offer our sympathies to the victims and their families" (Kurzman, online). On September 12, 2001, the Secretary-General of the Organization of the Islamic Conference, the only body representing all Muslim-majority countries, issued this statement:

> Following the bloody attacks against major building and installations in the United States yesterday, Tuesday, September 11, 2001, Dr. Abdelouahed Belkeziz, secretary-general of the 57-nation Organization of the Islamic Conference (OIC), stated that he was shocked and deeply saddened when he heard of those attacks which led to the death and injury of a very large

number of innocent American citizens. Dr. Belkeziz said he was denouncing and condemning those criminal and brutal acts that ran counter to all covenants, humanitarian values and divine religions, foremost among which was Islam. (Press Release, Jeddah, Saudi Arabia, September 12, 2001; Kurzman, online)

Shaykh Yusuf al-Qaradawi is perhaps the best known and most widely respected Sunni Muslim cleric in the world today. His television program, *Al-Shari`ah wa'l-Hayah* (*Sharia and Life*), is viewed by millions weekly. He is well known for his ardent defense of Palestinian rights, including their right to use guerilla tactics against Israelis. But in response to the 9/11 attacks, he issued the following statement:

> Our hearts bleed for the attacks that have targeted the World Trade Center, as well as other institutions in the United States, despite our strong opposition to the American-biased policy towards Israel on the military, political, and economic fronts. Islam, the religion of tolerance, holds the human soul in high esteem and considers the attack against innocent human beings a grave sin. This is backed by the Qur'anic verse which reads: "Whosoever kills a human being [as punishment] for [crimes] other than manslaughter or [sowing] corruption on the earth, it shall be as if he has killed all mankind, and whosoever saves the life of one, it shall be as if he had saved the life of all mankind ([5]:32)." (Press Release, Jeddah, Saudi Arabia, September 12, 2001; Kurzman, online)

Also known for his support of Palestinians and condemnation of US militarism is Ayatollah Ali Khamene'i, the supreme ruler of Iran. Following 9/11 he proclaimed:

> Killing of people, in any place and with any kind of weapons, including atomic bombs, long-range missiles, biological or chemical weapons passenger or war planes, carried out by any organization, country or individuals is condemned ... It makes no difference whether such massacres happen in Hiroshima, Nagasaki, Qana, Sabra, Shatila, Deir Yassin, Bosnia, Kosovo, Iraq or in New York and Washington. (Khamene'i, 2001)

Similarly, in a joint statement issued September 14, 2001, the leaders of Egypt's Muslim Brotherhood, Pakistan's Islamist group the Jamaat-i Islami, Bangladesh's Jamaat-i Islami, the Islamist Palestinian resistance movement HAMAS, the Tunisian Islamist Nahda Party, the Pan-Malaysian Islamic Party (PAS), and 40 other Muslim authorities proclaimed:

The undersigned, leaders of Islamic movements, are horrified by the events of Tuesday 11 September 2001 in the United States which resulted in massive killing, destruction and attack on innocent lives. We express our deepest sympathies and sorrow. We condemn, in the strongest terms, the incidents, which are against all human and Islamic norms. This is grounded in the Noble Laws of Islam which forbid all forms of attacks on innocents. (Kurzman, online)

Recognizing that the 9/11 terrorists claimed they were punishing Americans for their government's support of Israel's violation of Palestinian rights, the joint statement continues: "God Almighty says in the Holy Qur'an: 'No bearer of burdens can bear the burden of another.'" (MSANews, 2001).

Following the attacks in Madrid, London, and Boston, similar condemnations were issued. For example, the Fiqh [Islamic Law] Council of North America issued a fatwa (authoritative legal ruling) endorsed by the Council on American-Islamic Relations (CAIR), the Islamic Society of North America (ISNA), the Muslim American Society (MAS), the Association of Muslim Social Scientists (AMSS), the Association of Muslim Scientists and Engineers (AMSE), the Muslim Public Affairs Council (MPAC),

...and more than 130 Muslim organizations, mosques and leaders in the United States. We have consistently condemned terrorism and extremism in all forms and under all circumstances, and we reiterate this unequivocal position. Islam strictly condemns religious extremism and the use of violence against innocent lives. There is no justification in Islam for extremism or terrorism. Targeting civilians' life and property through suicide bombings or any other method of attack is haram—prohibited in Islam—and those who commit these barbaric acts are criminals, not "martyrs." (Kurzman, online)

Not only do Muslim authorities condemn terrorism but they also argue that Muslims have the responsibility to stop terrorists. The Islamic Commission of Spain issued a fatwa following the Madrid bombings, claiming, "Muslims ... are not only forbidden from committing crimes against innocent people, but are responsible before God to stop those people who have the intention to do so" (March 10, 2005; Kurzman, online). These and dozens of similar statements by Muslims condemning terrorism have been compiled by Professor Charles Kurzman at the University of North Carolina. They can be found online at Islamic Statements Against Terrorism (http://kurzman.unc.edu/islamic-statements-against-terrorism). Just one month after the 9/11 attacks, the North American Fiqh Council issued another fatwa, assuring

American military personnel who were Muslim that their responsibility to defend their country supersedes the traditional prohibition against killing Muslims. The fatwa states that "[a]ll Muslims ought to be united against all those who terrorize the innocents, and those who permit the killing of innocents without a justifiable reason." Therefore, "[I]t's acceptable for the Muslim American military personnel to partake in the fighting in the upcoming battles against whomever their country decides has perpetrated terrorism against them" (al-Qaradawi *et al.*, 2001).

Muslims do, therefore, speak out against terrorism. A 2011 Gallup Poll of Muslim Americans found that "[a]t least 7 in 10 American adults from all major religious groups agree that [terrorist] attacks are never justified, but Muslim Americans again are the most opposed, with 89% rejecting such attacks" (Naurath, 2011). Yet the myth that Muslims don't speak out against terrorism persists. Following the Boston Marathon bombing in April 2013, the question was raised again. In response, one exasperated Muslim, the author Qasim Rashid, posted a blog for the *Huffington Post* titled "Do You Even Hear Muslims When We Condemn Violence?" (Rashid, 2013).

References

al-Qaradawi, Y (2001) *Sheikh Yusuf Al-Qaradawi Condemns Attacks against Civilians: Forbidden in Islam*, Press Release, Jeddah, Saudi Arabia, September, 12.

al-Qaradawi, Y., al-Bishri, T., al-Awa, M.S., al-Khayyat, H., Houaydi, F. and al-Alwani, T. (2001) *Fatwa on Muslims in the Military*, September 27. Arabic original and authorized English translation posted at http://www.unc.edu/~kurzman/terror.htm (accessed January 11, 2014).

Arab League (1998) The Arab Convention on the Suppression of Terrorism, www.unodc.org/tldb/pdf/conv_arab_terrorism.en.pdf (accessed January 9, 2014).

Belkeziz, A. (2001) Secretary-General of Organization of the Islamic Conference, Press Release, Jeddah, Saudi Arabia, September 12, 2001.

Fiqh Council of North America (2005) "*Fatwa by U.S. Muslims against Religious Extremism*." Plainfield, Indiana, July 25.

Helfstein, S., Abdullah, N. and al-Obaidi, M. (2009) *Deadly Vanguards: A Study of al-Qa'ida's Violence against Muslims*, Combating Terrorism Center at West Point Occasional Papers Series, West Point, NY.

Islamic Council of Spain (2005) "*Fatwa against Osama bin Laden by the Islamic Council of Spain*", March 10.

Khamene'i, A. (2001) "*Leader Condemns Massacre of Defenseless People*". Islamic Republic News Agency, Jeddah, Saudi Arabia, September 16.

Kurzman, C. (online) *Islamic Statements against Terrorism*, http://kurzman.unc. edu/islamic-statements-against-terrorism (accessed January 10, 2014).

MSANews (2001) "*A Clear Criterion (Bayan) … Forty-six Leading Muslim Scholars and Intellectuals Condemn Attacks in New York and Washington*". September 14.

National Counterterrorism Center (2012) Country reports on terrorism 2011, Report July 31, 2012, Annex of Statistical Information, www.state.gov/j/ct/rls/ crt/2011/195555.htm (accessed January 10, 2014).

Naurath, N. (2001) *Most Muslim Americans See No Justification for Violence*, August 2, www.gallup.com/poll/148763/muslim-americans-no-justification-violence. aspx (accessed January 10, 2014).

Pasha, K. (2009) The big lie about Muslim silence on terrorism, *Huffington Post*, April 20, www.huffingtonpost.com/kamran-pasha/the-big-lie-about-muslim_ b_188991.html (accessed January 9, 2014).

Rashid, Q. (2013) *Do You Even Hear Muslims When We Condemn Violence?* April 22, www.huffingtonpost.com/qasim-rashid/do-you-even-hear-muslims-when- we-condemn-violence_b_3125564.html (accessed January 10, 2014).

10. American Muslims Want to Impose Islamic Law on the United States

The vast majority of the world's 1.4 billion Muslims adhere to a view of their religion that agrees on the need to impose Sharia, or Islamic law, on the world. (Michael Mukasey, Attorney General under President George W. Bush, March 16, 2013 (Seitz-Wald, 2013))

A web site titled "Creeping Sharia" (http://creepingsharia.wordpress.com) asked, "When will the world have the courage to defeat this scourge?" in response to the bombing of a church in Peshawar, Pakistan on September 22, 2013, which killed at least 75 people according to initial reports. A video titled "Islam's Global War on Christianity" posted on the site explains that Islam has been persecuting Christians and other minorities for centuries, in "the exact same patterns." The Peshawar atrocities provided more evidence, from the perspective of the web site, that Muslims are trying to take over America and replace its laws with Shariah. As it's "About" page claims, "'Creeping Sharia' is a scourge occurring across the free world. We'll define it as 'the slow, deliberate, and methodical advance of Islamic law (Sharia) in non-Muslim countries' … Another frequently used term is 'stealth jihad.'" (Creeping Sharia, online)

Many Americans seem to share this fear of Islamic law. In July 2013 North Carolina joined Arizona, Kansas, Louisiana, Oklahoma, South Dakota, and Tennessee, becoming the seventh state in the United States to ban Islamic law, "Sharia." The 2010 Oklahoma ban was overturned by a federal judge, finding that it violated the First Amendment's ban on "establishment" of any official religion. In order to avoid violating the First Amendment, the states that successfully banned Sharia changed the language of their bills, substituting "foreign" for "Sharia" law. Fifteen more states proposed anti-Sharia laws in 2012.

According to an August 2011 poll by the Public Religion Research Institute and the Brookings Institution, almost a third of Americans believe Muslims are trying to establish Sharia as US law (Marrapodi, 2011).

In the run-up to the 2012 US presidential election, two of the three Republican frontrunners encouraged Americans to fear a takeover of the American legal system by Sharia, Islamic law. Rick Santorum called Sharia an "existential threat" to America (Elliott, 2011). "We need to define it and say what it is," he said. "And it is evil. Sharia law is incompatible with American jurisprudence and our Constitution" (Benen, 2011) Candidate Newt Gingrich called for a federal law to ban Sharia. In a talk to the American Enterprise Institute in Washington in 2010, he said, "I believe Sharia is a mortal threat to the survival of freedom in the United States and in the world as we know it." There are violent jihadis such as al-Qaeda, he warned, but also "stealth jihadis" who use "political, cultural, societal, religious, intellectual tools ... They're both engaged in jihad, and they're both seeking to impose the same end state, which is to replace Western civilization with a radical imposition of Sharia" (McMorris-Santoro, 2010).

Concerns about Islamic law replacing US law reveal at least three mistaken beliefs about Sharia. The first two were addressed by the leader of the Islamic Center of Nashville, Imam Mohamed Ahmed, during the anti-Sharia debate in Tennessee. First, the imam pointed out that Islam teaches that followers must obey the laws of the land where they live (Smietana, 2011). This is an established position in Islamic law. In early days of Islam, when the vast majority of Muslims lived under governments ruled by Islamic law, the requirement that people obey the law of the land wherever they were, pertained primarily to travelers, such as merchants and students who were in a foreign land only temporarily. But in the modern world, when perhaps one third of the world's Muslims live as religious minorities, the law has been extended to include everyone, temporary or permanent residents in countries that are not ruled by Sharia.

The rule that Muslims must follow the law of the land is strengthened by rulings dealing with the modern notion of citizenship. Citizenship is considered a contract in Islam, with the obligation to abide by the laws of the country of which one is a citizen. In fact, in the modern world an entire branch of Islamic law has developed, known as the "minority jurisprudence." It addresses the traditional position that Muslims living in foreign lands should return as quickly as possible to regions ruled by Islamic law. In modern jurisprudence, this ruling is considered archaic. Today, Islamic law calls upon Muslims to participate fully and constructively in the democratic political process. This ruling comes from the Fiqh [Islamic law] Council of North America, which reassures Muslims that "[t]he United States is a country of freedom that looks primarily after the rights of all its citizens, of all religions and races, despite the problems in application that manifest themselves from time to time" (Verskin, 2013: 137).

Second, the imam points out that Islamic law is based on moral values that are shared by most religions, such as truth, justice, and respect for property rights. " 'What do you mean, really, by saying that I can't abide by Sharia law?' Ahmed asked. 'Sharia law is telling me don't steal. Do you want me to steal and rob a bank?'" (Smietana, 2011).

The commonality of Islamic values points of the third basic confusion about Sharia: that it comprises a set of fixed laws utterly inconsistent with the values modern societies consider humane. This perception stems in part, no doubt, from equation of Sharia with the practices of terrorists who claim to be justified by Islam. As we saw above, terrorism – including the attacks on the World Trade Center, the Pentagon, the Madrid trains, the London transport system, the Boston Marathon runners, and the Peshawar Church – are in violation of Islamic law. They do not represent it, no matter how often terrorists shout that God is Great ("Allahu Akbar").

The misperception that Sharia is antithetical to Western values may also reflect equation of Sharia with some traditional criminal punishments in Islamic law. It is important to recognize that the term "Sharia," the Arabic word for "route" or "path," refers most broadly to the overall moral and religious code of Islam. Ideally, it covers all aspects of life, from private matters such as prayer and fasting, to public matters such as marriage and divorce. There is enormous diversity in Islamic law, with four main schools of jurisprudence and endless debate about minutiae of specific legislation, as is found in all legal systems. But all of Islamic legislation is guided by the objectives or goals (*maqasid*) of Sharia: the preservation of life, religion, intellect, property, family, and dignity.

Traditional Islamic law does contain some specific punishments (called *hudud* punishments) that are startling compared to modern norms, including the norms of most Muslim-majority countries. While some outspoken traditionalists argue for the re-implementation of traditional punishments, there is lively debate among Muslim scholars over their status. Leading European Muslim scholar Tariq Ramadan recommends a "moratorium" on the implementation of hudud punishments (Ramadan, 2005). Like the threat of physical punishments in other pre-modern societies – before the development of the modern prison system – these laws were meant as deterrents to crime. But in today's society, as leading American Muslim scholar Ali Mazrui argued, we have more effective penal codes (Mazrui, 1997). Among the more controversial traditional laws is the prohibition of renouncing one's religion (apostasy). The former chief justice of Pakistan, Dr S.A. Rahman, argues that the prohibition of apostasy under threat of capital punishment violates the Qur'an's fundamental insistence on religious freedom and freedom of conscience (Rahman, 1972). Ali Gomaa, formerly Egypt's highest religious authority, also rejects the death sentence for apostasy, arguing that if punishment is due, it will come in the afterlife (personal interview with Tamara Sonn, 2012). Tunisian historian Mohamed Talbi explains that the law requiring capital punishment for apostasy resulted from a confusion of apostasy with treason (Talbi, 2006).

In any case, when Muslims refer to Sharia in general, they refer to following the overall moral principles of Islam, summarized in the popular Qur'anic verse:

> It is not a matter of piety that you [pray] toward the East or the West; pious is the one who believes in God, the Las Day, the angel, scripture and the prophets, and gives wealth, despite his love for it, to relatives, orphans, the needy, the wayfarer, and those who ask for it, and for freeing slaves, and who prays and gives charity, those who fulfill their promise when they make one, who are patient in poverty and hardship and battle. Those are the ones who are sincere; they are the righteous. (Qur'2:177)

That is why the majority see no conflict between Sharia and US law. As New York Imam Feisal Abdul Rauf says in his essay "Five Myths about Muslims in America,"

> For centuries, most Islamic scholars around the world have agreed that Muslims must follow the laws of the land in which they live. This principle was established by the prophet Muhammad in AD. 614–615, when he sent some of his followers to be protected by the Christian king of Abyssinia, where they co-existed peacefully. Not only do American Muslims have no scriptural, historical or political grounds to oppose the US Constitution, but the US Constitution is in line with the objectives and ideals of Sharia. Muslims already practice Sharia in the United States when they worship freely and follow US laws. (Abdul Rauf, 2011)

References

Abdul Rauf, F. (2001) Five Myths about Muslims in America, *Washington Post Opinions*, April 1, www.washingtonpost.com/opinions/five-myths-about-muslims-in-america/2011/03/30/AFePWOIC_story_1.html (accessed January 9, 2014).

Benen, S. (2011) *Political Animal*, March 15, www.washingtonmonthly.com/archives/individual/2011_03/028463.php (accessed January 10, 2014).

Creeping Sharia (online) *About Creeping Sharia*, http://creepingsharia.wordpress.com/about-2/ (accessed January 9, 2014).

Elliott, J. (2011) *Santorum Calls Sharia "Existential Threat" to US*, April 29, www.salon.com/2011/04/29/santorum_sharia_existential_threat (accessed January 10, 2014).

Marrapodi, E. (2011) *Poll: Many Americans Uncomfortable with Muslims*, September 8, http://religion.blogs.cnn.com/2011/09/06/poll-many-americans-uncomfortable-with-muslims/comment-page-1 (accessed January 10, 2014).

Mazrui, A.A. (1997) Islamic and Western Values, *Foreign Affairs*, September/Octoberwww.foreignaffairs.com/articles/53386/ali-a-mazrui/islamic-and-western-values (accessed January 15, 2014).

McMorris-Santoro, E. (2010) *Gingrich Calls for Federal Ban on Sharia Law in US*, September 18, http://talkingpointsmemo.com/dc/gingrich-calls-for-federal-ban-on-shariah-law-in-us (accessed January 10, 2014).

Sonn, T. (2012) Interview with Ali Gomaa, Cairo, January 9, 2012.

Rahman, S.A. (1972) *Punishment of Apostasy in Islam*, Institute of Islamic Culture, Lahore, Pakistan.

Ramadan, T (2005)*An International Call for Moratorium on Corporal Punishment, Stoning and the Death Penalty in the Islamic World*, http://tariqramadan.com/blog/2005/04/05/an-international-call-for-moratorium-on-corporal-punishment-stoning-and-the-death-penalty-in-the-islamic-world/ (accessed January 12, 2014).

Seitz-Wald, A. (2013) *Bush AG tells CPAC: " 'The vast majority' of Muslims want to impose Sharia law,"* March 16, www.salon.com/2013/03/16/bush_ag_tells_cpac_the_vast_majority_of_muslims_want_to_impose_sharia_law (accessed January 10, 2014).

Smietana, B. (2011) Tennessee Bill Would Jail Sharia Followers, *USA Today*, February 23, http://religionnerd.com/2011/02/23/tennessee-bill-would-jail-shariah-followers (accessed January 10, 2014).

Talbi, M. (2006) Religious liberty: a Muslim perspective, in *New Voices of Islam* (ed. Mehran Kamrava) I. B. Taurus & Co. Ltd., New York, p. 115.

Verskin, A. (2013) *Oppressed in the Land? Fatwas on Muslims Living under non-Muslim Rule from the Middle Ages to the Present*, Markus Wiener, Princeton.

6

Myths About Other Western Traditions

1. Zoroastrians Worship Fire
2. Voodoo Is Black Magic
3. Witches Worship Satan
4. Rastafarians Are Marijuana Abusers
5. Unitarian Universalists May Believe Whatever They Want

Introduction

When most of us think of Western religions, we think of Judaism, Christianity, and perhaps Islam. But those are not the only ones. In this chapter, we'll take a brief look at five smaller traditions that are utterly diverse, but that all have significant interactions with the mainstream Western traditions. In those interactions, we'll see more examples of xenophobia and imaginative storytelling.

1. Zoroastrians Worship Fire

I bless this sacrifice and invocation, and the good offering, the beneficent offering, the offering of assistance offered unto thee, O fire, son of Ahura Mazda… may you have the right wood – may you have the right incense – may you have the right food – may you have the right fuel! May you burn in this house, may you ever burn in this house, may you blaze in this house, may you

50 Great Myths About Religions, First Edition. John Morreall and Tamara Sonn.
© 2014 John Wiley & Sons, Ltd. Published 2014 by John Wiley & Sons, Ltd.

increase in this house, even for a long time, till the powerful restoration of the world, till the time of the good powerful restoration of this world. ...

Give me, O fire, son of Ahura Mazda, however unworthy I am, now and forever, a seat in the bright, all-happy, blissful abode of the holy Ones. May I obtain the good reward, a good renown, and long cheerfulness for my soul.

Hail unto you, O fire of Ahura Mazda, O beneficent and most great guardian spirit. ("Reverence to Fire," a prayer of Zoroastrians (Darmesteter translation))

Without further background, someone reading this blessing might get the impression that the people pronouncing it would be worshipping fire. They might get the same impression from watching Zoroastrian rituals in which fire is an important part. In fact, the claim that Zoroastrians worship fire became an accusation of idolatry that led to periods of persecution throughout Zoroastrian history.

The term "Zoroastrian" is not very familiar to most people in the West. But Christians are familiar with the name of the priests of Zoroastrianism: Magi. The Gospel of Matthew says that Magi "came from the East" to worship Jesus as "king of the Jews," bringing rich gifts of gold, frankincense and myrrh (2:1–11). None of the other gospels mention this incident, but it has become such a staple of traditional Christmas stories that no Christmas scene would be complete without it. And students of music and literature are familiar with the name of Zarathustra the prophet. German philosopher Friedrich Nietzsche uses it in the title of the famous novel, *Thus Spoke Zarathustra*, in which he discusses the death of God, as did German composer Richard Strauss in the tone poem inspired by Nietzsche's work. Zarathustra, the prophet of Zoroastrianism, is believed to have lived around 1100 BCE.

Less well known is that fact that Zoroastrianism is arguably the oldest monotheistic religion in the world. Its Persian origins are traced to at least the sixth century BCE. In a world where belief in multiple gods was the norm, Zarathustra ("Zoroaster" is the Greek pronunciation) taught that there is only one God, the Almighty, who calls upon all creatures to choose truth over deceit, goodness over evil, light over darkness. Known as Ahura Mazda, God will judge all humans when they die, and reward those who have chosen to have good thoughts, speak good words, and do good deeds.

Many elements of Zoroastrian teachings are similar to later traditions. Traditional stories claim that his mother was a virgin who conceived the child without a sexual partner. Tradition also tells of a miraculous journey to heaven during which the prophet was told that he had an enemy who would try to persuade people to choose evil instead of goodness. Ethical human choices are not only necessary for happiness but will result in the defeat of this diabolical figure, and will be rewarded accordingly. Those whose choices thwart that inevitable victory will fall into punishment when they die, while those whose choices neither helped nor impeded the triumph of goodness will be suspended between good and evil. Even after death, the souls being punished, and those who are suspended, may earn reward through the prayers of the living. At the end of time, when it looks as if evil has triumphed, and the skies darken, a savior will be born of a virgin. He will revive the dead and they will undergo a final judgment. Good will defeat evil, the world will be renewed, and people – purified of their misdeeds – will live in eternal bliss.

So familiar are some of these elements that many scholars believe Zoroastrianism actually influenced the development of Jewish, Christian, and Islamic thought. Some practices are familiar, too, such as the requirement that people confess their offenses to priests and resolve not to sin again, and the five-times daily prayer (*namaz*) preceded by washing of the face, arms, feet, and mouth. But other Zoroastrian practices remain quite unique.

Zoroastrian houses of worship are called fire temples. In them a ceremonial, consecrated fire is kept burning day and night. Keeping this wood-fueled fire burning is one of the tasks of the temple priests. The fire symbolizes purification and therefore righteousness, justice, and, ultimately, divinity. As well, Zoroastrians celebrate two festivals with fire. Sadeh marks the beginning of winter and is celebrated 50 days before the Zoroastrian New Year begins at the spring equinox. Lighting a large fire symbolizes the triumph of light and goodness over darkness and evil. Chaharshanbe Suri is the "fire-jumping" festival beloved by children and adults alike, which ushers in the celebration of New Year (Noruz). People wear costumes, build small bonfires and jump over them, and children go door-to-door for special treats of nuts and berries.

It is the prevalence of fires in worship and festivals that has led some to believe that Zoroastrians worship fire. Zoroastrianism was the official religion of Persia (modern-day Iran) from the third century CE to the seventh century, when their emperors were defeated by the newly formed Muslim forces. Many Muslim authorities recognized Zoroastrianism as a monotheistic religion like Judaism and Christianity, and therefore permitted its practice in return for loyalty and taxes. But some Muslim rulers proved intolerant. Under accusations of disbelief, Zoroastrians were harassed, and their temples and libraries destroyed. In some cases, they were persecuted. Gradually, the majority of Zoroastrians left Persia for India, where they are known as Parsees.

Reference

The Sacred Fire, September 13, 2012, http://archive.is/hbR4 (accessed January 12, 2014)

Further Reading

Boyce, M. (1975–1982) *A History of Zoroastrianism I and II*, Brill, Leiden/Küln.

2.   Voodoo Is Black Magic

Barely 18 hours after an earthquake devastated Haiti on Jan. 12, the Rev. Pat Robertson supplied a televised discourse on the nation's history, theology and destiny. Haiti has suffered, he explained, because its rebellious slaves "swore a pact with the devil" to overthrow the French two centuries ago. Ever since, he went on, "they have been cursed by one thing or another." (Samuel G. Freedman (2010))

Rev. Robertson is not alone in his perception of Voodoo. Freedman's article discusses the prevalence of "very degrading, derogatory" descriptions of Voodoo, and quotes Leslie G. Desmangles of Trinity College in Hartford, Connecticut, who traces it to nineteenth-century racism. In particular, the Catholic Church in Haiti undertook efforts to eradicate "superstition" – as it characterized Voodoo – beginning in the 1860s. The goal was to replace "sorcery and sacrilege" with "true" religion: Catholicism (Fernandez Olmos and Paravisini-Gebert, 2011: 119). These campaigns continued through the early 1940s and involved destroying temples and killing hundreds of Voodoo practitioners.

The practitioners of Voodoo (more regularly spelled Vodou or Vodu) do not consider it superstition or sorcery. Vodou is actually one of the official religions of Haiti, practiced by an estimated 80% of the island's population, along with Roman Catholicism. Fernandez Olmos and Paravisini-Gebert (2011: 120) report that Vodou and Catholicism flow "in and out of each other as the spiritual and healing needs of the Haitian people demand. For practitioners there is no conflict between Vodou and Roman Catholicism."

Vodou's origins are in Vodun, the religion of Gbe-speaking people from a region in West Africa stretching from modern Ghana eastward through Togo, Benin, and parts of Nigeria, who were taken as slaves to the French colony that would become Haiti. Under the impact of the intolerant and exclusivist religious policies of the French, and because of the tolerant and inclusivist nature of Vodun, the slaves' religion gradually incorporated elements of Catholicism into its system of gods and spirits. Given their living conditions, slave communities had little communication with one another, and gradually their traditions developed unique local characteristics. Thus there are now distinct forms of Vodun in Puerto Rico, Brazil, Cuba, Dominican Republic, and Surinam. A hybrid of Haitian Vodou and folk traditions is identified as Louisiana (or New Orleans) Voodoo.

Monotheism is represented in Vodou's belief in one God, known as Bondié, or Bondyé (from the French Bon Dieu), or Gran Met (the Good God). Serving as intermediaries between God and humans are the Loa (or Lwa, or L'wha), an array of powerful spirits known as *mystères, anges, saints,* or *les invisibles.* Each Loa is generally associated with a particular aspect of life, such as fertility, agriculture, or defense. Many of these spirits are also identified with specific figures honored in Christianity. The great keeper of the crossroads between the mundane and spiritual worlds, for example, Papa Legba, in charge of communication, is associated with St Peter, keeper of the "pearly gates" in folk Christianity. Erzulie Freda, the Loa of love and beauty who remains ultimately sad due to unrequited desires, is identified with the suffering Mary, mother of Jesus. Ayizan, Loa of the marketplace, is identified with St Clare, patron saint of goldsmiths.

The Loa are traditionally grouped into "nations," associated with the presumed ethnicities or regions of the slaves who brought them, such as Rada, Petwo (or Petro), Ibo (Igbo), Wangol (Angola), Siniga (Senegal), Ginen (Guinea), and Kongo. These may reflect the origins of Loa in ancient ancestral heritage. Traces of these associations remain in Vodou, with families sometimes treating specific Loa as their own.

In any case, just as some Catholic communities feel special bonds with the saints for whom their churches are named, Vodou congregations develop quite personal relationships with their chosen intermediaries. They learn their distinct personalities, powers and specific preferences for colors, foods, and other objects used in rites associated with them, and preserve their specific songs, rhythms, and dances. Vodou ceremonies then consist of invoking the presence of the Lwa and pleasing them with their favorite things. Indeed, practitioners of Vodou call themselves Sèvitè, "servants of the spirits."

Vodou ceremonies can be conducted within families at their homes or in temples (ounfo, or hounfour) by male and female ounfo leaders (oungan and manbo or mambo, respectively). Oungans (or houngans) and manbos, like priests, are believed to possess mystical understanding of the supernatural realm, the realm of the Loas, and to channel their power. Like pastoral figures in many traditions, they also provide counseling and advice to individuals, in addition, commonly, to herbal medicines for healing and protection.

To assist in pleasing and channeling the spirits' aid, oungans and manbos train temple assistants known as ounsis (or hounsies). The ounsis cook the food and prepare the objects preferred by the group's Loa, and play important roles in the extensive drumming – the "voice" summoning the presence of the Loa – as well as the dance and song involved in Vodou rites. Included among the ounsis' roles is channeling the Loa being invoked (although this type of channeling – often described as being "mounted" or "ridden" by the Loa – is not restricted to ounsis). Once identified on the basis of specific voice or behavior patterns exhibited in the individual being "ridden," the Loa is offered his or her favorite things and asked for favors by those present. In other words, as in a Catholic Mass, congregants offer gifts and pray for specific intentions.

Scholars of Vodou are careful to distinguish between Vodou and folk beliefs and practices that are often associated with it. Such practices are grouped under the category of sorcery called "black magic," rather than religion, and are not under the purview of oungans and manbos (although some oungans and manbos may practice it). Known by the West African terms Bo and Juju, this kind of sorcery includes casting spells on people and, most famously, creating zombies. Zombies, according to the *Encyclopedia of Death and Dying*, can be created with a poison extracted from puffer fish that results in a kind of coma that makes a person appear dead. The adept practitioner of this kind of trickery can then administer an antidote that reduces the effects of the poison and leaves the individual awake but "deprived of will, memory, and consciousness." (Ackerman and Gauthier, 1991: 474) In that condition, the individual appears to be under the control of the sorcerer, a possibility that terrifies those who believe in it, and thus gives sorcerers a kind of credibility.

Other, less spectacular claims made by such practitioners include the ability to cause harm to someone by damaging an image of her. But such practices fall outside the holistic way of life designated by the term Vodou. To its practitioners, Haitian Vodou is a way of life defined by service to spirits whose role is to protect and bring health and prosperity. Those blessed by the spirits are expected to behave with dignity as well as loyalty and generosity to the community. Those visited by tragedy are assumed to have failed to serve the spirits. In the words of Mambo Racine Sans Bout, "The [Lwa] do not prescribe moral behavior. They confer protection and power … Misfortune of any kind is always the fault, at least in part, of the person upon whom it falls, because that person failed to adequately protect himself" (Grey, 2000). The proper response, then, is commitment to service of the Lwa, not recourse to sorcery.

Because of the prevalence of misunderstandings about the true nature of Vodou, a number of scholars at the University of California at Santa Barbara founded an organization known as KOSANBA, dedicated to promulgating proper understanding of Vodou.. Among their first successful efforts was a petition to the Library of Congress to use "Vodou" rather than "voodoo" and "voodooism" to avoid further confusion between Vodou and folk practices.

References

Ackerman, H.W. and Gauthier, J. (1991) The ways and nature of the zombie, *Journal of American Folklore*, 104, 466–494.

Fernandez Olmos, M. and Paravisini-Gebert, L. (2011) *Creole Religions of the Caribbean: An Introduction from Vodou and Santeria to Obeah and Espiritismo*, 2nd ed, New York University Press, New York.

Freedman, S.G. (2010) Myths obscure Voodoo, source of comfort in Haiti, *International New York Times*, February 19, www.nytimes.com/2010/02/20/world/americas/20religion.html?_r=0 (accessed January 9, 2014).

Grey, K.S. (Mambo Racine Sans Bout) (2000) *Morality, Power, and the Vodou Tradition in Haiti* (December 3), available at www2.webster.edu/~corbetre/haiti/voodoo/morality.htm (accessed January 9, 2014).

KOSANBA A Scholarly Association for the Study of Haitian Voudou, http://www.research.ucsb.edu/cbs/projects/haiti/kosanba/ (accessed January 12, 2014)

3. Witches Worship Satan

Witches have good reason to be excited about Harry Potter. The book series is giving the 'craft' a huge boost. No wonder that when interviewed by *USA Today*, a warlock endorsed Harry Potter and bubbled with excitement at the series' wide acceptance by the mainstream. ("All Witchcraft Is Satanic!" (jesus-is-savior.com))

The concern expressed in this quotation is that Harry Potter, Sabrina the Teenage Witch, the *Twilight* series and other aspects of popular culture are not mere entertainment. They are dangerous means by which the devil himself is taking over the youth of today. If you are not dealing with the Holy Spirit, the jesus-is-savior web site explains, then "you are dealing with the devil." The devil's vehicles include "horoscopes, astrology, tarot cards, witchcraft, sorcery, magic, séances, psychics, palm readings, spiritism, fortune telling, necromancy (communicating with the dead), yoga, New Age meditation, the force, Chinese Zodiacs, burning candles, chants, spells, potions, charms, the Rosary, icon bracelets, et cetera." He uses such seemingly innocent devices, we are told, because "The Devil is a Beautiful Liar."

The equation of witchcraft with Satan worship was a common assumption in early modern Europe. It is from Satan, many thought, that witches got their supernatural powers. After a series of witch trials in Lancashire, England, in the summer of 1612, posters announced: "The Wonderfvll Discoverie of Witches in the Covnty of Lancaster". Over the words was an image of four ugly women dancing around a black male figure with horns, wings, and a spiked tail, as three monsters flew overhead (many such images can be found at www.pendlewitches.co.uk). Of the "Nineteene notorious WITCHES" mentioned in the poster, 10 were convicted and hanged, following the biblical injunction, "Thou shalt not suffer a witch to live" (Exodus 22:18).

Across the Atlantic in New England, Satan loomed large in the witch trials of 1692–1693 in Massachusetts. A common belief in that Puritan culture was that witches signed a contract with the Devil giving him permission to enter their bodies and take on their appearance, in order to harm other people. Though often called simply the Salem Witch Trials, the hearings took place not only in Salem Village and Salem Town but also in Ipswich and Andover. More than 200 people, mostly women, were accused. Most scholarly estimates of the number of people executed as witches between 1400 and 1800 range from 30,000 to 50,000 (CatholicCulture.org)

Five kinds of evidence were used in these witch trials. First, the defendant could be given an exercise to perform, such as saying the Lord's Prayer. If they refused, or if they made mistakes, that might indicate that they were witches. Second were physical marks such as moles and birthmarks, which were believed could be entry points for Satan. Third was the testimony of neighbors blaming some problem on a spell cast by the defendant. Fourth was "spectral evidence" – the appearance of a spirit or ghost in the form of the accused person. Because the Puritans thought Satan could assume the form of a particular human being only with that person's consent, they counted such an apparition as proof that the one being impersonated was a witch. The fifth kind of evidence was a confession from the defendant.

Curiously, in the Salem Witch Trials it was to a person's advantage to confess. Those who confessed were imprisoned and asked to name other witches; four died in prison awaiting trial, but none was executed. The 20 defendants who denied witchcraft and relations with Satan, however, were all convicted and executed. Nineteen were hanged, and one was "pressed" – crushed under a pile of stones. Two dogs were also convicted and put to death.

During the trials, Cotton Mather, a Puritan leader and son of the President of Harvard College, Increase Mather, was consulted by three of the five judges. After the executions, he was appointed to write a book to justify the trials to the higher powers in the Massachusetts Bay Colony. In that book, *The Wonders of the Invisible World*, he condemned several of those executed. Concerning Bridget Bishop, he wrote that there was "little occasion to prove witchcraft, it being evident and notorious to all beholders." He described Susanna Martin as "one of the most impudent, scurrilous, wicked creatures in the world." (Mather, 1693)

Though the witch trials of the 1600s are the most famous, the practice began in the late 1400s. The major impetus was Pope Innocent VIII's commissioning the Dominican friars Heinrich Kramer and James Sprenger to investigate rumors about Satan-worshippers in Germany casting evil spells, causing abortions, ruining crops, and doing other harm. In 1486, Kramer and Sprenger produced a document that was not just a report on witches and Satan-worship, but a handbook for spotting, investigating, and convicting witches. Its Latin title was *Malleus Maleficarum*. *Malleus* is Latin for "hammer"; *Maleficarum* means "of witches." The implied meaning of the title was that the book was a weapon to use against witches. It was so titillating that it was soon published, using the printing press invented a few decades earlier (Kramer & Springer, 2007).

The book has three parts. The first challenges those who doubt the threat of witches. In the fifth century, St Augustine had said that God alone could suspend the laws of nature, so neither Satan nor witches had supernatural powers. That view dominated through the early Middle Ages. In the eighth century, St Boniface declared that belief in the supernatural power of witches was pagan, not Christian. The Holy Roman Emperor Charlemagne made witch-burning a capital crime. So Kramer and Sprenger had to overcome a number of arguments. They did it by describing cases in which witches acted as Satan's agents, inflicting harm by his supernatural power. Satan's power is greatest, they said, in matters of sexuality. Women often become witches after having sex with him. Women's sex drive is greater than men's, the friars argued, and "all witchcraft comes from carnal lust, which is in women insatiable." The second part of the book describes witches and their spells, their recruitment techniques, and ways of foiling them. The third part is a guide for interrogating and trying witches.

Malleus Maleficarum focuses mostly on women because, it claims, it is easier for women to fall under Satan's power than for men, since females are more "carnal." Even the word "maleficarum" means female witches. (If the authors had wanted to refer to male and females in the title, they would have used "maleficorum.")

For two centuries, only the Bible sold more copies than *Malleus Maleficarum*. It went through thirteen reprints and twenty editions in just four decades. Its popularity no doubt resulted at least in part from the entertainment value of some of its accounts. For example:

> And what, then, is to be thought of those witches who in this way sometimes collect male organs in great numbers, as many as twenty or thirty members together, and put them in a bird's nest, or shut them up in a box, where they move themselves like living members, and eat oats and corn, as has been seen by many and is a matter of common report? It is to be said that it is all done by devil's work and illusion, for the senses of those who see them are deluded in the way we have said. For a certain man tells that, when he had lost his member, he approached a known witch to ask her to restore it to him. She told the afflicted man to climb a certain tree, and that he might take which he liked out of the nest in which there were several members. And when he tried to take a big one, the witch said: You must not take that one; adding, because it belongs to a parish priest. [*Malleus Maleficarum* Part II, Question I, Chapter VII]

The interrogation techniques laid out in the book included stripping the accused, shaving off all body hair, and searching for moles and other marks indicating a relationship with demons. If that turned up no convincing evidence, the suspected witch was tortured in the hope of getting a confession. *Malleus Maleficarum* recommends that on the day of the trial, defendants should be brought into court walking backwards, to reduce their opportunity to cast spells on the magistrates themselves.

In the centuries that followed its publication, *Malleus Maleficarum* became the leading authority on witches and their relations with Satan. As scholars have investigated the history of European witchcraft, however, they have discovered that there never was a link between real witches and Satan worship. Among today's witches, who also call themselves "Wiccans," the charge of Satanism is considered ludicrous. Wiccans do not even believe in Satan, they say – that's a *Christian* belief.

Witchcraft or Wicca is a tradition that traces its roots to pre-Christian nature religions in Europe. The core belief is that the divine is natural and immanent in nature rather than supernatural, transcending nature. The material world is alive with divine forces that can be accessed through spells and incantations. The chief deities are the Goddess and the Horned God. His horns may be what made Christians think of Satan, but the idea that Satan has horns is itself folklore invented by medieval Christians. The Bible and Christian theology books have no physical description of devils – no horns, goat legs, pointed tails, or pitchforks.

Wiccans today are both female and male, and come from all walks of life. They are organized into local groups called covens, usually headed by a woman. Rituals and holidays are attuned to the seasons and natural processes. At planting time, around May 1, is Beltane; at harvest time is Samhain, which coincides with the Christian Eve of All Hallows – Halloween.

While Wiccans do cast spells and work other "Magick," it is supposed to be for good only and not for harm. A basic principle is the Law of Threefold Return – what you do to others will come back to you three times.

A typical Wiccan meeting, in Rehoboth, Massachusetts, was described in the *New York Times*, October 31, 1999:

> An hour before sundown, 40 adults have formed a circle in a small backyard, the limbs of a barren tree overhead. Most are dressed in black, many in capes. But the occasion, a gathering of local witches' covens, is expectant, not somber. In their midst, a blond woman raises a sword above her head, points skyward and walks clockwise within the group. "I would like you to concentrate on raising a circle of energy around us, to turn the wheel of the year," says Cheryl Sulyma-Masson, high priestess of one coven in this town near Providence, R.I. After completing the circle, she adds, "We will change the future through tolerance, education and through love." All respond, "As a witch, I make this pledge."

Unlike the Christians who once held witch trials, Wiccans have no heresies to condemn, or theology to profess. There are no inerrant sacred scriptures, or central religious authorities. Many Wiccans accept beliefs and practice rituals from ancient Greek, Roman, and Celtic religions, but in Wicca, belief is not doctrinaire. It is a matter of individual perspective and preference.

Though Wiccans see themselves as inheriting an ancient tradition, many of their beliefs and practices were articulated in the 1950s by Gerald Gardner, a British civil servant who began writing books about Wicca as fiction to avoid prosecution under Britain's anti-witchcraft laws. In the year those laws were repealed, 1951, Gardner published Witchcraft Today (2004), and then *The* Meaning of Witchcraft (2004). Traditional covens had kept their beliefs and practices secret, to avoid prosecution, but Gardner's coven allowed him to write about some of theirs, now that they were no longer illegal.

Gardner's writings and later books on witchcraft confirm that Satan worship, and even belief in Satan, have no place in witchcraft. Wiccans do celebrate sex, as in the Great Rite, where the High Priestess and the High Priest may actually have intercourse, but none of the sex among witches is with Satan.

References

CatholicCulture.org., *Who Burned the Witches?* http://www.catholicculture.org/culture/library/view.cfm?recnum=4005 (accessed January 12, 2014)

Gardner, G. (2004) *The Meaning of Witchcraft*, Wheeler/Weiser, Boston.

Gardner, G. (2004) *Witchcraft Today*, Citadel, New York.

jesus-is-savior.com (online) *All Witchcraft is Satanic!* www.jesus-is-savior.com/False%20Religions/Wicca%20&%20Witchcraft/witchcraft_is_satanic.htm (accessed January 9, 2014).

Kramer, H. and Springer, J. (2007) *Malleus Maleficarum*, translated by Montague Summers. Cosimo Classics, New York, p. 121.

Mather, C. (1693) *The Wonders of the Invisible World. Observations as Well Historical as Theological, upon the Nature, the Number, and the Operations of the Devils.* Boston.

Niebuhr, G. (1999) "Witches Cast as the Neo-Pagans Next Door," *New York Times*, October 31.

Further Reading

Howard, M. (2010) *Modern Wicca: A History from Gerald Gardner to the Present*, Llewellyn Publications, Woodbury MN.

4. Rastafarians Are Marijuana Abusers

Rastas to Snoop Lion: Smoking weed does not a Rasta make. (Headline on *Newswire* (Bernhardt, 2013))

Many people became familiar with the LA rapper Calvin Broadus Jr in the 1990s, when he was known as Snoop Dogg. According to his web site, he is now Snoop Lion, and has produced a movie called *Reincarnated*. The marketing description for the film is: "In a cloud of smoke, *Vice* magazine's Andy Capper follows rapper Snoop Dogg on a pilgrimage to Jamaica, where he experiences a spiritual and commercial transformation, reemerging as Snoop Lion, a reggae artist." (Netflix, 2014) As the opening quote indicates, however, some observers are skeptical. Snoop has been known to enjoy marijuana; some observers seem to think his "reincarnation" is just an excuse to smoke more weed.

The skeptics include the Ethio-Africa Diaspora Union Millenium Council (or Rasta Millennium Council). According to *The Guardian*, the council has threatened to sue Snoop if he does not stop calling himself Lion, claiming, "Smoking weed and loving Bob Marley and reggae music is not what defines the Rastafari Indigenous Culture" (Petridis, 2013).

Undoubtedly, the connection between smoking marijuana, Bob Marley's music, and Rastafarianism is well known. Less well known is what the followers of Rastafarianism actually believe.

To begin, Rastafarians do not use the term "Rastafarianism." They refer to themselves as Ras Tafarians, followers of Tafari Makonnen. Born in Ethiopia in 1892 into a royal family that traced its heritage to King Solomon and the Queen of Sheba, Tafari was educated in the Ethiopian Orthodox Christian tradition. At age 18 he was appointed regional governor, giving him the title Ras. Ras Tafari was crowned emperor of Ethiopia in 1930, whereupon he took the name "Power of the Trinity," Haile Selassie in Amharic.

Meanwhile, in Jamaica, Marcus Garvey was emerging as an anti-racism activist. He formed the Universal Negro Improvement Association (UNIA) in 1914. The organization became widely popular in Jamaica and attracted international attention. Garvey embarked on a speaking tour of the United States in 1916, where he gained more followers, opened a branch of the UNIA, and launched a newspaper, *Negro World*. Advocating social development and economic independence, the Association's membership and success grew. The Association opened a number of businesses, including the Black Star shipping line. Garvey's reputation continued to grow and in 1920 he was able to hold an international convention of the UNIA in New York, filling Madison Square Garden.

Garvey remained in the United States for the next seven years. He became embroiled in a number of controversies with other Black leaders, including W.E.B. Du Bois, co-founder of the National Association for the Advancement of Colored People (NAACP). He also encountered legal problems. Convicted of mail fraud, he served two years in prison, and returned to Jamaica in 1927. There, it was his focus on God and homeland Africa that took root.

In particular, Jamaicans noticed a refrain in Marcus Garvey's popular speeches that predicted the imminent crowning of an African king. Rastafarian reports record Garvey saying, "Look to Africa, where a black king shall be crowned, for the day of deliverance is near." (Gallagher and Ashcraft, 2006: I:111). Ras Tafari's 1930 coronation in Ethiopia appeared to fulfill that prediction. Marcus Garvey achieved the status of a prophet. And when Haile Selassie took the title Lion of the Tribe of Judah (thus, Snoop's new name), he came to be seen as the fulfillment not only of Garvey's prophecies but those of the Hebrew Bible: "Do not weep! See, the Lion of the tribe of Judah, the Root of David, has triumphed" (Revelation 5:5). He appeared to be, in fact, the Messiah. As the "Power of the Trinity," he appeared to be divine.

Haile Selassie was an Orthodox Christian and denied being either the Messiah or divine. But his followers, now known as Ras Tafarians, developed a movement based on faith in him. Initially, it involved belief that he would release them from their involuntary diaspora and they would be able to return to dignified life in Africa. But Haile Selassie didn't even visit Jamaica until 1966. By then his followers focused less on immediate return to Africa and more on a way of life centered on clean living and belief in the oneness of humanity and God (Jah).

Rastafarians advocate a vegetarian diet devoid of processed foods, milk, coffee, and alcohol. Alcohol is seen as a tool used by white people to weaken and enslave Africans. "Babylon" is used by Rastafarians as a symbol of white people's greed and use of deceit to destroy people, just as Babylon the Great did in the Book of Revelation (chapter 17), where it is described as "the mother of harlots and abominations of the earth." By contrast to Babylon's values, Rastafarians believe in the unity of all humanity and the possibility of achieving eternal life in union with God on earth. Some of these beliefs are explained in the Holy Piby, "Black Man's Bible," published in 1924, which Rastafarians believe is an accurate version of the Christian Bible. Interestingly, however, the Rasta tradition of not cutting their hair derives from the Hebrew Bible's Book of Numbers: "All the days of the vow of his separation there shall no razor come upon his head: until the days be fulfilled … he shall be hold and shall let the locks of the hair of his head grow" (6:5, KJV). (The reason Rasta's characteristic hairstyle is called "dreadlocks" is disputed. Some explain that it reflects the fear inspired by white people when they see people wearing the style; others believe it reflects Rasta's righteous fear of God.)

When Haile Selassie arrived in Jamaica in 1962, he was welcomed as the Messiah, a manifestation of Jah, just as Jesus was. Rastas believe that the announcement of his death following a military coup in 1974 was a hoax, that he is still alive, and will become manifest again on the Day of Judgment.

Most Rastafarian holidays center around events in Haile Selassie's life (including his birthday, coronation and visit to Jamaica). Ordinary Rastafarian gatherings are called "reasonings," and focus on discussion. All Rasta events begin with smoking ganja (marijuana), the "holy herb" that Rastas believe is described in the Hebrew Bible (e.g., Psalm 104:14: "[God] causeth the grass for the cattle, and herb for the service of man." The Rastafarian understanding of this can be found at www.earthcultureroots.com/rastafarism.html) But ganja is not the focus of the events. Rather it is the importance of living in a way that reflects human dignity. As Bob Marley's iconic lyrics put it:

> Most people think,
> Great god will come from the skies,
> Take away everything
> And make everybody feel high.
> But if you know what life is worth,
> You will look for yours on earth
> And now you see the light:
> Stand up for your rights. Jah!
>   ("Get Up, Stand Up")

Snoop has not made clear whether or not he accepts this challenge, but it is clear that Rastafarians consider freedom, human dignity, and a healthy lifestyle central to their tradition. Marijuana remains, after all, technically illegal, even in Jamaica. Interestingly, it is only in Italy that Rastafarians have won the legal right to use marijuana, on religious grounds (Popham, 2008)

References

Bernhardt, A. (2013) Rastas to Snoop Lion: Smoking Weed Does Not a Rasta Make, *Newswire*, January 23, www.avclub.com/articles/rastas-to-snoop-lion-smoking-weed-does-not-a-rasta,91507 (accessed 9 January 2014)

Gallagher, E. and Ashcraft, W.M. (eds) (2006) *Introduction to New and Alternative Religions in America*, Greenwood Press, Westport, CN. http://dvd.netflix.com/ Search?v1=Reincarnated&oq=reincarnated&ac_posn=1 (accessed January 12, 2014)

Petridis, A. (2013) Is Snoop Dogg Taking His Rastafarianism Seriously? *Guardian*, January 24, www.theguardian.com/lifeandstyle/lostinshowbiz/2013/jan/24/ snoop-dogg-rastafarianism-seriously (accessed January 9, 2014.)

Popham, P. (2008) Rastas Can Use Cannabis, Italian Court Rules. *The Independent*, July 12, www.independent.co.uk/news/world/europe/rastas-can-use-cannabis-italian-court-rules-865829.html (accessed January 9, 2014).

Further Reading

Barrett, L.E. (1997) *The Rastafarians: Twentieth Anniversary Edition*, Beacon Press, Boston.

Hausman, G. (2013) *Rastafarian Children of Solomon: The Legacy of the Kebrea Nagast and the Path to Peace and Understanding*, Bear & Company, Rochester, VT.

5. Unitarian Universalists May Believe Whatever They Want

Unitarian Universalism is a scam! How can any organization claim to follow God, when they have NO set beliefs? Is God undefined? To say such a thing is to throw away the Word of God (which defines God). It is extremely odd for any religion to claim to believe *nothing* as a group. The only thing agreed upon is that anything goes. Tragically, you can believe anything you want. (*Unitarian Universalism EXPOSED!* (Stewart, online))

Most of the religious traditions we've considered in this chapter developed outside Judaism, Christianity, and Islam. But Unitarian Universalism has its Unitarian roots in the Protestant Reformation of the sixteenth century, and its members trace their Universalism – the belief that everyone will be saved – to early Christian theologians like Origen and Clement of Alexandria. In 1961, the American Unitarian Association, founded in 1825, and the Universalist Church of America, founded in 1866, merged to become Unitarian Universalism, or UU for short. Most of its members are still found in the United States.

Among the things that distinguish Unitarian Universalists from Christian denominations is their rejection of the doctrine of the Trinity – the teaching that God is three persons. Jesus, they say, may have been a great teacher who had a special relationship with God, but he was not God and he did not exist before his birth. Those UUs who believe in God tend to insist on God's unity, hence the term "Unitarian." We say "who believe in God" here because over half of UUs are atheists or agnostics – another major distinction between UUs and mainstream Christians. UUs also reject the standard Christian doctrine of Original Sin – the teaching that the first sin of Adam and Eve, and the punishment for that sin, are inherited by all human beings.

Though UUs do not consider Jesus divine, many regard him as a great religious teacher bringing a divine message. For those who consider themselves "Christian" in a broad sense, there is the Unitarian Universalist Christian Fellowship (UUCF). For those who don't believe in the Biblical God, there are other possibilities, such as the Humanist Unitarian Universalist Association (HUU, or HUUmanists), and the Covenant of Unitarian Universalist Pagans (CUUPS).

These examples of diversity among Unitarian Universalists reveal another distinction between UUs and mainstream Christianity: they do not enforce a theological creed, such as the Nicene Creed or Westminster Confession. However, Unitarian Universalists deny that they have no beliefs or can believe whatever they choose. For them what is important in religion is morality – how people treat each other – not theology. With great care and intellectual effort, the Unitarian Universalist Association has articulated their beliefs in the following Seven Principles:

- The inherent worth and dignity of every person
- Justice, equity and compassion in human relations
- Acceptance of one another and encouragement to spiritual growth in our congregations
- A free and responsible search for truth and meaning
- The right of conscience and the use of the democratic process within our congregations and in society at large
- The goal of world community with peace, liberty, and justice for all
- Respect for the interdependent web of all existence of which we are a part.

Unitarian Universalists find inspiration in diverse religious traditions, including Jewish, Christian, Muslim, Hindui, Buddhist, Taoist and Confucian, as well as other worldviews. The Unitarian Universalist Association of Congregations web site (http://www.uua.org/beliefs/principles/index.shtml) quotes Rev. Kathleen Rolenz saying, "Throughout history, we have moved to the rhythms of mystery and wonder, prophecy, wisdom, teachings from ancient and modern sources, and nature herself." The site lists the following as the sources for their "living tradition:"

- Direct experience of that transcending mystery and wonder, affirmed in all cultures, which moves us to a renewal of the spirit and an openness to the forces which create and uphold life
- Words and deeds of prophetic women and men which challenge us to confront powers and structures of evil with justice, compassion, and the transforming power of love
- Wisdom from the world's religions which inspires us in our ethical and spiritual life
- Jewish and Christian teachings which call us to respond to God's love by loving our neighbors as ourselves
- Humanist teachings which counsel us to heed the guidance of reason and the results of science, and warn us against idolatries of the mind and spirit
- Spiritual teachings of earth-centered traditions which celebrate the sacred circle of life and instruct us to live in harmony with the rhythms of nature.

It's just not true, then, that UUs may believe anything they want. In fact, they agree on a great deal and welcome only people who share their intellectual and moral principles. Someone who believed in nihilism – the principle that traditional morals and ideas have no value – would not be accepted. Nor would someone who believed there is only one true church offering salvation. Nor would a white supremacist, a neo-Nazi, or someone wanting to take away women's right to vote. Far from being indiscriminate in their beliefs, Unitarian Universalists have rather high standards.

References

Stewart, D.J. (online) *Unitarian Universalism EXPOSED!* www.jesus-is-savior.com/False%20Religions/Unitarianism/uu.htm (accessed January 9, 2014).
Rolenz, K. (online) *"Sources of Our Living Tradition,"* http://www.uua.org/beliefs/principles/index.shtml (accessed January 16, 2014).

Further Reading

Greenwood, A. and Harris, M.W. (2011) *An Introduction to the Unitarian and Universalist Traditions*, Cambridge University Press, Cambridge.
Morales, P. (2012) *The Unitarian Universalist Pocket Guide*, Skinner House Books, Boston.

7

Myths About Eastern Traditions

1. Hinduism Is a Single Religious Tradition
2. Hinduism Promotes the Caste System
3. Hindus Worship Idols
4. Buddha Is a God for Buddhists
5. The Laughing Buddha (Budai, Ho-Ti) Is Buddha

Introduction

As we mentioned in Chapter 2, the term "religion" does not apply neatly in all cultures. It works well for modern Christianity, which is identified as (a) a coherent body of beliefs and practices that (b) pertain to the sacred sphere of life and so can be distinguished from non-religious aspects of life. Neither of those characteristics works particularly well for Eastern traditions, but as Europeans tried to understand the traditions of India and the Far East, they naturally thought of them as similar to their own traditions. That led to some of the myths we'll look at in this chapter. Others result from simple misperception resulting from failure to understand the way practitioners of the traditions understand them.

1. Hinduism Is a Single Religious Tradition

"Hinduism is not a religion. It is a way of life." You can today hear it in every drawing room wherever youngsters are sitting and discussing Hindu culture and India. (*Hinduism: Religion or Way of Life?* (Veylanswami, 2013))

50 Great Myths About Religions, First Edition. John Morreall and Tamara Sonn.
© 2014 John Wiley & Sons, Ltd. Published 2014 by John Wiley & Sons, Ltd.

The author of the above quotation went on to call the claim that Hinduism is not a religion a "false statement." He continued, "No thinking man can accept it or give it any credit at all. What an abominable stupidity is wrapped up in such an attractive sentence!" Whether or not something is considered a religion can have significant tax implications and, in fact, that is the context for Veylanswami's vehement rejection of the claim that Hinduism is not a religion. But outside the realm of taxes, scholars argue that the term "Hinduism" should be used with caution. Hinduism is not a religion in the sense in which that term applies to Christianity, for example. It is not a single set of beliefs and practices accepted by all who are called "Hindus," and it is not readily confined to a sphere of life identifiable as "religious," as distinct from "secular" life.

The term "Hinduism" comes from *hindu*, a Persian and Arabic term referring simply to people who live on the eastern side of the Indus River (which today goes right through the heart of Pakistan). *Hindu* was strictly a geographic designation and had nothing to do with religious or ideological identity. The place where Hindus lived was called Hindustan by Persians, and al-Hind by Arabs. When the people of India used the term Hindu, it was only to distinguish themselves from foreign invaders. Again, the term did not designate a religious identity (O'Conell, 1973).

It was Europeans who began to use the term "Hindu" to refer to Indians that were not Christian, Muslim nor Jewish, thus giving the term its religious identity. It did not distinguish between Hindus and Jains or Sikhs, two other indigenous Indian religions. The term "Hinduism" – denoting a religious counterpart to Christianity or Islam or Judaism – was then coined. It is an English word, and came into usage only in the nineteenth century.

The term "Hindu" as it is now used excludes Jains and Sikhs, who follow indigenous Indian traditions, but do not recognize the authority of the Vedas, and it is that – accepting the authority of the Vedas – that has come to identify people as "Hindu."

The Vedas are collections of creation stories, stories about gods, hymns of praise to the gods, prayers, instructions for diverse rituals, and philosophical speculation. They are organized into four major collections: the Rig Veda, the Yajur Veda, the Sama Veda, and the Atarva Veda. The Vedas are believed to have been perceived in the ancient past by people who were extraordinarily attuned to cosmic realities, and indeed to Brahman, the formless Ultimate Reality. Brahman is thus credited as the source not only of the cosmos but also of the Vedas.

The gods of Hinduism are many and diverse. Some are considered to be personifications of natural phenomena like fire, storms, and the sky. Some have single personalities, while others have a number of personas. Shakti, for example, can be considered energy as such, or the energy of various gods, or a god herself. Some even consider her the energy of the creator and therefore the creator herself.

The Rig Veda describes 33 gods, some more familiar than others. Among them is Dyaus Pita, who is the Heavenly Father. That name and identity appear in Greek mythology as the great Zeus Pater, "Father Zeus," lord of all the gods. In Roman mythology he appears as Jupiter, the supreme Roman god.

The gods of Hinduism are many and diverse. Some are considered to be personifications of natural phenomena like fire, storms, and the sky. Some have single personalities, while others have a number of personas. "Shakti," the word for "power," for instance, can be used as the name of an individual goddess who is also called "Devi," or can refer to the energy of various male gods, who each "has his Shakti." In one Hindu tradition, Shakti or Devi is even the supreme being.

Some gods are known only in certain regions of India, while others are universally popular. Ganesha, the elephant-headed god known as the "remover of obstacles," is an example. He is so popular that even people who do not consider themselves Hindus count on him for good luck. The traditional number of gods and goddesses in Hinduism is 330 000 000.

Some Hindu gods are considered greater than others. The "great gods" (mahadevas) include Vishnu, the preserver, and Shiva, the destroyer and re-creator. Each is associated with a goddess, who can be called his Shakti. Saraswati, the goddess of knowledge, assists Brahma; Lakshmi, the goddess of prosperity, assists Vishnu. The great Shiva's consort is Devi, also called Shakti. An ancient tradition holds that Brahma is a third mahadeva, a god who creates on behalf of others—either Shiva, Vishnu, or a form of Devi.

But belief in a god or gods is not essential to being a Hindu. There is a profound philosophical tradition in Hinduism, based on another text, the Upanishads. Like the Vedas, the Upanishads are considered to have been perceived or "heard" by extraordinary individuals in the distant past, rather than being composed by them. They are therefore believed to be of divine origin and so, like the Vedas, ultimately authoritative. The Upanishads teach that all the gods are really manifestations of Ultimate Reality, the Eternal, the Real, which comprehends all that is: Brahman. All the gods and goddesses are ultimately no more than manifestations of Brahman, as is each individual existent, including each human being.

So profound is this teaching that the Upanishads are considered the last of the Vedas, or "Vedanta," and understanding this teaching can take countless lifetimes of experience and contemplation. When one achieves that understanding, one is released (achieves *moksha*) from the limitations of individual, material existence. No longer bound to the cycle of rebirths (*samsara*), the individual will become what one really always has been: One with the Real.

There are many schools of thought dealing with the wisdom presented in Vedic literature and its commentaries. They present Brahman in diverse ways – as divine, or beyond divinity, for example. So sublime is this Ultimate Reality, however, that words are inadequate tools in its pursuit. Instead, various kinds of actions (*yoga*) are recommended. These include ethical living and self-control, and also contemplation, meditation, and pious devotion.

But just as all Reality is Ultimately One, all Hindu practices recognize that the laws of the cosmos are fixed and unerring. To put it another way, all actions resonate throughout the cosmos. Thus, positive actions – such as carrying out family responsibilities, showing respect for the gods and goddesses, studying, and contemplating – have positive effects, including advancing the individual on the path to release from the cycle of rebirths. Negative actions, such as those motivated by greed and cowardice, have the opposite effect. It is therefore one's duty to act in accordance with cosmic law, so much so that the same term – *dharma* – is used for both "duty" and "cosmic law." The principle of cause and effect is known as *karma*.

As diverse as the Indian traditions collectively known as Hinduism are, they do share the worldview described by notions of Ultimate Reality, dharma, and karma, as well as respect for the scriptures that convey this "wisdom" or "knowledge" – the meaning of the Sanskrit term *veda*. So although there are no required beliefs or practices for Hindus, Hinduism as it is understood today may well be considered a religion. As Simon Weightman (1998: 264) puts it, Hindu self-identity affirms that Hinduism is a "single religious universe, no matter how richly varied its contents."

Reference

Veylanswami, S.B. (2013) Hinduism: Religion or Way of Life? *Hinduism Today*, April – May, www.hinduismtoday.com/modules/smartsection/item.php? itemid=5359 (accessed January 9, 2014).

O'Conell, J. (1973) The word 'Hindu' in Gaudiya Vaisnava texts, *Journal of the American Oriental Society* 93(3) 340–344.

Weightman, S. (1998) Hinduism, in *A new handbook of living religions* (ed J.R. Hinnells), Penguin, New York, pp. 261–309.

Further Reading

Flood, G. (2005) *The Blackwell Companion to Hinduism*, John Wiley & Sons, Ltd, Chichester.

2. Hinduism Promotes the Caste System

Broadly speaking, a caste system is a process of placing people in occupational groups. It has pervaded several aspects of Indian society for centuries. Rooted in religion and based on a division of labor, the caste system, among other things, dictates the type of occupations a person can pursue and the social interactions that she may have. Castes are an aspect of Hindu religion. Other religions in India do not follow this system (*Doing Business in India For Dummies* (Manian, 2007))

The explanation of India's caste system excerpted above goes on to describe "four main classes" of the caste system, noting that they are also called "varnas." The equation of castes with the varnas is a common misperception, as are the related assumptions that the castes are religiously mandated and exclusive to Hinduism. In fact, castes are not the same as varnas, and only varnas are rooted in Hindu scriptures. The caste system is a social construct that developed gradually over centuries, and is so widespread that it is even observable in some Christian and Muslim communities in India.

The varnas are four social categories characterized by the contributions people make to society. The Brahmins are priests and scholars, the Kshatriya are warriors and rulers, the Vaishyas are herders, farmers, craftsmen, and traders, the Shudras are those who work for others. Some scholars describe the defining characteristics simply as "how people make their living," but this does not reflect the richness of the scriptural basis for the varnas. Carrying out one's responsibilities as a scholar, priest, warrior, ruler, herder, farmer, craftsman, trader, or worker – which covered all the walks of life in traditional society – was a sacred duty. Each was essential to the successful functioning of society and therefore equally honorable.

The religious sanction of the varnas is found in one of Hinduism's best-known creation stories. Hinduism's sacred Rig Veda text describes how the world and its inhabitants were created from a primeval "self" or "human," Purusha. From his mouth come the priest scholars; from his arms come warriors; from his thighs come the herders, farmers, craftsmen and traders; and from his feet come the workers. These are the four varnas.

The castes, by contrast, number in the thousands. They are the jatis, and are not derived from the sacred Vedas. Their sanction is traditionally traced to the legal codes described in the Laws of Manu. Scholars date the Laws of Manu in the first centuries of the common era, a period of political upheaval in India in which there was understandable concern about the social order. The text presents itself on the authority of a student of a son of the god Brahma, a device sure to lend it credibility, but in Hindu thought, it belongs to a class of literature known as "traditional" (*smriti*) rather than of divine origin (*shruti*).

The Laws of Manu recall the creation of the varnas, and expand on their characteristics and duties, levels of purity, and diverse social issues such as the status of women. Over the centuries and through numerous commentaries on the Laws of Manu, Indian society developed the complex social stratification that became known to the modern world as the caste system.

That system involved a rigid system of social hierarchy that undoubtedly overlaps with the varnas. The Brahmins remain dominant, although there are countless distinctions even within the Brahmin varna, as there are in the other varnas. As well, there are people who are utterly outside the system – "out-castes" – a phenomenon not found in the varnas. Outcastes, commonly known as Dalits, comprise nearly one sixth of India's population. Dalits are marginalized from mainstream society, deprived of the right to study, worship, eat, or otherwise socialize with other Indians. They are, literally, "untouchable," another term for them.

The source of the Dalits' untouchability can be traced to archaic notions of pollution and purity. In traditional society, contact with bodily fluids or dead substances results in impurity. Any such contact must be remedied through purification rituals involving cleansing and prayer. This phenomenon is found in societies throughout the world. Even in modern Orthodox Judaism and Islam, menstrual blood and childbirth are sources of impurity, so women must ritually purify themselves before resuming normal life. But in the caste system, pollution is a permanent condition for anyone whose livelihood brings them into regular contact with such substances. That includes people who work as butchers, leather-workers, street cleaners, sewer workers, maids, and housekeepers.

Dalits' low status is also associated with notions of karma. As we saw above, Hindu sacred scripture teaches that all actions have cosmic consequences. Good actions will bring one closer to release from the cycle of rebirths and the joy of pure existence, while bad actions will have the opposite effect. Thus, those born in low social status may be assumed to have done something to deserve it.

In the modern world, however, many reformers reject the notion that the caste system is religiously sanctioned, and pay particular attention to the plight of the Dalits. In fact, India's constitution prohibits discrimination on the basis of religion, race, caste, sex, or place of birth, and makes discrimination based on "Untouchability" punishable by law. The leader of India's struggle for independence from England, Mahatma Gandhi, refused even to use the word "untouchable." He called the Dalits "children of God," *harijan*. Even among those who believe the caste system can be traced to religious sources are critics of its modern form. The revered Brahmin Swami Krishnananda (d. 2001) wrote that the system originally served the purpose of social stability, but over time "bigotry and fanaticism took its place through the preponderance of egoism, greed and hatred, contrary to the practice of true religion as a social expression of inner spiritual aspiration for a gradual ascent, by stages, to God Almighty." (http://www.swami-krishnananda.org/disc/disc_03.pdf, page 3 (accessed January 12, 2014)

Reference

Manian, R. (2007) India's Caste System, in *Doing Business in India For Dummies* John Wiley & Sons, Ltd, Chichester, www.dummies.com/how-to/content/indias-caste-system.navid-815477.html?print=true (accessed 9 January, 2014).

Further Reading

Dumont, L. (1981) *Homo Hierarchicus: The Caste System and Its Implications*, University of Chicago Press, Chicago.
Rao, A. (2009) *The Caste Question: Dalits and the Politics of Modern India*, University of California Press, Berkeley.

3. Hindus Worship Idols

[Benares] is a vast museum of idols – and all of them crude, misshapen, and ugly. They flock through one's dreams at night, a wild mob of nightmares. (Mark Twain (1989: 504), upon visiting Benares (now Varanasi), one of Hinduism's holiest cities, on the banks of the Ganges River)

What Twain described as a "wild mob of nightmares" were the thousands of images of India's multitude of gods. He was visiting Varanasi, but images of the gods and goddesses are found everywhere in India: in temples, in homes, in shops, in offices, in taxis, on buses, in theaters, on awnings, and walls.

As we saw above, the number of deities in Hinduism is virtually limitless, and so are their images. Each deity has characteristic features that are depicted – whether in statues or drawings and paintings on flat surfaces – with elaborate detail and exuberant color. We mentioned the elephant-headed Ganesha. He is usually depicted in vibrant orange, pink, purple, and blue, with a giant golden crown and lots of jewelry. The invincible Durga, is usually a lustrous gold. She has even more jewelry than Ganesha, at least four arms – each holding an iconic object, sometimes riding a tiger or a lion, but always with a sweet smile. Kali, on the other hand, Durga's alter-ego, is all purple or blue or even black. Her jewelry is made of human skulls, her tongue (or tongues) sticks out in a vicious sneer, sometimes revealing fangs. She stands on corpses, sometimes in the midst of flames.

Some images are less graphic. Lord Shiva, the great deity of the cycle of preservation and destruction, can be seen in a graceful pose as a man with four arms when he is depicted in his "Lord of the Dance" persona. In more symbolic form, he is represented by a simple stone shaft known as a *lingam* (or *ling*). It is often presented with a *yoni* (or *pitha*), a wedge-shaped shallow vessel with a drain, symbolizing "passage" or "origin" or "birthplace." The lingam may be considered simply the ever-emergent force of Shiva. Viewed in tandem with its yoni, which may be seen as a representation of female sexual organs, the lingam may be seen as a phallic symbol. Together they may represent creative energy.

Worship of Shiva and Shakti, symbolized in the lingam and yoni, involves offerings of milk or honey or clarified butter, and flowers, among other things, poured over or rubbed on the lingam, then draining through the yoni. Similar kinds of *puja* are offered to other deities. Another aspect of worship is called *darshan*. It is "seeing" and "being seen by" a deity. *Darshan* can take place when people present offerings to the images of the deities in temples, or on pilgrimages to places where there are famous images of a deity, or celebrate a deity's feast-day by joining the crowds to witness a special image along a parade route.

Viewed from the outside, the spectacular array of images of deities, the offering of gifts to the images, and the clamoring to be in the presence of these images could easily look like idol worship. That is, it could look as if people are worshiping "graven images," as the Hebrew Bible has it: "You shall not make for yourself an image in the form of anything in heaven above or on the earth or in the waters below" (Exodus 20:4). The reason for this prohibition in the Bible was that the people were worshiping things like the "golden calf" – statues that they allegedly believed had divine power. To this day, Jews and Muslims reject the practice of making paintings or statues of sacred figures for fear of confusing the image for the Divine itself.

The importance of visual contact with the deity is manifested in the representations of eyes in Hindu images. Many deities are depicted with a third eye, some with even more; and even when only two eyes are evident, they are often given exaggerated size and color. As Hinduism scholar Diana Eck (1996: 7) puts it, "The gaze of the huge eyes of the image meets that of the worshiper, and that exchange of vision lies at the heart of Hindu worship."

With Hinduism, however, the allegation of idol worship is misplaced. Worshipers believe that the sculpted form is only the embodiment of the deity, not the deity itself. Thus it is the deity that is being honored, not the image. What appears as an image or "idol" is actually a concrete manifestation of the deity, in Hindu perspective. However, as we saw above, in Hindu thought, each of the multiplicity of deities is but a manifestation of Ultimate Reality, Brahman. And no number of deities or images could contain Brahman. Brahman is formless and without limiting characteristics. But the formless and limitless Ultimate Reality is manifest in the endless variety of things in the visible world. This unity in multiplicity is expressed in the sacred Hindu text, the Upanishads, in a dialogue between a student and one of the "seers" (*rishi*) who "perceived" the wisdom of the Vedas. It begins with the student asking how many gods there are.

> "Three thousand three hundred and six," [the sage] replied.
> "Yes," said [the student], "but just how many gods are there…?"
> "Thirty-three."
> "Yes, said he, "but just how many gods are there…?"
> "Six."
> "Yes," said he, "but just how many gods are there…?"
> "Three."
> "Yes," said he, "but just how many gods are there…?"
> "Two."
> "Yes, said he, "but just how many gods are there…?"
> "One and a half."
> "Yes, said he, "but just how many gods are there…?"
> "One."
>
> (Eck, 1996: 27)

If no single deity or embodiment ("image") of a deity can comprehend Ultimate Reality, each can allow a glimpse of an aspect of Ultimate Reality. But in ordinary life we rarely focus on the Ultimate. Celebrating a unique embodiment allows us that opportunity. As the traditional manual of Vishnu worship explains:

> Without a form, how can God be meditated upon? If (He is) without any form, where will mind fix itself? When there is nothing for the mind to attach itself to, it will slip away from meditation or will glide into a state of slumber. Therefore the wise will meditate on some form, remembering, however, that the form is a superimposition and not a reality. (Eck, 1996: p. 45)

References

Eck, D. (1996) *Darshan: Seeing the Divine Image in India*, Columbia University Press, New York.

Swami Krishnananda, *Religion and Spirituality*, http://www.swami-krishnananda.org/disc/disc_03.pdf, page 3 (accessed January 12, 2014)

Twain, M. (1989) *Following the Equator*, American Publishing Co., Hartford CN.

4. Buddha Is a God for Buddhists

> Like deceived Roman Catholics, Buddhists claim and are taught that they do not worship Buddha, saying that they only "pray" to his statue. The truth of the matter (as you will see in the numerous photos on this webpage) is that Buddhists do bow in worship and praise of Buddha. *Buddha Devil Worship* (Stewart, 2011)

As we saw in Chapter 1, people familiar with only Western monotheistic religions tend to think that the essence of religion is worship. Seeing statues such as the Tian Tan Buddha in Beijing, which measures 34 meters (112 feet) in height, people might well assume that Buddha is a god being worshipped. After all, some Christians note similarities between Buddha and Jesus, and Jesus is worshipped. Both first preached to a small group of followers, and then to larger and larger groups. After their death, their followers became missionaries spreading their message far and wide. They built churches and temples with statues of Buddha and Jesus, and created orders of monks and nuns. But that is where the similarities end. While

Jesus is worshipped as divine, the Buddha is not. He was a wise teacher with a "great soul" – symbolized in the enormity of some of his statues – but he was only a teacher, and what he taught was therapy to end life's suffering.

"Buddha" is a title, not a name. It means "awakened" (sometimes translated as "enlightened"). The title "Buddha" was given to a man who lived in northern India in the fifth century BCE. His name was Siddhartha Gautama and he grew up as a prince. According to Buddhist tradition, before his birth it was predicted that he would be either a king or a religious leader. His royal father wanted him to follow in his footsteps, and so shielded him from the problems in life, because they often lead people to religion. Siddhartha was wed to his cousin, a beautiful princess, and lived in his father's palace, unaware of the suffering in the world outside. In his late 20s, however, Siddhartha wandered away from the palace to find out what the world was like. Outside his cloistered palace he witnessed people bent with old age, suffering sickness, and mourners grieving over the death of loved ones. These experiences so moved the young man that he left his family and the comfort of the palace, and set out to discover the cure for suffering.

Siddhartha spent years studying with traditional Hindu teachers, devouring their wisdom and following their practices, including the most extreme forms of self-denial. But none of the traditional ways provided the release from suffering he was seeking. Eventually, he decided to stop going from teacher to teacher, and to simply sit and meditate until he figured it out. After some time, he emerged from his meditation "awakened;" he had discovered both the cause of suffering and its cure. He became the "Buddha." As we saw in Chapter 2, his teaching is contained in the Four Noble Truths: that life is characterized by suffering, suffering is caused by desire (or attachment), suffering can be avoided by ending desire, and the way to end it is to follow the Eightfold Path:

> right views – having a proper understanding of the world,
> right aspirations – commitment to ending desire,
> right speech – not lying or speaking angrily, but speaking with compassion,
> right action – behaving peacefully and honestly,
> right way of living – not harming any other living creature,
> right effort – being steadfast in one's efforts,
> right mindfulness – paying full attention to what is going on and what one
>   is doing,
> and right concentration – being at peace in any situation by focusing deeply
>   on it.

In other words, by wanting nothing, and living in simplicity and with compassion for all living things, one can accept life as it comes, avoid suffering, and find peace. This teaching was the heart of the Buddha's first sermon. He preached it to the five ascetics he had lived with, who became the first *sangha* – community of Buddhist monks – and set about spreading the message so that others could be released from suffering. Unlike Christian missionaries, Buddha and his followers did not preach about God or gods. Their focus was entirely on the practical matter of human suffering and how to overcome it.

As Buddhism spread through Asia, some communities tried to remain close to the Buddha's original teaching. Their traditions, found today in Sri Lanka, Myanmar, Thailand, Cambodia, and Laos, are called *Theravada* or *Hinayana* (Lesser Vehicle) Buddhism. But about five centuries after the Buddha's death, as Buddhism entered China, then Korea, and Japan, new ideas and practices were added to create traditions called *Mahayana* (Greater Vehicle) Buddhism. Mahayana traditions have figures who act as saviors, and people pray to them for help, though they are not gods but human beings. These figures are called *bodhisattvas*.

Like Hindus, Buddhists believe that people are reborn again and again until they become "awakened." Then they cease reincarnations and enter the blissful condition of existence known as *nirvana*. A *bodhisattva* is someone who has reached "awakening" and is poised to enter *nirvana*, but out of compassion for all those still struggling in the cycle of suffering and rebirth, forgoes *nirvana* to help others reach enlightenment. One of the most important *bodhisattvas* is Avalokitsvara, sometimes called the Buddha of Compassion. He is said to live in a special heavenly realm, to which he will bring those who ask him for assistance. In Japan, there is a female version of Avalokitsvara called Kannon. Like other *bodhisattvas*, she is not a god, though it may look that way when Buddhists pray in front of a statue of Kannon.

In a kind of Mahayana Buddhism called "Pure Land," it is said that a monk named Dharmakara once vowed that if he reached *nirvana*, he would create a blissful Pure Land, similar to the Western idea of heaven, to which he would bring people who asked him for help, by calling his name at the moment of their death. This figure is called *Amitabha* in Sanskrit, and *Amida* in Japanese. His role as a savior to those who pray to him is something like that of Jesus in Christianity, but, unlike Jesus, he is not a god.

One Mahayana tradition that shows clearly that the Buddha is not a god is Zen Buddhism. Following the Buddha, Zen masters emphasize non-attachment as a way to eliminate desire. We should be non-attached not only to possessions and social status, they say, but to concepts and systems of thought; and so they try to derail ordinary logical thinking by asking students *koans* – baffling questions such as "What is the sound of one hand clapping?" In derailing familiar trains of thought, they even encourage disrespect for Buddhist scriptures and the Buddha himself. According to one Zen story, the master Tanka (d. 824) visited a monastery in the middle of winter, when the snow had covered up the monks' supply of firewood. Shivering from the cold, Tanka walked up to the altar and took down one of the wooden statues of the Buddha, smashed it into chunks, and used them to start a fire to warm himself. There is even a Zen saying, "If you meet the Buddha, kill him."

The Buddha, then, is the founder of a great religious tradition, but he is not a god. Today there are thousands of Buddhist temples throughout the world, and even more statues of the Buddha. But statues of the Buddha are not part of worship. They are there to help people focus their attention on the Buddha's very practical teachings regarding the nature of suffering, and inspire them in their efforts along the Eightfold Path.

Reference

Stewart, D.J. (2011) *Buddha Devil Worship*, www.jesus-is-savior.com/False%20 Religions/Buddhism/satanic.htm (accessed January 9, 2014).

Further Reading

Keown, D. (2013) *Buddhism: A Very Short Introduction*, Oxford University Press, New York.

Dalai Lama (2002) *How to Practice: The Way to a Meaningful Life*, Simon and Schuster, New York.

5. The Laughing Buddha (Budai, Ho-Ti) Is Buddha

Lucky Wish Buddha Bring Peace and Happiness to Your Home

If you want to attract more wealth, good health and joy, make sure you rub the Laughing Buddha's belly every day and make a wish for yourself and your family. Laughing Buddha is also known as Buddha of Wealth and Happiness…

> We specialize in high quality buddha statues and we pay attention to detail
> and focus on fine quality craftsmanship. All of our buddha statues are
> HANDMADE and each item is unique. (Advertisement for Laughing Buddha
> statues sold by Wealth Buddha, Inc. of New York and Vancouver)

With the current popularity of meditation, feng shui, and other phenomena
associated with Buddhism has come the popularity of images of the Buddha,
or at least images that people call the Buddha. The trouble is that some of
these are not the Buddha. One of the most popular images is that of a fat,
bald, bare-chested male figure laughing heartily. He is often called the
Laughing Buddha. Many Chinese restaurants display such statues, and the
staff may tell patrons that rubbing his stomach brings good luck, wealth,
and prosperity. One popular gift catalog (http://acacialifestyle.com/six-little-
buddhas/p/51068) recently offered "Six Little Buddhas" in a gift box.
Customers are told that "[s]ix little laughing Buddhas (an auspicious
number) symbolize health, happiness, prosperity and longevity." However,
the so-called Laughing Buddha is not, in fact, the Buddha.

The "Laughing Buddha" first appeared in China. The proper Chinese
name for him is *Budai*, the Loving or Friendly One. In Vietnam, he is called
Bo Dai, and in Japan *Hotei*. He is a patron of restaurateurs and bartenders.
When someone has eaten or drunk too much, friends may jokingly blame
his influence.

Budai means "cloth sack" and refers to the bag this character carries. In
the sack he brings forth rice plants, food, and candy for the children who
often surround him. His kindness makes him a patron of children, and
weak and poor people.

Historians tell us that Budai is modeled on a Buddhist monk in the Chan
(Zen) tradition named Qieci, who lived in China in the tenth century – over
1500 years after the Buddha. A kind and jovial man, he got tired of life in
the monastery and set out to live as a wandering beggar. His kindness to the
people he met on the road eventually made him legendary, and a cult grew
up around him.

In some Asian traditions, Budai has been identified with Maitreya
Buddha, a savior predicted to come in the distant future when the human
race has degenerated. The Buddha is said to have predicted that after five
thousand years, people would forget his message. Steeped in selfishness,
jealousy, and hatred, their health and lifespan would decrease, and they
would go through long periods of famine, disease, and war. The Buddhist
scripture *Cakavatti Sutta*, in *Digha Nikaya* 26, says:

At that time, brothers, there will arise in the world an Exalted One named Maitreya, Fully Awakened, abounding in wisdom and goodness, happy, with knowledge of the worlds, unsurpassed as a guide to mortals willing to be led, a teacher for gods and men, an Exalted One, a Buddha, even as I am now. (Davids and Carpenter 1995)

In the *Maitreyavyankarna*, "The Prophecy Concerning Maitreya" (Conze, 1959: 239), the Buddha describes this savior as a huge, handsome, kingly figure:

He will have a heavenly voice which reaches far; his skin will have a golden hue, a great splendor will radiate from his body, his chest will be broad, his limbs well developed, and his eyes will be like lotus petals. His body is eighty cubits [120 feet] high, and twenty cubits [30 feet] broad.

Perhaps it is Maitreya's enormous size that accounts for confusing him with the Laughing Buddha, but neither is actually considered the Buddha.

Reference

Conze, E. (1959) *Buddhist Scriptures*, Penguin Books, New York.
T.W. Rhys Davids and J.E. Carpenter (1995) *Digha Nikaya*. Pali Text Society, Melksham, U.K.

8

Myths About Nonbelievers

1. Nonbelievers Are Ignorant about Religion
2. Nonbelievers Have no Basis for Morality
3. Without Religious Belief, Life Has No Purpose
4. Atheism Is Just as Much a Matter of Faith as Religion Is

Introduction

In a book on myths about religions, why would we include a chapter on people who are *not* religious, specifically those who lack belief in God? The answer is that "nonbelievers" have traditionally seemed threatening to some religious believers, especially Christians and Muslims. As with any group perceived as threatening, myths have grown up about them, and all the myths have been unfavorable.

1. Nonbelievers Are Ignorant about Religion

ATHEISM
Like a fish denying the
existence of water
(words under a photograph of a goldfish in a fish bowl, in article
Atheism is Stupid (Sacerdotus, 2013))

Religious people often assume that they know a lot about religions while nonbelievers don't. But numerous studies refute both assumptions. As we

50 Great Myths About Religions, First Edition. John Morreall and Tamara Sonn.
© 2014 John Wiley & Sons, Ltd. Published 2014 by John Wiley & Sons, Ltd.

saw in Chapter 4, according to Stephen Prothero's *Religious Literacy: What Every American Needs to Know – and Doesn't* (2007), a shocking majority of Christians are unable to name any of the four Gospels. On tests taken by American high school seniors, half identified Sodom and Gomorrah as a married couple. *Tonight Show* host Jay Leno wanted to test claims like these and asked the hundreds in his studio audience to name one of the twelve apostles. No one in the audience could (Hardiman, 2001).

About religions other than their own, Americans are even more ignorant. In one study with high school students, just 36% identified Ramadan as the Islamic holy month; 17% chose "Jewish Day of Atonement." Prothero concludes that "Americans are both deeply religious and profoundly ignorant about religion" (2007: 1).

In the United Kingdom, where religious affiliation is lower than in the United States, there is a similar level of "religious illiteracy." In a 2003 Mori poll, only 55% of Britons could name one of the four Gospels. A few more could name the sacred book of Muslims, the Qur'an. One study concluded, "The British public, both adults and children, are almost wholly ignorant of the basic facts surrounding Christians and other world religions." (Crabtree, 2007) The 2007 Ofsted report on Religious Education in British schools noted problems with teachers' poor knowledge of religion at primary school level and with recruiting specialists at secondary school level.

What about nonbelievers? Are they as ignorant of religious facts as the general population polled by Prothero? On the issue of how much people know about religion, a report of the Pew Research Center's Forum on Religion & Public Life (2010) is revealing. It said that "Atheists and agnostics ... are among the highest-scoring groups on a new survey of religious knowledge, outperforming evangelical Protestants, mainline Protestants and Catholics on questions about the core teachings, history and leading figures of major world religions." Jews and Mormons also scored higher than evangelical Christians and mainline Christians (such as Lutherans, Methodists, and Episcopalians).

The Pew Report was based on a quiz with 32 questions about religion. The average participant got 16 correct. Atheists and agnostics, however, averaged 20.9 correct answers. Jews and Mormons did almost as well, averaging 20.5 and 20.3, respectively. Protestants averaged 16 correct answers and Catholics 14.7. So atheists and agnostics scored 42% higher than Catholics on a test of religious knowledge.

In the view of Gregory Smith, a senior researcher at the Pew Research Center's Forum on Religion and Public Life, there is a correlation between atheism and the greater knowledge of religion shown by atheists. The vast majority of people are brought up with some kind of religious training. To be an atheist therefore requires a conscious choice; while even non-observant or non-practicing members of various religious denominations frequently still consider themselves "believers" in some sense, individuals must deliberately choose to become atheists. As Smith says, "That decision presupposes having given some thought to these things," which is strongly associated with religious knowledge (CNN, 2010).

If you would like to test your own knowledge of religion, the Pew Forum on Religion and Public Life offers a 15-question quiz online at http://features.pewforum.org/quiz/us-religious-knowledge/?q=16

References

CNN Belief Blog, (2010) *Don't know much about religion? You're not alone, study finds,* September 28. http://religion.blogs.cnn.com/2010/09/28/dont-know-much-about-religion-youre-not-alone-study-finds/ (accessed January 12, 2014)

Crabtree, V. (2007) July 05, *Religion in the United Kingdom: Diversity, Trends and Decline,* section 5: Ignorance of Religion. http://www.stanwell.org/downloads/religious_education/religion_and_community/Religion%20in%20the%20United%20Kingdom.pdf (accessed January 12, 2014)

Hardiman, C. (2001) *Bible literacy slipping, experts say,* Newshouse News Service, March 28.

Ofsted (2007) *US Religious Knowledge Survey: Making Sense of Religion,* Ofsted, Manchester, UK, www.ofsted.gov.uk/resources/making-sense-of-religion-0 (accessed January 9, 2014).

Pew Research Center's Forum on Religion & Public Life (2010) *Who Knows What About Regligion?* www.pewforum.org/2010/09/28/u-s-religious-knowledge-survey-who-knows-what-about-religion (accessed January 9, 2014).

Prothero, S. (2007) *Religious Literacy: What Every American Needs to Know – And Doesn't,* HarperCollins, New York.

Sacerdotus (2013) *Atheism is Stupid,* January 23, www.sacerdotus.com/2013/01/atheism-is-stupid.html (accessed January 9, 2014).

2. Nonbelievers Have no Basis for Morality

Think about it, in atheism, there is no moral right and wrong. There is no moral "should and shouldn't". Why? Because when you remove God, you remove the standard by which objective moral truth is established. In atheism morality is up for grabs. (*The Failure of Atheism to Account for Morality* (Slick, 2009))

There is undeniably a social stigma attached to atheism. Not believing in God isn't like not believing in ghosts or UFOs. For the vast majority of Americans, it is simply not an acceptable worldview. A 2007 *USA Today/Gallup Poll* showed how negatively Americans view atheists. All ten questions on the survey were in this format:

> If your party nominated a generally well-qualified person for president who happened to be _____, would you vote for that person?

When the question had the word "Catholic" in it, 95% of Americans said yes. For a "Jewish" candidate, 92% said yes. Even "Mormon" yielded 72% yes answers. But when the pollster asked people if they would vote for a well-qualified candidate chosen by their party who happened to be "an atheist," only 45% of respondents said yes, and 53% said no (Goodnough, 2012).

If we turn from politicians to neighbors, Americans attach even more stigma to nonbelievers. In 2010, Jessica Ahlquist, a freshman at Cranston High School West in Cranston, Rhode Island, noticed that on the wall of the school auditorium, near the stage, there was a sign, eight feet high, titled "School Prayer." It had been there since 1963. The prayer began "Our Heavenly Father," and asked God to "Grant Us Each Day" the desire to do our best, be kind, etc. Jessica was not opposed to the ideals expressed, but did object to the prayer format, because she is an atheist. "It seemed like it was saying, every time I saw it, 'You don't belong here,'" she commented. When a parent at the school filed a complaint with the American Civil Liberties Union (ACLU) about the prayer sign, the school board held a series of public hearings and Jessica spoke at all of them. She also started a Facebook page requesting the removal of the sign. In March 2011 the Cranston School Board voted 4–3 to keep the prayer on the wall of the auditorium. The Rhode Island Chapter of the ACLU then asked Jessica to be the plaintiff in a lawsuit to get the prayer removed. She agreed. Early in January 2012 a federal judge ruled that having the sign in a public school was unconstitutional because it violated the principle of government neutrality in religion. Within days Cranston residents came to school board meetings to demand an appeal to the ruling. Jessica received so many threats online that police were assigned to escort her to school. On a popular talk-radio show, State Representative Peter Palumbo from Cranston called Jessica "an evil little thing." Three florist shops refused to deliver roses sent to her from The Freedom From Religion Foundation, an atheist group. One 2009 graduate of the high school called Jessica "an idiot," noting that no one had been forced to say the prayer. "If you don't believe in that [the prayer sign]," she said, "take all the money out of your pocket, because every dollar bill says, 'In God We Trust.'" (Goodnough, 2012).

It is highly likely that the prejudice against nonbelievers stems from the association of morality with religion. One of the basic features of religions is that they provide guidance about what is right and wrong. They provide a "moral compass." The three Western monotheistic religions – Judaism, Christianity, and Islam – teach that God has issued commands or laws. The most familiar of God's laws are the Ten Commandments, shared in various forms by all monotheists. Jews identify 613 mitzvot, laws given by God. Muslims have no set number of laws but recognize five obligations: acknowledging God and Muhammad's prophecy, prayer, charity, fasting, and pilgrimage, as well as other obligations and prohibitions encompassed in Sharia. It is a natural conclusion, then, that those who recognize no divine authority would be living without moral guidelines. John Calvin, the Reformation leader, wrote, "We know that there is such perversity in human nature, that everyone would scratch out his neighbor's eyes if there were no bridle to hold him." (Calvin, 1885: col. 211). In the early 1700s, the essayist Joseph Addison (1965: 460) wrote about the need to have people attend worship services regularly:

> It is certain that country people would soon degenerate into a kind of savages and barbarians, were there not such frequent returns of a stated time, in which the whole village meets together with their best faces, and in their cleanliest habits, to ... have their duties explained to them, and join together in adoration of the supreme Being.

As Dmitri Karamazov, a character in nineteenth-century Russian novelist Fyodor Dostoevsky's *Brothers Karamazov*, put it, "If there's no God and no life beyond the grave, doesn't that mean that men will be allowed to do whatever they want?" (Dostoevsky, 1983)

Despite the popularity of the idea that being moral requires being religious, many scholars disagree. Harvard psychologist Steven Pinker (2008) argues that there is general agreement about morality among the world's cultures that is independent of religion. He says that agreement can be explained by human evolution. All cultures say that lying, theft, and murder are bad, and that caring for your family members is good. All cultures reflect these values and incorporate them into their ideological systems, whether those ideologies are identified as religious or not. Pinker says that's because early human groups that had these values were more likely to survive and flourish, and so they produced more offspring. Over time, they came to dominate the planet. If there ever were human groups that did not encourage people to take care of their family members, and did not discourage lying, theft, and murder, they would have been so dysfunctional that they would have died out in competition with groups that had morality. Drawing on the research of another psychologist, Jonathan Haidt, Pinker explores five moral principles found in cultures around the world.

- Avoid harming people.
- Promote fairness – pay back favors, reward benefactors, punish cheaters.
- Be loyal to the group.
- Respect leaders.
- Promote purity.

Pinker theorizes that having these values conferred an evolutionary advantage on early human beings, and so they became part of our inherited human nature.

Furthermore, if atheists are naturally immoral, then we should find that they violate moral laws at a higher rate than Christians and other believers. Statistics indicate, however, that the number of atheists convicted of crimes is significantly lower per capita than religious believers. Only 0.2% of those in US prisons are atheists. The American state with the highest rate of church attendance, Louisiana, has double the national murder rate, while states with low rates of church attendance, like Vermont and Oregon, have low murder rates. Japan, with less than 10% of the population claiming certainty that God exists, has the lowest homicide rate among industrialized countries. Norway, Britain, Germany, and the Netherlands demonstrate similarly low crime rates, yet less than one third of their populations claim faith in God. By contrast, the United States has the highest rate of religious belief among industrialized countries – and the highest crime rate. (Zuckerman, 2009).

References

Addison, J. (1965) *The Spectator*, 112, July 9, 1711 (ed, D. Bond), Clarendon Press, Oxford, 460.

Calvin, J. (1885) Sermons on Deuteronomy, Sermon 142, in *Corpus Reformatorum*, Vol. 56, C.A. Schwetschke & Sohn, Brunswick, CA, col. 211.

Dostoevsky, F. *Brothers Karamazov*, trans. Andrew R. MacAndrew (New York: Bantam Books, 1983), 788.
Goodnough, A. (2012) Student Faces Town's Wrath in Protest Against a Prayer. *New York Times*, January 26.
Pinker, S. (2008) The Moral Instinct. *New York Times*, January 13.
Slick, M. (2009) *The Failure of Atheism to Account for Morality*, Christian Apologetics and Research Ministry (CARM), June 18, http://carm.org/failure-of-atheism-to-account-for-morality (accessed January 9, 2013).
Zuckerman, P. (2009) Atheism, secularity, and well-being: How the findings of social science counter negative stereotypes and assumptions. *Sociology Compass*, 3 (6), 94–971.

Further Reading

Epstein, G. (2009) *Good Without God: What a Billion Nonreligious People Do Believe*, William Morrow, New York.
Harris, S. (2010) *The Moral Landscape: How Science Can Determine Human Values*, Simon & Schuster, New York.
Zuckerman, P. (2008) *Society Without God: What the Least Religious Nations Can Tell Us About Contentment*, New York University Press, New York.

3.   Without Religious Belief, Life Has No Purpose

You were made by God and for God and until you understand that, life will never make sense. (Rick Warren (2002), American evangelical preacher and best-selling author of *The Purpose-Driven Life: What on Earth Am I Here for?*)

Dr Rick Warren's *The Purpose-Driven Life: What on Earth Am I Here for?* (2002) has sold over 30 million copies. In 2003, according to *Publishers Weekly*, it was the top-selling book – not just the top-selling religious book, but the top-selling book of any kind in the world. Warren is founding pastor of Saddleback Church in Lake Forest, California, the fourth largest church in the United States, drawing 22 000 people a week to his services. The quotation above expresses Warren's central idea. The main purpose of human life, he says, is to glorify God. Each individual must find her own way to do that, and that will comprise the purpose of her life and source of her happiness.

Warren's book sales and church attendance numbers attest to the huge appeal of the idea that "You were designed to worship God." Even when they imagine themselves in heaven after death, many Christians picture themselves singing hymns and praising God for ever and ever.

If someone does not believe in God, of course, they are not going to believe that God has assigned them a purpose. So if the only way for a human life to have a purpose is for God to give it one, then atheists would not believe their life has a purpose. But is that the only way for a person's life to have a purpose?

Imagine an eight-year-old cellist who plays a Bach suite in a recital and feels so good about her performance that she decides to devote her life to becoming the next Yo Yo Ma. Imagine a college student in a biology lab making an exciting discovery about the suppression of tumor cells, and deciding that he will spend his life working on cures for cancer. Couldn't we say that these two young people have purposes for their lives? It seems that we could.

Now suppose that these two are atheists. Couldn't we still say that each has a purpose for their life? Isn't having a purpose for your life having some overall goal that organizes your time and efforts? If each of these young people has chosen an overall goal and organizes their time and efforts around that goal, then don't they have a purpose for their life, whether or not they believe in God?

Rick Warren would say that these young people have *not* found a purpose for their lives. He writes:

> The search for the purpose of life has puzzled people for thousands of years. That's because we typically begin at the wrong starting point – ourselves. We ask self-centered questions like What do I want to be? What should I do with my life? What are my goals, my ambitions, my dreams for my future? But focusing on ourselves will never reveal our life's purpose. (2002: 17)

Here Warren seems to be restricting the phrase "our life's purpose" to a purpose that is assigned by God rather than given by the person whose life it is. But why should we go along with that restriction? Usually when we talk about the purpose of someone's actions, we allow for the possibility that they have chosen that purpose. If you and I are going for a walk and you notice that with each step I am lifting and lowering two dumbbells, you might ask, "What's the purpose of doing that?" If I say, "To tone the muscles in my arms," you wouldn't say, "That can't be the purpose, because that's something *you* chose." Of course, the purpose of one of my actions can be a purpose I choose. And the same goes for the purpose of my life.

So while Warren is right that *one* way for life to have a purpose is for it to have a purpose assigned by God, that is not the *only* way, at least if we use the word *purpose* in the ordinary sense. A purpose for someone's life doesn't have to be assigned from the outside; it could be chosen by the person whose life it is.

If we think about these two ways for life to have a purpose, another issue comes up: is it necessarily good to have a purpose assigned to your life by someone else – even if that person is God? A purpose is a goal or function. Consider a carpenter's hammer. What is its purpose? To pound nails into wood. Consider a dishwasher or a lawnmower – their purposes are obvious in their names.

Now let's move up to living things. What is the purpose of a cow? To give milk, bear calves, and ultimately become steaks, roasts, and ground beef. Is it a good thing for the cow that its life has been assigned these purposes by its human owners? Would the cow be worse off if it had been born into a wild herd and spent its days doing what it wanted to do?

We can move up one more step to a human being who has been assigned a purpose by someone else. What if I walked up to you at a party and asked, "What is your purpose here?" To ask that would be to presume that you are not at the party because you wanted to be, but instead are, say, part of the kitchen staff or clean-up crew. If you are in fact a guest at the party, you would probably react negatively to the question, "What is your purpose here?" It implies that you are merely serving a function, that, like a dishwasher or floor polisher, you are a *device*, a piece of machinery.

Comparing a person's purpose to a machine's purpose may sound odd, but that is exactly what Rick Warren does in his book:

> You didn't create yourself, so there is no way you can tell yourself what you were created for! If I handed you an invention you had never seen before, you wouldn't know its purpose, and the invention itself wouldn't be able to tell you either. Only the creator or the owner's manual could reveal its purpose. (2002: 22)

Back to the party. Not only might you resent my asking, "What is your purpose here tonight?" but you would probably be more insulted if I asked what purpose has been assigned to *your whole life*. There is a word for a person who is alive to serve the goals of another person. That word is *slave*. Just as I own my lawnmower and so can use it for whatever I want, slave-owners thought of themselves as owning human beings, and so able to use them for whatever they wanted. In the United States before the Civil War, slave owners made careful calculations of how long slaves would live under various conditions. In cotton-growing areas like Mississippi, some figured that they could get two years of hard work out of a slave before they would die of exhaustion or illness. If they didn't assign them such hard work, they would probably live longer, but then they would not pick as much cotton per year, and they would consume more food over their lifetime. This kind of cost-benefit analysis sounds cruel, but it was a natural part of slavery, which was based on one person owning other persons and assigning their lives purposes.

Someone like Rick Warren who believes God assigns a purpose to our lives might protest here that God is not like a slave owner. But there are similarities. Like the slave owner, God is said to own human beings; we are his property. That is the traditional Christian reason for why suicide is wrong: your body and your life belong to God, not to you, so it is up to God – not to you – when you will die. If you take your own life, you violate God's property rights, just as you would violate the property rights of a slave owner if you killed one of his slaves.

But isn't there one big difference between God and the slave owner: while slaves did not *like* having their lives assigned a purpose by the slave owner, many people *like* the idea that they exist to praise God. They look forward to worship rituals; indeed, as we said, they think of heaven as praising God for ever and ever. Here we should point out that not all slaves hated their masters. Unlike "field slaves," "house slaves" were not assigned to back-breaking labor in the hot sun. Some of them came to accept their status as property and the jobs they were given. Some even came to like their masters, especially if they were not treated cruelly.

We might ask about those slaves who accepted the purposes they had been assigned and accepted the idea that someone else owned them. Was it a bad thing that they had a purpose assigned to their lives by someone else, when they accepted that purpose? Opponents of slavery would point out that because slavery was the only condition these people had ever known, and they had been systematically prevented from thinking about the value of human freedom, they had been brainwashed into accepting a morally unacceptable system.

Even if we can justify a system in which one person is assigned a purpose by another person, however, it seems that the person being assigned the purpose must, like the contented slave, embrace that purpose. And that, of course, is true of Christians like Rick Warren. They choose the purpose they believe God has assigned their lives. In their minds, it's not just God's purpose for them, but also their purpose for themselves.

If they changed their mind, however, and decided that they wanted to devote their lives to other purposes than glorifying God – say curing cancer – what then? The two quotations from Rick Warren above say that it is a mistake to try to determine your own goals for your life. But many people would say that determining your own goals is the essence of human freedom. It's what the Declaration of Independence means in its famous sentence about our natural God-given rights to "life, liberty, and the pursuit of happiness."

In any case, the only way it seems good for your life to have a purpose is if you embrace that purpose. Rick Warren embraces the purpose of glorifying God. Naturally, atheists don't embrace that purpose, but their lives can still have a purpose if they choose one for themselves.

There are no statistics available that measure the extent to which atheists believe their lives have meaning or purpose. It is clear, however, that atheists in general do not believe their lives are meaningless. Consider some of the more famous atheists: Charles Darwin, Marie Curie, Albert Einstein – each of whom made enormous contributions to science. As anyone who has spent countless hours toiling at research can attest, such labor is not undertaken for its own sake. Their work was undoubtedly in the service of their fellow humans. Lists of "famous atheists" reveal numerous scientists, scholars, artists, entertainers, and business people. Interestingly, these lists include only two famous criminals: Bavrilo Princip, the man who assassinated Archduke Ferdinand of Austria, thus precipitating World War I; and Jared Lee Loughner, who shot US Representative Gabrielle Giffords of Arizona and killed six others. Loughner, a diagnosed schizophrenic, pled guilty and is serving a life sentence in prison. Let us assume that neither of these infamous individuals, as despicable as their acts were, considered his life purposeless.

Some scholars believe that excessive emphasis on divine purpose, particularly when it is focused on the expected reward in the afterlife, can have a detrimental effect on purposeful living. New York University philosopher Samuel Scheffler argues in his recent book *Death and the Afterlife* (2013) that we must derive our purpose in life from recognition that our lives are finite but that others live on after us. Scheffler acknowledges that many people claim belief in the afterlife is what makes their earthly lives meaningful. But he suggests just the opposite. If we acknowledge that our own deaths are final but that our families and friends will live on, as will their families and friends, we can find purpose in working to ensure the world they inherit is a healthy one.

References

Scheffler, S. (2013) *Death and the Afterlife*, Oxford University Press, New York.
Warren, R. (2002) *The Purpose-Driven Life: What on Earth Am I Here for?* Zondervan, Grand Rapids, MI.

Further Reading

Frankl, V., Winsslade, W. and Kushner, H. (2006) *Man's Search for Meaning*, Beacon Press, Boston.

4. Atheism Is Just as Much a Matter of Faith as Religion Is

> Atheism is every bit of a religious commitment as Christianity itself. It represents the latest version of the human assault on God, born out of resentment that we do not in fact rule the world and that God calls on us to submit our lives to him. It is a form of idolatry in which we worship ourselves. (Archbishop Peter Jensen of Sydney, Australia, Good Friday Sermon, April 2, 2010)

In debates about atheism, many people say that while it may be impossible to prove that God exists, it's also impossible to prove that God *doesn't* exist. The above quotation reflects a common conclusion: that those who believe in God are on an equal footing with those who don't believe in God. Each accepts something for which there is no proof, and that's what faith is.

Some believers extend this line of reasoning to claim that belief in God is in fact preferable to atheism because it's easy to find evidence for the existence of God – just look at all the design in the natural world – while it's hard to argue for the non-existence of something, especially an invisible God. In a book titled *I Don't Have Enough Faith to Be an Atheist*, for example, Norman Geisler and Frank Turek (2004: 32) argue that:

> conclusions such as "God exists" and "the Bible is true" are certain beyond reasonable doubt. Therefore it takes a lot more faith to be a non-Christian than it does to be a Christian.

On the cover of Geisler and Turek's book, Phillip Johnson says, "Atheism requires gobs of blind faith while the path of logic and reason leads straight

208 *50 Great Myths About Religions*

to the gospel of Jesus Christ." The web site of Let Us Reason Ministries (online) argues the same way:

> No matter how strenuously some may try to deny it, atheism is a belief system. It requires just as much faith (believing) to embrace that God does not exist, even more belief than a Christian would need to believe he does exist. Atheism has made a secular belief system (religion/philosophy) of having no God and their focus is usually nature. God's creation has replaced the one who made it. An atheist must assume that personal, unique, intricate living organisms arose from impersonal, disorderly chaos. Something had to come from nothing. They have no explanation for a beginning of when or why. There is no purpose in what we see and call creation. Atheism assumes that the potential gives rise to the actual. Reality shows that something actualized the potential itself. All potentials have an actualizer. Scrap iron from a junk yard does not form itself into an airplane or a building without some thing that is able to put it to order. All designs have a designer, and the universe has proven to be incredibly designed. Even the minutest organism is more complex than the space shuttle. ...To be an atheist one would have to be omniscient, knowing all things, having a perfect knowledge of the universe, to say they absolutely know God does not exist. For one to do this they would have to have personally inspected all places in the present known universe and in all time, having explored everywhere seen and unseen things of matter or things invisible.

The problem with this position is that it confuses not making an assertion with making an assertion. Some atheists make their nonbelief into an assertion: "I believe (or know) that there is no God." But most atheists do not make nonbelief into an assertion. They simply do not believe in God. That's something negative, not positive, and it's all it takes to be an atheist.

The distinction between positively claiming that there is no God, and not claiming to believe in God is captured nicely in Carl Sagan's (1985: 168) novel *Contact*, where Dr Ellie Arroway says:

> The question [Do you believe in God?] has a peculiar structure. If I say no, do I mean I'm convinced God doesn't exist, or do I mean I'm not convinced he does exist? Those are two very different questions.

Picture a tribe on a Pacific island who have never heard of any gods, including the God of the Bible. They would not believe in gods or God, because they could not even think about gods. So they would never say, "I believe that there is no God." But they would be atheists.

Most adults in our culture, of course, have heard of God and other gods. Millions believe in the God of scriptures, and over a billion believe in gods like Shiva and Vishnu, the Goddess and the Horned God of Wicca, and so on. But many do not believe in any gods. A survey by BBC News (2004) found that the proportion of people in the United Kingdom "who don't believe in God" was 39%. To be an atheist, people do not have to take a stance and make a positive assertion. They simply have to lack belief in God. Some of them were raised by nonreligious parents, and when they learned in school about the God of the Bible, the gods of India, and others, nothing prompted them to believe that any of them are real. Such lack of belief doesn't require faith, because faith is belief in something, and a lack of belief isn't belief in anything.

Atheists, then, don't have to say "I *know* that there are no gods" or even "I *believe* that there are no gods." All it takes is something negative – *not believing* that there are gods or a single God. This lack of belief is something we all have towards literally millions of gods. Through history there have been tens of thousands of religions. The *World Christian Encyclopedia* counts 10 000 in the world today. One of them, Hinduism, has 330 000 000 gods, about whom everyone except Hindus is an atheist. In an early use of the term "atheist," second-century Christians such as Polycarp were punished by Roman authorities for being "atheists" because they did not believe in Jupiter, Juno, Mars, and other state gods. Today, the whole world is atheist about the gods of Rome.

No one believes in the Norse god Thor anymore, either. We are all "a-Thorists." But how many of us have ever felt compelled to insist, much less prove, that Thor doesn't exist? For an atheist, the lack of belief may be like the a-Thorism we all share – not a kind of faith, but a lack of faith.

References

BBC News (2004) *UK Among Most Secular Nations*, 26 February.

Anthony Fisher, A. (2010) *Atheists hit back at clergy criticism of non-belief*, April, 2. http://www.smh.com.au/national/atheists-hit-back-at-clergy-criticism-of-nonbelief-20100402-rjmr.html#ixzz2qCxgfxTh (accessed January 12, 2014)

Geisler, N. and Turek, F. (2004) *I Don't Have Enough Faith to Be an Atheist*, Crossway, Wheaton, IL.

Let Us Reason Ministries (online) *There are No Atheists*, www.letusreason.org/Apolo7.htm (accessed January 9, 2014).

Sagan, C. (1985) *Contact*, Pocket Books, New York.

Bonus Myths

1. The Bible says "Cleanliness is next to Godliness," "The Lord works in mysterious ways," "Hate the sin, love the sinner," "God helps those who help themselves," "Money is the root of all evil," "Spare the rod and spoil the child," "To thine own self be true," "This too shall pass," "To err is human, to forgive divine," and "Idle hands are the Devil's workshop."
2. The Bible Forbids Eating Pork Because It Causes Illness
3. The Apocalypse Is the End of the World Foretold in Scripture
4. Satan and His Devils Torture People in Hell
5. Cherubs Are Cute, Childlike Angels
6. Christians Were Systematically Persecuted by the Romans
7. There Was a Female Pope Named Joan
8. Saint Patrick Drove the Snakes out of Ireland

50 Great Myths About Religions, First Edition. John Morreall and Tamara Sonn.
© 2014 John Wiley & Sons, Ltd. Published 2014 by John Wiley & Sons, Ltd.

1. The Bible says, "Cleanliness is next to Godliness," "The Lord works in mysterious ways," "Hate the sin, love the sinner," "God helps those who help themselves," "Money is the root of all evil," "Spare the rod and spoil the child," "To thine own self be true," "This too shall pass," "To err is human, to forgive divine," and "Idle hands are the Devil's workshop."

There are many sayings that only *sound* Biblical. Once they are repeated often enough, especially by people in authority, they can become widely accepted as being from the Bible.

"Cleanliness is next to Godliness."

The first statement of something like this saying in English was by Francis Bacon (1561–1626) in *The Proficience and Advancement of Learning*: "Cleanness of body was ever deemed to proceed from a due reverence to God." (Bacon, 2001) By the time of John Wesley (1703–1791), one of the founders of Methodism, the expression must have been widespread, since Wesley put it in quotation marks: "Slovenliness is no part of religion. 'Cleanliness is indeed next to Godliness.'" (Outler, 1986)

If we search through the Bible for something similar, we find Psalm 19:9 in the New King James Version: "The fear of the Lord is clean, enduring forever." The Hebrew word translated as "clean" here is *tahowr*, which means ceremonially and morally unpolluted.

"The Lord works in mysterious ways."

This saying comes from a hymn by William Cowper (1734–1800), *God Moves in Mysterious Ways*. The first verse is:

God moves in a mysterious way,
His wonders to perform;
He plants his footsteps in the sea,
And rides upon the storm.

According to legend, this was the last hymn Cowper ever wrote, and he was inspired to write it after almost committing suicide. One night in a fit of depression, Cowper decided to drown himself in the Thames River. He summoned a cab and told the driver to take him to the river, but a thick fog made it hard to navigate the streets of London. After driving around lost and frustrated for some time, the cabby gave up and stopped to let Cowper out. Unbeknownst to either man, they were back at Cowper's house. In his mind, the heavy fog was God's mysterious way of saving his life.

"Hate the sin, love the sinner."

This charitable motto sounds like something Jesus or Paul might have said, and it shows up occasionally in Christian sermons. But it's actually 19 centuries newer than Jesus and Paul. In his 1929 autobiography, Mohandas Gandhi wrote "Love the sinner but hate the sin." There is something like the motto in the writing of St Augustine of Hippo, too: in his Letter 211, he uses the phrase "Cum dilectione hominum et odio vitiorum," "with love of men and hatred of sins."

"God helps those who help themselves."

This saying is ancient but it's not in the Bible. In fact, it goes against the Biblical idea that God intervenes in the world to do for people what they cannot do for themselves. One of the first appearances of the saying is in Aesop's fable of Hercules and the Wagoner, a story that also includes the expression, "Put your shoulder to the wheel:"

> A wagoner was once driving a heavy load along a very muddy road. At one place the wheels sank half-way, and the more the horses pulled, the deeper the wagon sank. The wagoner dropped to his knees and prayed to Hercules the Strong," "O Hercules, help me in my hour of distress." But Hercules appeared and said, "Don't sprawl there, man. Get up and put your shoulder to the wheel. The gods help them that help themselves." (Jacobs, undated)

Over two thousand years later, in 1736, the saying, with "God" in the singular, appeared in Ben Franklin's *Poor Richard's Almanac*. The idea resonated with Franklin because he was a deist rather than a Christian. Deists believe that God created the world and the scientific laws by which it operates, but then let it operate on its own after that. Because God does not intervene in the world, Franklin thought, prayers to ask God for help are pointless. In times of trouble, people have to rely on their own skills and ingenuity.

"Money is the root of all evil."

This saying is probably an exaggerated version of something that does appear in the Bible. Paul's First Letter to Timothy 6:10 says, "For the love of money is the root of all evil: which while some coveted after, they have erred from the faith, and pierced themselves through with many sorrows" (King James version). Many modern translations render the Greek plural πᾶς κακός as "all kinds of evil" or "all sorts of evil" rather than "all evil." That allows for some kinds of evil for which the love of money is not the cause. But in all translations, it is the *love* of money, and not money by itself that is the problem.

"Spare the rod and spoil the child."

People who believe in physical punishment for children have often cited this saying as Biblical. While not in the Bible, it is similar to four passages in the Book of Proverbs:

He who withholds his rod hates his son,
But he who loves him disciplines him diligently. (Proverbs 13:24)

Foolishness is bound up in the heart of a child;
The rod of discipline will remove it far from him. (Proverbs 22:15)

Do not hold back discipline from the child,
Although you strike him with the rod, he will not die.
You shall strike him with the rod
And rescue his soul from Sheol. (Proverbs 23:13–14)

The rod and reproof give wisdom,
But a child who gets his own way brings shame to his mother. (Proverbs 29:15)

So although the saying is not in the Bible, the idea that children need physical discipline is there.

"To thine own self be true."

The advice to be honest with yourself and not engage in self-deception is morally upright and follows the values of the Bible. Further, the word order of this saying and the "thine" make it sound like the English of four centuries ago, the language in which the King James version of the Bible was written. That's because this line was penned by William Shakespeare around the time the King James Bible was written. It is in his tragedy *Hamlet*, Act 3, Scene 1. As advice to his son Laertes, Polonius says:

> This above all: to thine own self be true,
> And it must follow, as the night the day,
> Thou canst not then be false to any man.

Just before this, Polonius says another line that is sometimes thought to be from the Bible: "Neither a borrower nor a lender be."

"This too shall pass."

No matter how bad some experience is, it will come to an end sometime, and no matter how good some experience is, it too will end. In the Middle East, there are proverbs like "This too shall pass" in Hebrew, Persian, Arabic, and Turkish. Some trace them to Persian Sufi poets in the Middle Ages. Jewish folklore has stories in which the wise king Solomon says the proverb. There is also a fable in which the saying is inscribed on a ring. Making its wearer realize that everything is temporary, the ring makes sad people happy, but also makes happy people sad. This fable and the proverb became popular in the nineteenth century, as Westerners became enamored of things from Persia and the Orient. An early version of the saying in English is in the tenth century poem *Deor*. The main character, Deor, laments losing his job as court poet. Comparing his troubles to those of several heroes from Old English folklore, he ends each comparison with the line "Þæs ofereode, þisses swa mæg" – "That passed, this will too."

"To err is human, to forgive divine."

In the Gospel of Matthew, when Peter asks Jesus if he should forgive his brother as many as seven times, Jesus tells him to forgive "seventy times seven times" (Matthew 18:22). And the Lord's Prayer, composed by Jesus, asks God to forgive us as we forgive each other (Matthew 6:9–13, Luke 11:2–4). With this emphasis on forgiveness in the New Testament, it is understandable that people might think that "To err is human, to forgive divine" is from something like the Sermon on the Mount. But it isn't. It was written seventeen centuries after Jesus, by Alexander Pope (1688–1744), British poet and satirist, in "An Essay on Criticism." That essay also has a famous line that helps explain how some of these sayings got attributed to the Bible: "A little learning is a dangerous thing."

"Idle hands are the Devil's workshop."

This saying has been popular in English-speaking America since the Puritans brought their Protestant work ethic to the shores of New England. American Christians have often treated hard work as a virtue on a par with faith, hope, and charity. In this worldview, idleness and play – not working – are at least dangerous, if not themselves vices. The rulebook of an eighteenth-century Methodist residential school in Connecticut shows this attitude:

> The student shall rise at 5 o'clock summer and winter, at the ringing of the bell. ... The student shall be indulged in nothing which the world calls play. Let this rule be observed with strictest nicety, for those who play when they are young will play when they are old. ("Student Restriction 1796.") (*Northwestern Christian Advocate*, 1916)

Decades before this rule was written, Isaac Watts, English pastor and hymn writer, put this line into one of his hymns for children (*Divine Songs for Children*, 1715): "In Works of Labour or of Skill I would be busy too: For Satan finds some mischief still for idle Hands to do." Variations of the saying include "Idle brains are the Devil's workhouses" in the 18th century, and a line from Merideth Willson's *The Music Man* in the 20th: "Friends, the idle brain is the devil's playground."

Despite the popularity of the saying, it is not in the Bible in any form. In fact, the whole valorization of hard work is quite unbiblical. There is no record in the Gospels of Jesus ever doing a day's work, and the Old Testament has strict rules against work on the Sabbath, rules that survive today in Judaism. Exodus 31:15 says that "Whoever does any work on the Sabbath day must be put to death."

What do these examples say about the ease with which we ascribe Biblical origins to words of wisdom?

References

Bacon, F. (2001) *The Proficience and Advancement of Learning*, ed. Stephen Jay Gould, Book 2 X, Random House, New York. p. 11

Franklin, B. (1736) *Poor Richard's Almanac*, New Printing Office, Philadelphia.

Gandhi, M. (1929/2009) *An Autobiography: The Story of My Experiments with Truth*. The Floating Press, Auckland, New Zealand, p. 439.

Jacobs, J. (Undated) The Fables of Aesop, Selected, Told Anew, and Their History Traced. The Edward Publishing Co., New York, http://archive.org/stream/fable saeso00aesouoft/fablesaeso00aesouoft_djvu.txt (accessed January 10, 2014).

Leinenweber, J. (1992) *Letters of St. Augustine*, ed. John Leinenweber. Baker Books, Ada, MI, Letter 211.

Northwestern Christian Advocate (1916) Volume 64. Available at: http://books. google.co.uk (accessed January 10, 2014).

Pope, A. (2008) *Essay on Criticism*, Forgotten Books, London, Part II, line 15.

Outler, A.C. (1986) Sermons 88 and 98, in *The Works of John Wesley*, III: Sermons iii ed. Albert C. Outler, Abingdon, Nashville TN, pp. 249, 392.

Further Reading

Lang, S, (2003) *What the Good Book Didn't Say: Popular Myths and Misconceptions about the Bible*, Kensington, New York.

Watts, I. (1866) *Divine and Moral Songs for Children*. Hurd & Houghton, New York, Song 20, p. 65.

2. The Bible Forbids Eating Pork Because It Causes Illness

> God knows what's best for us, and back in the Bible days the pig was considered unclean … One of the main reasons why, was that the pig will eat anything. A pig eats waste and garbage … a pig will eat its own dead child! A pig will eat other sick and infected animals. They're scavengers. (Joel Osteen, pastor of Lakewood Church, Houston, Texas (Osteen, online))

The Hebrew Bible (the Christian Old Testament) has hundreds of rules governing daily life. Among the best known are those about "clean" and "unclean" animals in Leviticus and Deuteronomy. The "clean" animals, such as the cow and the sheep, are acceptable as food. But "unclean" species, such as the pig and the lobster, are "an abomination" and should never be eaten. In Hebrew they are called *trefa*, meaning they were not slaughtered in accordance with the law and, more generally, forbidden.

Pastor Osteen, commenting above on those Biblical prohibitions of certain kinds of food, falls into the common error of presenting a modern rationale for an ancient injunction. He explains that "unclean" means "lives in filth and garbage," and God banned "unclean" animals as food because they would make us sick. The "clean" animals, such as cattle and sheep, by contrast, do not scavenge for food, but eat fresh vegetation, Osteen says. "Would you rather eat an animal that eats waste and filth," he asked the congregation and TV audience, "or an animal that eats fresh, clean vegetation?" Osteen gives the same explanation for God's calling sea creatures such as lobster and shrimp "unclean." They live at the bottom of the ocean, he says, where they eat the waste of other animals.

Today we associate unclean food with germs that cause illness, but germs were not discovered until the seventeenth century, and their link to illness became clear only in the nineteenth century. Even if the writers of the Bible didn't know about germs, however, might they have thought that "unclean" animals are the ones that cause illness, as by carrying parasites? Pastor Osteen is not the first to assume so. Anthropologist Mary Douglas (2002) identifies an early expositor of this position. In his 1841 *The Expositor's Bible* (London), S. H. Kellog wrote that

> It is probable that the chief principle determining the laws of this chapter [Leviticus] will be found in the region of hygiene and sanitation ... The idea of parasitic and infectious maladies, which has conquered so great a position in modern pathology, appears to have greatly occupied the mind of Moses, and to have dominated all his hygienic rules. (Douglas, 2002: 31)

As rational as the sanitation theory of Biblical dietary laws may seem, Douglas points out that it is anachronistic and that, in fact, there is another explanation that was perfectly rational in the Biblical context. The books of Leviticus and Deuteronomy declare some animals "unclean" and "an abomination" because they don't meet Biblically established criteria for animals of their kind. In those books, as in Genesis, animals are categorized into three groups: those that live on the land, those that live in the water, and those that fly in the air.

For land animals, there are two criteria for being acceptable: they must have split hooves and they must "chew the cud" – regurgitate their food to chew it again.

> The Lord said to Moses and Aaron, "Say to the Israelites: 'Of all the animals that live on land, these are the ones you may eat: You may eat any animal that has a divided hoof and that chews the cud. There are some that only chew the cud or only have a divided hoof, but you must not eat them. The camel,

though it chews the cud, does not have a divided hoof; it is ceremonially unclean for you. The hyrax, though it chews the cud, does not have a divided hoof; it is unclean for you. The rabbit, though it chews the cud, does not have a divided hoof; it is unclean for you. And the pig, though it has a divided hoof, does not chew the cud; it is unclean for you." (Leviticus 11:1–7. See Deuteronomy 14:3–8.)

There are different rules for animals that live in the water. To be acceptable, they must have fins and scales.

Of all the creatures living in the water of the seas and the streams you may eat any that have fins and scales. But all creatures in the seas or streams that do not have fins and scales – whether among all the swarming things or among all the other living creatures in the water – you are to regard as unclean (Leviticus 11:9–10. See Deuteronomy 14:9–10).

So salmon, tuna, and other fish are acceptable food, but shrimp, lobsters, clams, and other water creatures that lack fins and scales are not.

What makes some animals "unclean" in the Bible, then, is not that they cause illness but that they lack features considered essential to being a land animal or a water animal. Pigs are declared "unclean" for the same reason as camels and rabbits are declared "unclean:" they meet only one – not both – of the Biblical criteria for land animals. What makes lobsters unclean is that they lack both essential features of water creatures – fins and scales.

Why would the writers of the Bible use the word "unclean" in this way? Douglas points out that in declaring certain species acceptable as food and other species unacceptable, God repeatedly says, "You shall keep yourselves holy, because I am holy" (Leviticus 11:45 and 19:1–2, for instance).

Since each of the injunctions is prefaced by the command to be holy, so they must be explained by that command. There must be contrariness between holiness and abomination which will make over-all sense of all the particular restrictions. (Douglas, 2002: 51–52)

What is holiness, and how could it apply to animals? The root meaning of "holy," Douglas says, is "set apart." What is holy is distinct and separate from other things. To be set apart, something has to be whole and complete: it has to have all the features that define its kind of thing. God is holy in the ultimate way – by being perfect and utterly distinct from everything else.

No creature is perfect and utterly distinct from all other creatures, of course, but creatures can be holy by having all the features that things of their kind should have, and by not having features that belong to other kinds of creatures.

We see the idea of holiness as completeness in Leviticus, where it says that any animal offered as a sacrifice to God, and any priest offering a sacrifice, must be perfect and unblemished.

> None of your descendants throughout their generations who has a blemish may approach to offer the bread to God. For no one who has a blemish shall draw near, a man blind or lame, or one who has a mutilated face or a limb too long. Or, a man who has an injured foot or an injured hand, or a hunch-back, or a dwarf, or a man with a defect in his sight or an itching disease or scabs, or crushed testicles (21:17–20).

Anything that makes a creature less than a perfect example of its kind, in other words, makes it less than complete, and so not holy.

Another way for things to not be set apart is for different kinds of things to get combined. Mixtures are impure, and, so, unholy. Leviticus 19:19, therefore, says, "You shall not allow two different kinds of beast to mate together. You shall not plant your field with two kinds of seed. You shall not put on a garment woven with two kinds of yarn." Even today in Orthodox Judaism, there are men whose career is inspecting garments for forbidden *shatnes*, the mixing of fibers such as linen and wool.

How does all this insistence on distinctness and completeness apply to the animals that may be eaten and those that may not be eaten? First, if humans are striving for holiness, then the food they eat should be holy. They should eat only things that are complete, that is, perfect examples of their kind. The Israelites were predominantly herders, so for them the paradigms of land animals were the ones they raised: sheep, goats, and cattle. What made those species distinct from other creatures is that they had split hooves and they chewed the cud. So the writers of the Bible classified land animals with those two features as whole and complete, hence holy and clean. Animals that did not have both those features, such as the pig, were unclean. In classifying water animals, the Biblical writers also took as the paradigm the creatures that they knew best – fish. What make fish distinct from other sea creatures are their fins and scales. So those are the necessary features of a complete water animal. Clams have neither fins nor scales, so are incomplete as water animals. Lobsters are even more troubling, since

220

they not only lack fins and scales, but move in a way that is more like land animals – by walking. So not only are lobsters incomplete, but their features overlap with those of land animals. Even more than pigs, they are not distinct and separate, and so not holy.

Douglas' conclusion is that the Bible's rules banning the pork and shellfish are not about avoiding illness but about avoiding unholiness, just as the Bible says.

References

Douglas, M. (2002) *Purity and Danger: An Analysis of Concepts of Pollution and Taboo*, Taylor and Francis, London.
Osteen, J. (online) *Joel Osteen Teaches Christians Clean Unclean Foods! No Pork*, YouTube Video uploaded February 27, 2012, www.youtube.com/watch?v=7dYheb6OwVQ (accessed January 10, 2014).

3. The Apocalypse Is the End of the World Foretold in Scripture

> So I looked, and behold, a pale horse. And the name of him who sat on it was Death, and Hades followed with him. And power was given to them over a fourth of the earth, to kill with sword, with hunger, with death, and by the beasts of the earth. (Description of the Fourth Horseman in Revelation 6:8, New King James version)

The belief in the coming end of the world as we know it is common to all monotheisms (Zoroastrianism, Judaism, Christianity, Islam, and Baha'i), and they all teach that the end of the world will be marked by specific signs. The Book of Daniel of the Hebrew Bible, for example, tells of the coming of four great beasts, the last one of which will be really hideous. It will have ten horns and crush the entire earth and then eat it. But believers don't have to worry, Daniel says, because many of the dead will be brought back to life, "some to everlasting life, some to shame and everlasting contempt" (Daniel 12:2).

Christian scriptures refer to the Book of Daniel and reiterate that the "end times" will be marked by "abomination of desolation" and the coming of "great tribulation such as has not been seen since the beginning of the world" (Matthew 24:15–22; Mark 13:14–20). The Gospel of Luke provides more detailed indicators or "signs" so that readers will be able to prepare themselves: "There shall be signs in the sun, and in the moon, and in the stars; and upon the earth distress of nations, with perplexity; the sea and the waves roaring" (21:2–33)

The Qur'an's descriptions of the end times are similarly striking:

[T]he sun will be darkened, when the stars will be thrown down, when the mountains will be set in motion, when the pregnant camels will be abandoned, when the savage beasts are herded together, when the seas boil over, when the souls are sorted into classes, when the baby girl buried alive is asked for what sin she was killed, when the record of deeds are spread open, when the sky is stripped away, when Hell is made to blaze, when Paradise brought near, then every soul will know what it has brought about. (81:1–14)

But it is Christians who place the greatest emphasis on the imminent coming of the end of the world and its signs. The signs are detailed in the last book of Christian scripture (the New Testament), a book often called the Book of Revelation but originally known as *The Apocalypse of John*. It tells of the "book with seven seals." With the opening of the first four seals, four riders appear, one each on a white, red, black, and "pale" horse – the "four horsemen of the apocalypse." Opening the fifth seal reveals a vision of those who were slain for their loyalty to the "word of God." The sixth seal releases a great earthquake, "and the sun became black as hair sackcloth, and the whole moon became as blood, and the stars of heaven fell upon the earth… and the heaven was removed as a scroll rolled up, and every mountain and island were removed out of their places." This happens on a day described as "the great day of wrath" (Revelation 6). Given the vivid nature of these descriptions, the term "apocalypse" has come to mean cataclysmic events marking the end of the world. "Apocalyptic" is usually used to describe doomsday scenarios, and "apocalyptic literature" is that dealing with events associated with the End Times. An Internet search for quotations about the Apocalypse results in hundreds of references to the end of the world – or to movies and games about the end of the world (such as www.goodreads. com/quotes/tag/apocalypse and www.brainyquote.com/quotes/keywords/ apocalypse.html).

Taking the descriptions in scripture literally, many people have predicted the end of the world in astonishing – though, thankfully, inaccurate – detail. These predictions have often come in the context of political turmoil, so that tyrants and others considered to be enemies have been identified with various figures mentioned in John's Apocalypse, and the troubles they caused were interpreted as signs that the end was near. Ironically, such interpretations brought comfort to some, because the horrors of the End Times were to be followed by the Second Coming of Jesus, the Messiah, who would do battle with the Anti-Christ and usher in a period of peace and tranquility. Hilary of Poitiers, for example, struggling against Arianism – an interpretation of Christianity deemed heretical by the Council of Constantinople in 381 – predicted the world would end in 365 (www.religioustolerance.org).. Pope Innocent III identified Muslims as the cause of doom, and predicted the world would end 666 years after the rise of Islam – which he put at 1284 (Schwartz, 1996)Why 666 years? Because the name of one of the beasts described in John's Apocalypse – the one with seven heads and ten horns (Revelation 13:1–10) – has a numerical value (determined through calculations using numbers corresponding to letters) of 666 (Revelation 13:18; 15:2). That number is therefore called "The Mark of the Beast." The diaries of Puritan leader Cotton Mather (online), a devotee of John's Apocalypse, saw the Antichrist at work in Catholic missionaries in India, and predicted the end would come in 1697, then 1716, and then 1736. (He died in 1728.)

However, in fact, the term "apocalypse" does not mean the end of the world or anything associated with it. It means "revelation," from the Greek *apocalypsis*, uncovering or disclosing what had been hidden. Furthermore, scholars generally see in "apocalyptic literature" reflections of the anxieties of the times in which it was produced. Many scholars think that the apocalyptic passages in the books of Daniel and Isaiah were written while the Jews were being persecuted by the Greeks. The Book of Revelation (John's *Apocalypse*) was written after Jerusalem was attacked by the Romans, the temple destroyed, and Jews evicted (70 CE). Today, scholars generally interpret its descriptions as symbolic references to current events, rather than predictions of the future. And the descriptions had to be symbolic because they were so negative. They conveyed harsh criticism of ruling powers; to present them openly would have invited severe retribution. For example, the great Beast of the Sea's identification number happens to be the numerical equivalent of Nero, the Roman emperor so despised by Christians (Corey 2006: 61). Cory explains that 666 is based on numbers assigned to Hebrew letters used to transliterate "Nero.") The book itself claims that "the seven heads are seven mountains" (17:9). This could be another reference to Rome, a city built on seven hills, or else a reference to Jerusalem, also built on seven hills. Similarly, the Whore of Babylon – who is described in Chapter 17 as being destroyed by the great Beast of the Sea – is often understood as those who worked for the Roman administration, which controlled Jerusalem at the time.

This scholarly interpretation of the references in the Book of Revelation is reflected in mainstream Christian interpretations. The Catholic Church, for example, holds that the book's purpose was not to predict a distant future but to encourage first-century Christians, living under an oppressive Roman regime. Through symbolic language it indicated that Rome would soon fall and they would be amply rewarded for their faith and fortitude. Their oppressors would be punished. In any case, mainstream theologians reject the idea that people can predict the end of the world, stressing the Gospel of Matthew's claim that no one can know when Jesus will come again. Nevertheless, it is clear that many people take comfort in the idea that political turmoil and other disasters need not be the cause of undue anxiety. Rather, they signal that reward for righteousness is just around the corner.

References

Cory, C. (2006) *The Book of Revelation*. Liturgical Press, Collegeville, MN.

Mather, C. (online) *An American on Patmos*, www2.lib.virginia.edu/exhibits/brimstone/mather.html (accessed January 10, 2014).

Ontario Consultants on Religious Tolerance, (2011) *"46 failed end-of-the-world predictions that were to occur between 30 & 1920 CE, but didn't"* June 14 http://www.religioustolerance.org/end_wrl2.htm (accessed January 11, 2014)

Schwartz, H. *Century's End: An Orientation Manual Toward the Year 2000*. Doubleday, New York, p. 181.

Further Reading

Browne, Silvia. (2008). *End of Days: Predictions and Prophecies about the End of the World.*: Dutton/ Penguin. New York.

McIver, Tom. (1999). *The End of the World: An Annotated Bibliography*. McFarlane & Co. Jefferson NC.

Weber, Eugen. (1999). *Apocalypses.*: Harvard University Press. Cambridge MA.

4.   Satan and His Devils Torture Humans in Hell

Satan has been a popular figure in literature, art, and folklore for a thousand years. In a common image, he has horns, black or red wings, goat legs, and a pointed tail. Often he carries a trident, a three-pronged weapon sometimes called a pitchfork. At Arizona State University, the athletic teams are called the Sun Devils, and the mascot, Sparky the Sun Devil, carries a trident.

A lot of Satan-imagery comes from medieval Christianity, when painters and sculptors produced hundreds of representations of hell with devils in charge of torturing people. Many were featured on low-relief sculptures of the Last Judgment over the entrances to churches. As people walked under these portals, they could look up to reinforce their fear of hell. In 1416, three artist brothers – Paul, Hermann, and Jean Limbourg – made a miniature painting of hell that became part of the *Book of Hours*, a prayer book, of Duke Jean de Berry, brother of King Charles V of France. In the painting, Satan is center stage, lying on a huge fiery grill, under which people are being roasted. One either side of the grill, his fellow demons operate large bellows to fan the flames. In each hand, Satan squeezes the contorted bodies of a naked couple. Out of his large mouth, he vomits a burning geyser of over a dozen more naked victims. His feet trample others who are being tortured by snakes too. In front of the grill, other devils torture more people, while in the background, tall conical mountains serve as boilers to cook still more.

Hieronymus Bosch's *Hell*, painted around 1500, is a larger version of the same theme, with devils engaging in ingenious torture techniques.

All of this imagery works well in fantasy paintings, in *New Yorker* cartoons, and in Halloween costumes, but it's not from the Bible and not part of the teachings of Christian churches.

What *does* the Bible say about Satan? The Hebrew Bible/Old Testament says little except that he was a "son of God" – that is, an angel – whose name means "Accuser." In the Book of Job, Satan is an agent of God who patrols the earth and reports back about what people are doing.

The New Testament presents quite a different picture of Satan. He is not an agent, but an enemy of God. Much of the evil that he does is tempting people to sin. According to the Gospels of Matthew, Mark, and Luke, he even tempted Jesus. After being baptized, Jesus fasted in the desert for 40 days, and then he was tempted by Satan three times (Matthew 4:1–11; Mark 1:12–13; Luke 4:1–13). It was in response to the third temptation – to worship Satan in return for being given all the kingdoms of the world – that Jesus said, "Get behind me, Satan."

As for the popular idea of Satan living in hell, that has two sources in the Bible. In Matthew 25:41, Jesus says that at the Last Judgment, the King will separate the sheep from the goats—the good people from the bad – and say to the bad people, "Depart from me, ye cursed, into everlasting fire, prepared for the devil and his angels."

The other Biblical source for the idea of Satan in hell is the Book of Revelation, Chapter 20. It says that after being bound for a thousand years, Satan will be set free to deceive the nations of the earth.

> Then I saw an angel coming down from heaven, holding in his hand the key to the bottomless pit and a great chain. He seized the dragon, that ancient serpent, who is the Devil and Satan, and bound him for a thousand years, and threw him into the pit, and locked and sealed it over him … When the thousand years are ended, Satan will be released from his prison and will come out to deceive the nations … And fire came down from heaven and consumed them. And the devil who had deceived them was thrown into the lake of fire and sulfur, where the beast and the false prophet were, and they will be tormented day and night forever and ever (20:1–3, 7–8, 9–10).

What the New Testament says about Satan and his angels, then, is that they are evil, they tempt people to sin, and hell was created as a place of eternal punishment for them. It says that evil human beings will be condemned to hell, too, at the Last Judgment. What it does not say is that Satan and his angels are in hell now – before the Last Judgment. Nor does it say that hell is their domain or that in hell they torture human beings.

The vision of the devil being thrown into the lake of fire from the Book of Revelation is of a future event. It's something that will happen at the end of the world. That implies that Satan has not yet been put in hell. If Satan were already in hell, moreover, how could he be roaming the earth tempting people?

Thinking about the second two myths – that Satan and his demons are in control of hell and torture human beings there – we can see that they are confused in at least three ways.

The first problem with the idea of Satan punishing evil people is that evil people are the ones who do what he wants them to do. They go along with his plans and do things that please him. Why, then, would he want to punish them forever? Wouldn't he instead want to reward them for their loyal service? Picture Hitler and Stalin entering hell. Wouldn't Satan welcome them with open arms, as colleagues? How could he enjoy punishing these agents of his?

A second problem with the common picture of devils torturing people in hell is that it makes devils into God's agents. It is God, not Satan, who wants people to be punished for doing evil. If Satan and other devils are opposed to God and want to frustrate his plans, why would they help him – indeed, work for him for all eternity punishing evil people?

The third thing wrong with the myth of devils torturing people in hell is that they are thought to enjoy their work. Indeed, in many Christian paintings, they are shown gleefully hurting people with pitchforks, hot pokers, and so on. Their activities in hell looks like fun for them. But could hell really be a place where devils have a good time? The Bible says that hell was created as a place of punishment, not a Club Med for sadists. Jesus describes it in Matthew 25:41 as the "everlasting fire, prepared for the devil and his angels." If Satan and the devils ran operations in hell, strolling around trying out new forms of torture on human beings, hell wouldn't be punishment for them.

If the appearance and activities of Satan and his devils are not from Scripture, where did they come from? Scholars speculate that both arose in the Middle Ages from several sources. The horns, goat legs, and tail of Satan may have come from ancient Greek descriptions of the god Pan, or descriptions of satyrs, who were part goat and part man. The wings and the tail may have come from descriptions of the dragon in the Book of Revelation (above), who is associated with The Beast and the False Prophet. As for the trident or pitchfork, many scholars have pointed out that it was originally used for fishing, and so was associated with the sea gods Poseidon and Neptune, but then as a weapon in war and gladiatorial combat. Once all these images of evil were in place, and Satan was thought of as living in hell alongside human beings, it was only natural that someone would imagine Satan continuing his evil ways by torturing the human beings there. The trident may have seemed like an ideal tool for such work.

5.   Cherubs Are Cute, Childlike Angels

The traditional popularity of angels in Christian cultures has spiked in the last three decades. Evangelist Billy Graham's (1977) book *Angels: God's Secret Agents* went through several editions and sold over three million copies, creating a niche for dozens of angel books since. Angel stories became a staple on American television starting with *Highway to Heaven* in 1984. Another series, *Touched by an Angel* ran from 1994 to 2003. And angels had been popular in movies long before Rev. Graham's book. The classic Christmas movie *It's a Wonderful Life* (1946), has an angel who talks the lead character out of suicide. It was so popular that discussions of a sequel are currently under way in Hollywood. In *The Bishop's Wife*, also from 1946 and starring Cary Grant and Loretta Young, an angel helps save the lead characters' marriage. It was remade in 1996, this time starring Denzel Washington and Whitney Houston. In the 1951 *Angels in the Outfield*, angels help a baseball team break their losing streak. It was remade in 1994. In the 1996 movie *Michael*, John Travolta stars as an unconventional archangel. In the movie *Fallen* (2006), a teenager who is half-angel and half-human tries to save fallen angels and return them to Heaven.

Obviously, the popular modern versions of angels are the product of creative imaginations. But creative images of angels are not just a product of the modern entertainment industry. In the Renaissance, artists began painting cherubs as sweet, chubby children with wings – the kind of cherubs still popular at Christmas and Valentine's Day, and who so influenced our thinking that the adjective "cherubic" now means "having the childlike innocence or plump prettiness of a cherub."

If we consider what the Bible says about cherubs, however, we get a very different picture. They first appear in Genesis after God discovers that Adam has eaten of the tree of the knowledge of good and evil.

> Then the Lord God said, "See, the man has become like one of us, knowing good and evil; and now, he might reach out his hand and take also from the tree of life, and eat, and live forever" – therefore the Lord God sent him forth from the garden of Eden, to till the ground from which he was taken. He drove out the man; and at the east of the Garden of Eden he placed the cherubim [plural of *cherub*], and a sword flaming and turning to guard the way to the tree of life. (Genesis 3:22–24)

The New Oxford Annotated Bible (1994) comments that

> The *cherubim*, guardians of sacred areas (1 Kings 8:6–7), were represented as winged creatures like the Sphinx of Egypt, half-human and half-lion (Ezekiel 41:18–19). A divine sword (compare Jeremiah 47:6) was placed near the cherubim to warn banished human beings of the impossibility of overstepping their creaturely bounds (compare Ezekiel 28:13–16).

The Fourth Edition of *The New Oxford Annotated Bible* (2010) adds that "Representations of them guarded sanctuaries like the one in Jerusalem (1 Kings 6:23–28, 32, 35)."

Psalm 18:7–10 describes a terrifying God riding on a cherub:

> Then the earth reeled and rocked; the foundations also of the mountains
> trembled and quaked, because he was angry. Smoke went up from his nostrils,
> and devouring fire from his mouth; glowing coals flamed forth from him.
> He bowed the heavens, and came down; thick darkness was under his
> feet. He rode on a cherub, and flew; he came swiftly upon the wings of the
> wind. (Compare 2 Samuel 22:8–11)

When King Solomon built the Temple in Jerusalem in the 10th century BCE,
he used large sculptures of cherubs covered with gold for visual impact:

> In the inner sanctuary he made two cherubim of olivewood, each ten cubits
> high. Five cubits was the length of one wing of the cherub, and five cubits the
> length of the other wing of the cherub; it was ten cubits from the tip of one
> wing to the tip of the other." (1 Kings 6:23–24)

A cubit is about 18 inches, so these cherubs were about 15 feet tall with
15-foot wingspans. Stretching from one wall of the sanctuary to the opposite
wall, their wings alone would have seemed overpowering.

Besides the wings, what did the rest of a cherub look like? The Book of
Ezekiel 10: 20–22 describes them as "living creatures ... Each had four
faces, each four wings, and underneath their wings something like human
hands. As for what their faces were like, they were the same faces whose
appearance I had seen by the river Chebar." Earlier the author of Ezekiel
had described those faces this way: "The four had the face of a human
being, the face of a lion on the right side, the face of an ox on the left side,
and the face of an eagle" (Ezekiel 1:10).

In the Middle Ages, Christian theologians gave a lot of thought to angels.
For his careful examination of angels and their place in God's plan, Thomas
Aquinas acquired the title "Angelic Doctor." He said that there are nine orders
of angels, grouped into three hierarchies. In descending order, they are:

1. Seraphim, Cherubim, and Thrones
2. Dominations, Virtues, and Powers
3. Principalities, Archangels, and Angels.

The Cherubim are near the top, just below the Seraphim. Satan, Aquinas
said, was a cherub who fell from grace, and most theologians consider Satan
one of God's greatest creatures, if not *the* greatest. By comparison, the good

angels named in the Bible – archangels Michael, Gabriel, and Raphael – are second from the bottom in the lowest hierarchy.

In the Bible and Christian teaching, then, cherubs are among the greatest of all God's creatures – fearsome guardians represented in the Temple as 15 feet tall with 15-foot wingspans. So how did we end up with the idea that cherubs are harmless, chubby children with tiny wings? We do not know for sure, but we do know that the modern conception of a cherub is actually a secular figure known as a *putto* (plural *putti*), made popular by Renaissance painters. In Raphael's *Sistine Madonna*, for example, Mary stands in the clouds holding the baby Jesus, flanked by Saints Sixtus and Barbara. Two baby angels at the bottom of the painting look up at the Madonna. When Renaissance artists painted Cupid and other figures representing love, they often painted them as *putti*. For the central panel of his altarpiece in the Freiburg Cathedral, Hans Baldung Grien (1484–1545) painted *Coronation of the Virgin*, which features over a dozen putti playing lute, viol, harp, trombone, and crumhorn. Bohemian Wenzel Hollar (1607–1677) painted a group of winged babies playing musical instruments, and titled the work *Concert of Putti in the Clouds*. But Aurelio Luini (1530–1593) painted a similar work and called it *Musical Angels*. Without doing an exhaustive search of similar paintings, it would be difficult to pinpoint the origin of the confusion of putti with angels, but Luini's title is perhaps a starting point.

Reference

Graham, B. (1977) *Angels: God's Secret Agents*, Pocket Books, New York.

Further Reading

New Catholic Encyclopedia (1967) Angels, McGraw-Hill, New York.

6. Christians Were Systematically Persecuted by the Romans

"Though beheaded, and crucified, and thrown to wild beasts, and chains, and fire, and all other kinds of torture, we do not give up our confession; but the more such things happen, the more do others in larger numbers become faithful." (Justin Martyr, Dialogue with Trypho 110 (Schaff, 1885))

Second-century Justin Martyr's description of pagan Rome's persecution of Christians is chilling. There are hundreds of Christian saints identified as martyrs, many from the first three centuries. Fourth-century Emperor Constantine, who legitimated Christianity and ended the persecution, is considered by many denominations a saint. Many scholars have commented on the centrality of the theme of suffering for one's faith in Christianity. It is not surprising, therefore, that many people assume pagan Rome systematically tortured Christians in an effort to eliminate the new religious movement. However, there is actually very little historic evidence to support these claims. There were periods of persecution – often for political reasons – but also significant periods of security for Christians. Scholars believe the popular martyr and miracle stories date from the fourth century and later, and were no doubt exaggerated.

Candida Moss, in *The Myth of Persecution: How Early Christians Invented the Story of Martyrdom* (2013), explains how victims of hideous violence against random victims can be transformed from merely terribly unlucky people into sacred icons for an aggrieved group. Moss gives the example of 22-year-old Mariam Fekry, who was among the 20 people killed in an attack on a Coptic Church at Midnight Mass in Alexandria on New Year's Day 2011. The identity of the attackers was never found; their specific rationale for choosing that church on that date remains a mystery. But Mariam was identified as a martyr by remaining members of her family (several were killed with her), friends, and eventually even by then-President Hosni Mubarak.

What made her a martyr? A martyr is someone who is killed because of her religion. Mariam hadn't chosen to make a public avowal of her Christian identity; she was simply participating in a community tradition. According to her Facebook page, she was looking forward to another excellent year. And she wasn't targeted as Mariam Fekry. She was simply a random Christian to those who bombed her church. But identifying her as a martyr sacralized her death. It took it from the realm of the random and therefore utterly impersonal, to the special, the individual, the holy. As Moss puts it, "No longer was the attack simply an act of horrifying violence perpetrated by a terrorist group. Nor was it the unfortunate result of local religious, political, and social tensions. It became a direct and outright attack on Christianity as a whole" (2013: 2). Mariam became a symbol for all those killed for no other reason than that they were Christians. She became part of "a battle between good and evil" (2013: 3). What could be more ennobling?

All cultures valorize those who die rather than compromise the principles for which the group stands. Christians are no different in this regard. The language of martyrdom developed in early Christian history. Moss argues that it was a result of Jesus' followers trying to come to terms with his execution at the hands of a Roman official who himself, according the Gospel of John (19:4), believed he was innocent. Whether Jesus' death was interpreted as a choice or a sacrifice – both of which are represented in Christian discourse – it became purposeful. It also provided the core of a narrative of Christian persecution, and thus became a model to emulate. Moss notes that the New Testament describes the death of the first Christian to follow that model, Stephen (Acts of the Apostles, ch. 6–7).

By the second century, the valorization of martyrs was a significant part of Church teaching. The theologian Tertullian (d. 225) claimed that "the blood of martyrs is the seed of the church" (*Apologeticum*, online), and the third and fourth centuries were dubbed "the Age of the Martyrs."

There is no doubt that people were killed because of their religious identity. But it's the proliferation of martyr stories that is at issue here – the notion that Christians were constantly persecuted, specifically and only because of their religious identity – that Moss questions. Marshaling evidence drawn from archaeological records and Roman and Christian sources, Moss (2013) demonstrates that "the traditional history of Christian martyrdom is mistaken. Christians were not constantly persecuted … Very few Christians died, and when they did, they were often executed for what we in the modern world would call political reasons." Moss acknowledges that the laws under which Christians were prosecuted may have been unfair, but legal prosecution "is very far from the myth of how Christians were treated by the Romans." She finds no evidence in Roman history that the Christians prosecuted even under the strictest rulers were targeted for their religious identity. People who failed to acknowledge the gods in whose names the Romans claimed to rule were, of course, politically suspect. But Roman records reveal that the targeting of Christians was infrequent. The evidence to the contrary, Moss demonstrates, is from Christian sources dating years after the fact. By that time they had been transmitted orally within the community, accruing religious interpretations. "There are literally hundreds of stories describing the deaths of thousands of early Christian martyrs, but almost every one of these stories is legendary … In some of these cases, scholars are not even sure that the people described … even existed, much less that they were martyred." (2013: 15–16)

Moss cites the scholarly research of a group of researchers convened by seventeenth century priest John Bolland to sift through the thousands of stories about saintly people. The project continued for three centuries. The result: "[The researchers] decided that only a handful of stories were historically reliable." (2013: 16)

So why did the stories get exaggerated? For a number of reasons. Most obviously, they served as inspiration for others. It is easy for people in positions of power to become role models; they have high public profiles and automatically attract wannabes. But martyrs were usually just simple people; martyrdom made them even more admirable than rulers, and anyone could be like them. Christianity has always been a proselytizing tradition, attempting to attract as many followers as possible. Martyr stories, complete with the emotional appeal of high drama and violence, were effective in recruiting people to join Christianity.

Moss identifies another reason for the proliferation of martyr stories. Martyrs were usually associated with specific locations, and it was common for communities to erect shrines to their local heroes. As well, as the recent canonization of deceased popes John XXIII and John Paul II shows, Roman Catholicism maintains a vibrant tradition of intercession. Saintly people are believed to be not only in heaven with God, but able to intercede with God on behalf of earthly petitioners. (The usual requirement for canonization is two miracles. John Paul II is believed responsible for the cure of a French nun's Parkinson's Disease and a Costa Rican woman's brain injury. John XXIII is credited with the cure of an Italian nun's internal hemorrhaging, and this was deemed sufficient by Pope Francis; John XXIII was exempted from the need for a second miracle.) Villages and towns that otherwise would have been visited only by random salespeople thus became pilgrimage sites. The more interesting the martyr's story, the more likely it was to spread – and attract visitors who would spend money on local accommodations and food. "Thus," Moss concludes, "from the fourth century on, there was a veritable explosion in the production of stories about martyrs."

References

Apologeticum (online) Available at: www.tertullian.org/works/apologeticum.htm (accessed January 10, 2014).

Moss, C. (2013) The Myth of Persecution: How Early Christians Invented the Story of Martyrdom, HarperCollins, New York.

Schaff, P. (1885) *Ante-Nicene Fathers, Volume 1: The Apostolic Fathers with Justin Martyr and Irenaeus*, Christian Classic Ethereal Library, www.ccel.org/ccel/schaff/anf01.viii.iv.cx.html (accessed January 10, 2014).

Further Reading

Boyarin, D. (1999) *Dying for God*, Stanford University Press, Palo Alto CA.

Castelli, E.A. (2004) *Martyrdom and Memory: Early Christian Culture Making*, Columbia University Press, New York.

Perkins, J. (1995). *The Suffering Self: Pain and narrative Representation in the Early Christian Era*, Routledge, New York.

Ricciotti, G. (2009) *The Age of the Martyrs: Christianity From Diocletian (284) to Constantine (337)*, TAN Books. Charlotte, NC.

7. There Was a Female Pope Named Joan

As we saw in the Introduction, high drama, emotion, and graphic depictions of sex and violence give myths staying power, and the story of Pope Joan is a great example. In this story, a single woman is up against the leaders of the powerful medieval Roman Church.

The most influential version of the story is found in manuscripts attributed to Martin Polonus, who wrote in the latter part of the thirteenth century. Dozens of retellings followed. Giovanni Boccaccio (d. 1375), famous for the *Decameron*, also wrote *Concerning Famous Women*, which has a chapter on the female pope. While both Martin and Boccaccio used "John" as the Pope's name, Boccaccio (1964: 231) mentions that "there are some who say that it was Giliberta." Other writers used names such as "Jutta" and "Glancia." The reformer Jon Hus called her "Agnes." But the name that would eventually become standard was "Joan," the feminized form of "John." "Pope Joan" was especially popular with Protestants trying to show how corrupt the Papacy was, in books like Alexander Cooke's *Pope Joane. A Dialogue Between a Protestant and A Papist* (1610), and the anonymously penned *The History of Pope Joan and the Whores of Rome* (1687).

In the fourteenth and fifteenth centuries, Pope Joan was generally thought to be an historical figure. She was even included in a series of terra cotta papal busts installed in Siena Cathedral, with the inscription "Johannes VIII, Foemina de Anglia" ("John VIII, Woman from England"). Around 1680, the Theatre Royal in London staged a play: *The Female Prelate: Being the History of the Life and Death of Pope Joan. A Tragedy*, by Elkanah Settle. The story is also retold in Emmanuel Rhoides's 1866 novel, *The Papess Joanne*. In our own time, Pope Joan has spawned a stage play, two films, a best-selling novel, and a TV mini-series. The 1972 movie *Pope Joan* starred Liv Ullman and Maximilian Schell. Pope Joan appears in the opening scene of Caryl Churchill's 1982 play *Top Girls*. The 1997 novel *Pope Joan*, by Donna Woolfolk Cross, sold two million copies in Germany, and was then made into an award-winning movie in 2009. The trailer bills it as an "astonishing true story" and begins: "She changed the face of religion and became Pope. Two years later she was erased from history."

Martin Polonus, mentioned above, dates the reign of the female pope to the ninth century, between the reigns of Leo IV and Benedict III. In the *Chronicon Pontificum et Imperatum* (*MGH:SS*, XXII, 1265, p. 428), he refers to her as John Anglicus ("English John"), born in Mainz (in modern Germany), but says: "It is claimed that this John was a woman, who as a girl had been led to Athens dressed in the clothes of a man by a certain lover of hers." Martin describes her as so highly educated that she was able to return to Rome and teach. Her reputation as a great scholar grew to the extent that "she was the choice of all for pope." But then the trouble started: "While pope…she became pregnant by her companion. Through ignorance of the exact time when the birth was expected, she was delivered of a child while in procession from St Peter's to the Lateran, in a narrow lane between the Colisseum and St Clement's church." Martin claims that Joan's grave is located in the precise spot where she gave birth and that that's why subsequent popes make a detour around that spot when they make the procession to the Lateran Palace.

Thirteenth-century historian Jean de Mailly refers to the episode, with slightly different details, placing it in the year 1099:

> One day, while mounting a horse, she gave birth to a child. Immediately, by Roman justice, she was bound by the feet to a horse's tail and dragged and stoned by the people for half a league. And where she died, there she was buried, and at the place is written: *Petre, Pater Patrum, Papisse Prodito Partum* ["O Peter, Father of Fathers, Betray the childbearing of the woman pope"]. At the same time, the four-day fast called the "fast of the female pope" was first established. (Jean de Mailly, p. 514.)

de Mailly's version was followed by his contemporary Stephen of Bourbon, but in *De Diversis Materiis Praedicabilibus; Scriptores Ordinis Praedicatorum*, he adds even more detail:

[U]nder the Devil's direction, she was made a cardinal and finally pope. Having become pregnant she gave birth while mounting [a horse]. But when Roman justice was informed of it, she was dragged outside the city, bound by her feet to the hooves of a horse, and for half a league she was stoned by the people. And where she died, there she was buried, and upon a stone placed above her, this line was written: *Parce, Pater Patrum, Papisse Prodere Partum* ["Forbear, Father of Fathers, to betray the childbearing of the female pope"]. Behold how such rash presumptuousness leads to so vile an end. (Quetif and Echard, 1719:367)

And so the story circulated through the centuries. In the 14th century, the famous humanist poet Francesco Petrarch (d. 1374) expanded the demonic side of the Pope Joan scandal. After she was exposed, Petrarch (1534: 72) writes,

in Brescia it rained blood for three days and nights. In France, there appeared marvellous locusts which had six wings and very powerful teeth. They flew miraculously through the air, and all drowned in the British Sea. The golden bodies were rejected by the waves of the sea and corrupted the air, so that a great many people died.

What Pope Joan had done, according to Petrarch, was unleash two of the seven plagues described in the Book of Revelation – the rain of "hail and fire mingled with blood" (Revelation 8:7) and the locusts with "the teeth of lions" (9:3–11).

Some retellings of the story weren't as harsh with the woman pope as Stephen and Petrarch were. In versions that arose at the end of the fifteenth century, Joan deliberately chose public disgrace as a penance for her sins. In his tourist guidebook to Rome, *Marvels of the City of Rome* (*Mirabilia Urbis Romae*), written about 1500, Stephan Blanck writes,

We then proceed to a certain small chapel between the Colisseum and St Clements; this derelict church is situated at the place where the woman who became Pope died. She was heavy with child, and was questioned by an angel of God whether she would prefer to perish forever, or to face the world openly. But, not wanting to be lost for eternity, she chose the embarrassment of public reproach. (Wolfius, 1671: 231)

This guidebook also mentions a "stone which is carved with an effigy of the female pope and her child" (Wolfius, 1671: 231). After that statue was first cited in a *Marvels of the City of Rome* edition of around 1375, it was mentioned by many writers. When Martin Luther visited Rome in the early 1500s, he described it as representing a woman in a papal cloak holding a baby and a scepter. Luther notes his surprise that the popes had allowed the display of such an embarrassing object (Müntz, 1900, part 2: 333).

Another detail was added to the tale by Gaufridus de Collone, a French monk writing at the end of the 13th century: "[I]t is said that the Romans derive the custom of checking the sex of the pope-elect through a hole in a stone seat." (Burchard, part 1, vol.1: 83) This was repeated by Bartolomeo Platina, Prefect of the Vatican Library, in his 1479 *Lives of the Pope*, where he added that it was "the most junior deacon present" assigned to the genital-checking task (see Müntz, 1900, part 2:330). A few years later, Felix Haemerlein (Ca. 1490, f. 99) added that when the junior cleric accomplishes his task, he shouts, "He has testicles." And all the clerics present reply, "God be praised." Then they proceed joyfully to the consecration of the pope-elect.

In the late Middle Ages, part of the appeal of this story was that it connected Pope Joan to something that visitors to Rome could see – red marble chairs in the place where popes were crowned. At that time, two chairs with holes in them were used in the investiture ceremony: the new Pope first sat on one, then on the other. They are almost identical, and look like they were made in ancient Rome. Some scholars say they came from an old Roman bath; others speculate they were used by women giving birth. In any case, many scholars suggest that their beauty and classical origins are what got them included in the papal consecration; the holes in the seats were irrelevant.

The use of the chairs in the papal ceremony continued until Pope Leo X's coronation in 1513. His successor, Hadrian VI, abolished their use. Though the story of the sex-check had become very popular, there is nothing in the *Ordo Romanus*, the handbook for conducting such ceremonies, about the procedure. The ritual was already considered a myth by some in the fifteenth century. After the investiture of Pope Gregory XII in 1406, Jacobo d'Agnola di Scarperia called it a "senseless popular fable" (Von Döllinger, 1871: 50)

Nor is there any evidence in Vatican records that there ever was a Pope Joan. Martin Polonus's *Chronicon* says that she reigned "for two years, seven months and four days" after Leo IV and before Benedict III. But historians tell us that Leo IV ruled from 847 to his death on July 17, 855; and Benedict III was consecrated on September 29, 855, to reign until 858. The gap of two-and-a-half months between Leo and Benedict is hardly enough for a two-and-a-half-year reign.

There was a Pope named "John" who took the throne in 872, but he ruled for ten, not two years, and was known as a "warrior pope" for the ruthless way he dealt with his many enemies. John is said to have been beaten to death after an attempt at poisoning him had failed. If this John had been unmasked as a woman, her enemies would not have had to go to all that trouble to get her off the throne.

The later dates given by Jean de Mailly and Stephen of Bourbon – around 1100 – seem more plausible, since that was a time of political intrigue surrounding the papacy. A number of competitors claimed to be Pope, including those now called "antipopes." Pope Gregory VII died in 1085, having lost the support of almost all the clergy in Rome. Most had gone over to favor Clement III, the antipope chosen by Emperor Henry IV. On Gregory's death, there was no official Pope in Rome, but Clement stayed on in his unofficial role. In 1086 Victor II became Pope for a year, and was succeeded by Urban II, who is famous for calling the First Crusade. Because Emperor Henry IV controlled much of Italy, however, Urban's coronation had to be conducted one hundred kilometers southeast of Rome. He was finally able to get established in Rome in 1097, and then he died in July 1099. Two weeks later the new Pope, Paschal II, was consecrated. Though he had trouble with antipopes Clement III (1080–1100), Theodoric (1100–1102), Albert (1102), and Sylvester IV (1105–11), he held on to the papacy until his death in 1118. So, as with the earlier dates for Pope Joan, there was no time around 1100 for her to have reigned.

The story of Pope Joan, then, is debunked by historical records. But still it is told. As the Prefect of the Vatican Library, writing to a friend in 1479, commented (ChurchinHistory Information Centre, online), "These things that I have mentioned are popularly told, though by obscure and untrust-worthy authors, therefore I have related them briefly and plainly, so that I should not be thought obstinate and pertinacious in omitting that which almost everyone asserts to be true." And so we expect the tale will continue to be told.

References

Anonymous. (1687) *The History of Pope Joan and the Whores of Rome.* London

Boccaccio, G. (1964) *Concerning Famous Women,* translated by Guido Guarino, George Allen & Unwin, London.

Burchard, J., *Liber Notarum; in* L.A. Muratori, ed., *Rerum Italicarum Scriptores* (Milan 1723–1751), XXXII.

ChurchinHistory Information Centre (online) *Pope Joan*, www.churchinhistory.
   org/pages/booklets/pope-joan%28n%29.htm (accessed January 10, 2014).
Cooke, A. (1610) *Pope Joane. A Dialogue Between a Protestant and A Papist*. London.
Cross, D.W. (1997) *Pope Joan*, Ballantine, New York.
Rhoides, E. (2000) *The Papess Joanne*, translated and adapted by Lawrence Durrell.
   Peter Owen, London.
Von Döllinger, J.J.I. (1871) *Fables Respecting the Popes of the Middle Ages*.
Graydon F. Snyder, (2002) *Irish Jesus Roman Jesus* Trinity Press International,
   Peabody, MA, p. 129
Haemerlein, F. (c. 1490) *De Nobilitate et Rusticitate Dialogus*.
de Mailly, J. (1879) *Chronica Universalis Mettensis*, in G. Waitz, ed., *Monumenta
   Germaniae Historica: Scriptores*, Vol. 24. Hahn, Hannover.
Müntz, Eugène, (1900) "La Légende de la Papesse Jeanne dans l'illustration des
   Livres, du XVe au XIXe siècle," La Bibliofilia, (Firenza: Leo Olschki), Vol. 2,
   325–39.
Petrarch, F. (1534) *Chronica de le Vite de Pontefici et Imperadori Romani*.
Polonus, M. (1872) *Chronicon Pontificum et Imperatum, in Monumenta Germaniae
   Historica: Scriptores*, Vol. 22. Hahn, Hannover.
Quetif, J. and Echard, I. (1719), eds., Stephen of Bourbon, *De Diversis Materiis
   Praedicabilibus; in Scriptores Ordinis Praedicatorum*, Vol. I.
Wolfius, J. (1671) *Lectionum Memorabilium et Reconditarum Centenarii XVI*, I.

Further Reading

Boureau, A. (2001) *The Myth of Pope Joan*, translated by Lydia Cochrane, University
   of Chicago Press, Chicago.
Pardoe, R. and Pardoe, D. (1988) *The Female Pope: The Mystery of Pope Joan. The
   First Complete Documentation of the Facts behind the Legend*, Crucible, Bath.

8.   Saint Patrick Drove the Snakes out of Ireland

Among the most common images of Saint Patrick is that of a pious looking
man with slithering snakes at his feet. Saint Patrick was undoubtedly a real
person, but the snakes are a part of mythology. Patrick was born in Roman
Britain in the fifth century. According to some historians, when he was
about 16 he was captured in Britain by Irish raiders and taken to Ireland as
a slave, where he lived for six years. Then he escaped and returned to
Britain. Later, after becoming a Christian, he went back to Ireland as a
missionary.

There is evidence of other Christian missionaries in Ireland in the late fourth century, and in 431 Pope Celestine sent Palladius to minister to "the Irish who believe in Christ." Whoever came before Patrick, though, paled in comparison to him in their success at converting local Celtic tribes to Christianity. And so by the seventh century, Patrick was revered as the patron saint of Ireland. Today, Saint Patrick's Day is celebrated on March 17, the supposed date of his death, not just in Ireland but around the world. For Catholics in Ireland it is a holy day requiring their attendance at Mass, and outside of Ireland it is a day to celebrate Ireland and Irish culture.

Only two of Patrick's letters have survived, and few details about his life have been confirmed by historians. Nonetheless, as often happens with important religious figures, many stories grew up about Patrick and were passed on to succeeding generations. From the early centuries to the present, Christians have written hagiographies (biographies of saints), many of which feature stories of amazing deeds showing the saints' supernatural powers. The story of the vanishing snakes is one of the best known in Patrick's hagiographies.

Driving the snakes out of Ireland can be interpreted literally or metaphorically. The literal interpretation is that Patrick got rid of all the legless reptiles on the island. According to one version, he fasted for 40 days atop a hill, and at the end of his fast, snakes attacked him. With his staff he herded them all into the sea, and from that day on, there have been no snakes in Ireland. In a variant of this story, one old serpent resisted Patrick, but the saint made a box and invited him to get inside. The serpent insisted that the box was too small to hold him, but Patrick argued that it wasn't. To prove Patrick wrong, the old snake squeezed into the box to show what a tight fit it was – whereupon Patrick slammed the lid shut and tossed the box into the sea.

How might the story of Patrick driving the snakes out of Ireland be interpreted metaphorically? Some of the Druidic religions from which Patrick converted the Irish had snakes as symbols. So driving the snakes out of Ireland can be interpreted as getting rid of those Druidic religions.

But snakes symbolize more than Druidism. In many cultures they symbolize evil, so Patrick's driving the snakes out of Ireland can be a metaphor for his conquering evil on the Emerald Isle. The association between snakes and evil runs deep in the human psyche. Think of the temptation of Eve by the serpent in Genesis, the opening book of the Bible. Most Christians think of that snake as Satan, who is evil in its purest and strongest form.

And think of the Pentecostal Christian churches in the Appalachian region of the United States that handle poisonous snakes as a religious ritual, following Bible verses such as Luke 10:19: "Behold, I give unto you power to tread on serpents and scorpions, and over all the power of the enemy: and nothing shall by any means hurt you." Here, too, snakes are close to an embodiment of pure evil.

The symbolism of snakes and metaphorical interpretations of Patrick's driving them out of Ireland are interesting, but symbols and metaphors are not true or false, and so cannot be considered myths, in this book's sense of myth – a widely believed story of questionable authenticity. But, what about the literal interpretation of the claim that St Patrick drove all the snakes out of Ireland? What evidence might someone give for this claim? One thing they could say is that if we scour the Emerald Isle today, there are no snakes to be found in the wild. That's true, but scientists have a simpler explanation than St Patrick for today's absence of snakes: there *never were* any snakes in Ireland. Nigel Monaghan, of the National Museum of Ireland in Dublin, has done extensive research through Irish fossil collections and records. He concludes, "At no time has there ever been any suggestion of snakes in Ireland, so [there was] nothing for St Patrick to banish." (Quoted in James Owen, "*Snakeless in Ireland: Blame the Ice Age, Not St. Patrick*," March 13, 2008, http://news.nationalgeographic.com/news/2008/03/080313-snakes-ireland.html")

Snakes evolved from earlier kinds of lizards about 100 million years ago, the same time as *Tyrannosaurus rex*. Early snake fossils are found only on southern continents. At this time, the area that would become Ireland could not have had snakes because it was completely under the ocean. Starting about 65 million years ago, the Earth began to get drier, and large open habitats such as grasslands appeared across the northern hemisphere. The big dinosaurs like *Tyrannosaurus rex* became extinct, opening up ecological niches for smaller animals such as mammals and snakes. By 50–35 million years ago, the predecessors of boa constrictors and pythons were spreading through the northern hemisphere. About 25 million years ago, vipers and cobras evolved. Eventually, there were varieties of snakes virtually everywhere in the Northern and Southern hemispheres; everywhere, that is, except the islands of New Zealand, Iceland, Greenland, Antarctica, and Ireland.

New Zealand split off from Australia and Asia before snakes ever evolved. Today, 1300 miles of open ocean separate New Zealand and Australia, a distance no snake could swim. Ireland is much closer than that to Scotland – only

12 miles at one point – but that's 12 miles of icy water. There haven't been many snakes in Scotland, anyway. Only four land reptiles are native to Scotland today – the adder, the slow-worm, the common lizard, and the grass snake, which, though common elsewhere, is rare in Scotland.

As the oceans have risen and fallen over the geological ages, land bridges have appeared between Ireland and other parts of Great Britain, which allowed humans and other animals to cross. But if any snakes had made the trip, they would not have survived the ice ages that followed. The most recent ice age started three million years ago and still continues. Between warm periods such as we are now in, there were glaciers advancing and declining more than 20 times. Ireland was often completely covered with ice. Snakes are cold-blooded, and so can't survive where the ground is frozen year-round. The last thaw in Ireland was only 15 000 years ago. Since that time, there have been periods when snakes could have lived in Ireland, and only 12 miles of ocean separating Ireland from Scotland; but, as we said, none of the small snakes in Scotland would have been up for the trip across the icy-cold North Channel.

Additional bonus myths can be found at **wiley.com/go/50Great mythsaboutreligions**

Index

Abraham, 20, 35
accuracy, historic and scientific, 2, 6, 54, 66
Adam and Eve, 2, 19–20, 56, 87, 103, 179, 227
Adams, John, 116, 119–120
Addison, Joseph, 200
Age of Reason, The, 118
agnostics, 179, 197
Ahlquist, Jessica, 199–200
Ahura Mazda, 163–4
Al-Qaeda, 154, 159
Ali, Ayaan Hirsi, 142, 143
All Saints Day, 88–89
All Souls Day, 88–89
Allah, 126–9, 132, 139
American Family Association, 97–98
American Muslim Alliance, 154
Amida Buddha, 192
angels, 18, 20, 21, 23, 149, 226–9
animals, unclean, 216–220
animism, 19, 22
anthropomorphism, 55–56
anti-Semitism, 3, 7, 62, 63, 66–67
apocalypse, 220–3
Aquinas, Thomas, 18, 106, 108–9, 228
Arab Convention on the Suppression of Terrorism, 153–4
Arab League, 153–4
Arab Spring, 150–1, 152
Arabic language, 24, 124–5, 127
Armstrong, Karen, 3

Asherah, 46–49
Atheism, 54, 196, 197, 198, 203
    Richard Dawkins, Daniel Dennett, Sam Harris, Christopher Hitchens, 35–36
    famous atheists, 206
    Jewish, 38
    morality, 198–201
    as requiring faith, 207–9
    social stigma of, 199–200
    Unitarian Universalists, 179
Augsburg, Peace of, 13–14
Augustine of Hippo, 18, 88, 103, 106, 107–108, 171, 212
Avalokitsvara, 192

Baal, 46, 47–48, 49
Bacon, Francis, 211
Bangladesh, 124, 155
Baptist Confession of Faith, 111
Baptists, 32, 59, 111–114
Bauckham, Richard, 81
Beard, Charles A., 72
belief(s), 1–2, 8, 16, 23–27, 38
Beltane, 173
Benares, 187
Benedict XVI (pope), 66, 114
Bethlehem, 85, 89, 91–92
Bhagavad Gita, 141
Bible, 19–21, 33, 50–53, 53–59, 86–89, 120, 132, 211–15, 216–20, 226, 227
Bin Laden, Osama, 71

50 Great Myths About Religions, First Edition. John Morreall and Tamara Sonn.
© 2014 John Wiley & Sons, Ltd. Published 2014 by John Wiley & Sons, Ltd.

Birthday of the Unconquered Sun, 90
black magic, 166, 168
blood libel, 68–69
Boccaccio, Giovanni, 233
bodhisattva, 192
Bolland, John, 232
Boniface (saint), 171
Book of Hours, 224
Boorstin, Daniel, 105
Brahman (Ultimate Reality), 10, 26, 182,
    183, 184, 189
Brahmins, 185, 186
Brothers Karamazov, 200
Buddha, 14–15, 22, 26, 30, 31, 190–3,
    193–5. See also Amida Buddha,
    Laughing Buddha, Maitreya Buddha,
    Pure Land Buddhism, Siddhartha
    Gautama, Zen Buddhism
Buddhism, 10–11, 12, 14–15, 16, 26, 30, 39,
    192–3
Bush, George W., 128

Calvin, John, 58, 104, 200
Cambridge, University of, 108
Campbell, Joseph, 3
caste system, 185–7
Catholicism, Roman, 43, 57, 63, 66, 74, 106,
    107, 109, 110–114, 166–7, 232
Catholics, Roman, 39, 43
Cavanaugh, William, 41, 42
Chaharshanbe Suri, 16
Charlemagne, 103, 171
cherubs, 226–9
China, 15–16, 19, 22, 26–27, 30–31, 33,
    124, 192, 194
chosen people, 60
Christ, 81, 84
Christianity, Christians, 9, 12, 13, 14, 21, 33,
    37, 173
    afterlife, understanding of, 86–89
    atonement theory, 103, 104
    beliefs as essential, 24–26
    Catholics as not, 110–114
    crucifixion, 101–104
    dualism, 18, 21
    Eastern religions, contrasted with, 10–11
    Fundamentalist, 53–55
    Jesus as a Christian, 93–96

Jews, understanding of, 60, 63–69
    laws in Old Testament, 100
    Muslims, understanding of, 126–34, 158
    U.S. as Christian country, 115–121
    world religion, as model for, 12
    worship, 28–30
Christmas, 77–79, 89, 90, 91, 164, 227
Church of Jesus Christ of Latter Day Saints
    (Mormons), 9, 120–1, 197
Churchill, Caryl, 234
clash of civilizations, 129, 150
Cleanliness is next to Godliness, 211
Clinton, Hillary Rodham, 150–51
compassion, 22, 26, 30, 179, 180, 191, 192
Comte, Auguste, 35
Confucianism, 12, 14, 15, 16, 19, 22, 23,
    26–27, 30, 31, 33
Constantine (emperor), 24–25, 230
Constitution of Medina, 133
Cooke, Alexander, 233
Cowper, William, 211–212
Creation Museum, 53–54
creation stories, 2, 3, 4, 45, 56, 58, 182, 185
creationism, 3–4, 55
crusade, 131, 135, 237

Daniel, Book of, 87–88, 220, 222
Dante, 131–2
darshan, 188
Dawkins, Richard, 3, 35, 36
death, life after, 9, 10, 11, 86–89, 95,
    192, 203
De Collone, Gaufridus, 236
deism, 117–120
de Mailly, Jean, 234, 237
demons, 18, 20, 23, 126, 172, 224–6
Dennett, Daniel, 35
Deor, 214
Deuteronomy, 50, 51, 52, 137, 216, 217–18
Devi, 183
devil(s), 20, 166, 170, 172, 173, 215, 224–6
dharma, 184
Dialogue with Trypho, 63–64, 229
Divine Comedy, 131–2
Documentary Hypothesis, 52–53
Doniger, Wendy, 3
Douglas, Mary, 217–220
dowry, 144

Draper, John William, 105–106
Druids, 239
dualism, 18, 88
Durga, 188
Durkheim, Émile, 31
Dyaus Pita, 183

earth, flat, 55, 105, 106
Eck, Diana, 189
Elijah, 47–48
emotion, 6–7, 16, 33, 37, 232, 233
evolution, 3–4, 36, 45, 53–59
Ezekiel, Book of, 227, 228

faith, 23–27, 54, 107, 113, 207–209
Family Research Council, 98
Family Values, 97–100
Fekry, Mariam, 230
Fiqh Council of North America, 156–7
fire, in Zoroastrianism, 163–6
folklore, 7, 173, 214, 224
Ford, Henry, 75–76
Four Noble Truths (Buddhism), 15, 22, 191
Franklin, Benjamin, 70–72, 117–118, 212
Frazer, James, 90
freedom of religion, 32–33
Freud, Sigmund, 7, 35
Fundamentalist Christians, 53–55

Galileo Goes to Jail and Other Myths, 106
Gandhi, Mohandas (Mahatma), 187, 212
Ganesha, 183, 188
Gardner, Gerald, 174
Garvey, Marcus, 175–6
Geisler, Norman, 207
Genesis, 2, 3, 20, 50, 51–52, 53–59, 227
Ghannouchi, Rachid, 152
Gingrich, Newt, 55, 159
God, 46–49, 164, 207–209
God helps those who help themselves, 212
A God Who Hates, 143
gods, 10, 15, 16, 22, 23, 26, 30, 35, 46–49,
    128, 164, 209
  Hindu, 182–3, 187, 189–90
goddesses, 46–47, 128, 173, 183, 187
Gomaa, Ali, 161
Gospels, 20, 81–85, 89–90, 91, 95, 96, 99,
    120, 136, 197

gossip, 6, 7
Graham, Billy, 86, 226
Graves, Philip, 76
Greek Orthodox Church, 9, 63
Grien, Hans Baldung, 229

Haemerlein, Felix, 236
Haidt, Jonathan, 201
Haile Selassie, 175, 176, 177
Haiti, 166, 167, 168, 169
Halloween, 173
Hamlet, 214
hanifs, 133
Hanukkah, 77–79
Harris, Sam, 3, 34, 35–36
Harry Potter, 169–70
Hate the sin, love the sinner, 212
heaven, 10, 11, 14, 20, 47, 55, 86–89, 111,
    147–8, 192, 203, 205, 232
Heilbron, John, 109
hell, 11, 18, 86, 131–2, 149, 224–6
Hell, by Hieronymus Bosch, 224
Hercules, 212
heretics, 25, 27, 112, 130, 131
Hilary of Poitiers, 222
Hinayana Buddhism, 192
Hinduism, 10, 11, 12, 14, 22, 26, 209
  caste system, 185–7
  idol worship, 187–90
  as a single tradition, 181–4
hirabah (unlawful warfare), 137–8, 139, 148
Hitchens, Christopher, 3, 35, 36, 39, 40
Hitler, Adolf, 65, 71, 75
Hizb ut-Tahrir, 150–1
holiness, 218–220
Hollar, Wenzel, 229
homosexuality, 98, 100
Horned God, 173
houri, 149
Hubal, moon god, 126, 127
hudud punishments, 160–1
Hugh, Little Saint, 68–69
Huguenots, 41–42
Huntington, Samuel, 150
Hus, Jon, 233

Idle hands are the Devil's workshop, 215
idolatry, 46, 64, 131, 164, 187–90, 207

ignorance about religion, 196–8
illness, from eating pork, 216–20
impurity, 186, 218–19
India, 12, 14, 22, 124, 166, 181–7
Indonesia, 124
infanticide, female, 144
Inferno (by Dante), 131–2
Innocent III (pope), 222
Intelligent Design, 55, 109
International Judge the Qur'an Day, 130
Iran, 125, 151, 152, 155, 165
Ireland, 39, 43, 238–41
Islam, 27, 28, 29–30, 44, 124, 126, 129–31,
    132, 136, 138, 139
  suicide, 147–8, 156, 205
  terrorism, 139, 147–8, 156
Islamofascism, 129
Islamophobia, 7, 123
Israelites, 46–49, 60, 61–62, 87, 137, 219

Jains, 182
Jama'a Islamiyya, 154
Jamaica, 175, 176, 177
James, William, 31
jatis, 186
Jefferson Bible (*The Life and Morals of Jesus
    of Nazareth*), 120
Jefferson, Thomas, 23, 32, 116, 119–20
Jerry Falwell Ministries, 116
Jesus, 29, 33, 63–67, 68, 111, 117, 178,
    224, 226
  birth, 78, 89–92
  as a Christian, 93–96
  crucified, 101–104
  death, understanding of, 88
  in deism, 117, 119, 120
  and Family Values, 97–100
  in Gospels, 81–85
  a Jew, 67
  in Qur'an, 133
Jews, 45–49, 60–79, 94–96, 125, 128,
    133–4, 136, 189, 197
jihad, 43, 135–8, 139, 148, 158, 159
Joan (pope), 233–7
Job, Book of, 87, 224
John Chrysostom, 64, 103
John of Damascus, 130–1
John Paul II (pope), 57, 66, 232

John XXIII (pope), 66, 232
Johnson, Phillip, 207–8
Jones, Terry, 130
Josiah (King), 46–47, 48
Judaism, 9–10, 12, 26, 28, 38, 50, 51, 57, 69,
    79, 96, 129–30, 132, 136, 186
Juergensmeyer, Mark, 39, 40
Justin Martyr, 63, 229–30

Kaaba, 128
Kali, 188
Kaplan, Mordechai, 38
karma, 11, 184, 186
Kellog, S.H., 217
Kennedy, John F., 31, 32, 34
Khamene'I, Ayatollah Ali, 155
Khatami, Mohamed, 152
Kimball, Charles, 40
koans, 193
KOSANBA, 169
Kramer, Heinrich, 171–2
Krishnananda, Swami, 187
Kshatriya, 185
Kurzman, Charles, 156

Lakshmi, 183
Lancashire, England, 170
Last Judgment, 11, 33, 88, 94, 224, 225
Laughing Buddha (Budai, Ho-Ti), 193–5
Law of Threefold Return, 173
law, Islamic (Shariah), 158
Leviticus, 50, 51, 100, 216–20
Limbourg, Paul, Hermann, Jean, 224
Lincoln, Bruce, 3
lingam, 188
A little learning is a dangerous thing, 215
Loa, 167–8, 169
Lord of the Dance (Shiva), 188
The Lord works in mysterious ways, 211
Luini, Aurelio, 229
Luther, Martin, 60, 65, 104, 236
lying, 191, 200, 201

Maccabees, 78–79
Madison, James, 116–120
magic, 7, 166, 168, 173
Mahayana Buddhism, 16, 192–3
Maitreya Buddha, 194–5

Magi, 164
Malleus Maleficarum (*Hammer of Witches*), 171–2
Manu, laws of, 186
marijuana, 175, 177
Marley, Bob, 175, 177
Marty, Martin, 40
martyr, 68, 156, 230–1, 232
Marvels of the City of Rome, 235
Marx, Karl, 35
Mather, Cotton, 171, 222
Mather, Increase, 91
Mazrui, Ali, 161
McCain, John, 115, 124, 126, 130
McVeigh, Timothy, 125
Mecca, 128, 140
Medina, 133, 140
Messiah, 10, 81, 92, 93, 94–95, 133, 176, 177
Milosevic, Slobodan, 43
misbelief, 2, 4, 8
Mithra, 90–91
moksha, 184
Monaghan, Nigel, 240
Money is the root of all evil, 213
monotheism, 9–10, 28, 29, 46–49, 129, 132, 133, 136, 164, 167, 220
morality, 11, 179, 198–201
Morey, Robert, 127
Moses, 49, 50–53, 61
Moss, Candida, 230–2
Muhammad, 126–127, 128, 130–133, 140–1, 145–6
Mukasey, Michael, 158
Müller, Max, 11, 12
Muslims, 1, 59, 117, 123, 135, 139, 142, 146
    Arabs, 124–129
    Bosnians, 39, 43
    democracy, 150–2
    shariah, 158–61
    terrorism, opposition to, 44, 153–7
    myth, meanings of, 2–4
Mythbusters, 7

Nazarenes, 94
Nero, 222
Nicaea, Council of
Nichols, Terry, 125

Nilus, Sergyei, 73–74
Nirvana, 10, 22, 30, 192
Noble Eightfold Path (Buddhism), 15, 22
Noruz, 165

Obama, Barack Hussein
Oberammergau Passion Play, 64
Oklahoma City bombing, 125
Ong, Walter, 6
Oshri, Aviram, 92
Osteen, Joel, 216–17
Ounfo, 168
Ounsis, 168
Oxford, University of, 108

Paine, Thomas, 118–119
Pakistan, 124, 182
Pan, 226
Pantokrator, 29
The Papess Joanne, 234
Parliament of the World's Religions, 12
Parsees, 166
Parsley, Rod, 126, 130
passion plays, 64, 66–67
Patrick, Saint, 238–40
Paul (saint), 63, 83, 93–94, 145
Pelley, William Dudley, 71
Pentateuch, 50–53
People of the Book, 132, 136
persecution, 7, 78, 164, 166, 229–32
Persia, 125, 149
Petrarch, Francesco, 235
Pharisees, 88, 95, 96
Picasso, Pablo, 3
Pinker, Steven, 200–201
Plato, 18, 84, 88, 107, 109
politics, 13–14, 31–32, 41–44, 115–116, 231
Polonus, Martin, 233, 234, 236
polygamy, 98
Poor Richard's Almanac, 212
pope as antichrist, 112
Pope Joan (film), 234
Pope Joan (novel), 234
Pope, Alexander, 214–215
pork, 100, 216–20
Principe, Lawrence, 109
Prothero, Stephen, 81, 197

Protocols of the Learned Elders of Zion, 73–76
Proverbs, Book of, 213
psychopomp, 149
puja, 188
punishment, 88, 89, 100, 101, 104, 130, 136, 137, 160–1, 213, 225
Pure Land Buddhism, 192
purgatory, 89, 111
purity, 186, 201
The Purpose-Driven Life, 202
purpose of life, 202–206
Purusha, 185
puto (putti), 229

quiz on religion, of Pew Forum on Religion and Public Life, 197, 198
Qur'an, 1, 13, 24, 44, 128, 129–34, 136–50, 197, 221

Rahman, S. A., 161
Ramadan, Tariq, 160–1
Raphael, 229
Rastafarians, 175–7
rationality, 5
rationalizing, 7
Rauf, Feisal Abdul, 161
Reagan, Ronald, 115
reincarnation, 10, 11, 22, 88, 175, 192
religion
  belief, 23–27
  definitions, 16–17, 41
  faith, 23–27
  ignorance about, 196–8
  personal matter, 31–34
  politics, 41–44
  science, 34–38
  spiritual, 18–21
  supernatural, 21–23
  universality, 12–17
  violence, 39–44
  worship, 28–31
Religious Studies, 2, 12
resurrection, 83, 87, 88, 94, 95
revenge, 140
Rhoides, Emmanuel, 234
Rig Veda, 182, 183, 185
Robertson, Pat, 126, 127, 166

Robinson, John, 38
Roman Empire, 24–25, 33, 90, 92, 95–96, 229–32
Rubenstein, Richard, 38

Sabbath, 100, 131, 215
Sabians, 127, 132, 133
Sadducees, 88, 95, 96
Sadeh, 165
Sagan, Carl, 105, 106, 208
Salem Witch Trials, 170–1
Sallustius, 2–3
Samhain, 173
samsara, 184
sangha, 192
Santorum, Rick, 34, 55, 159
Saraswati, 183
Satan, 64, 103, 174, 215, 239
  torturing humans in hell, 224–6
  and witches, 169–73
Saturnalia, 91
Scheffler, Samuel, 206
Schirach, Baldur von, 75–76
science, 23, 34–38, 57–58, 105–109, 206
Second Coming Project, 8
Segal, Alan, 96
September 11, 2001, 39, 43, 125, 130, 154
Shakespeare, William, 214
Shakti, 183, 188
shatnes, 219
Shudras, 185
Siddhartha Gautama, 10, 14–15, 22, 26, 191
Sikhs, 125, 182
Sistine Madonna, 229
slavery, 65, 98, 145, 161, 167, 204–205
Smart, Ninian, 16, 33, 37
Smith, Wilfred Cantwell, 14, 16, 24, 26
Smyth, John, 112
snakes, 238–41
Snoop Dog (Snoop Lion), 175, 177
Snopes, 7
social animals, humans as, 5, 123
Solomon (King), 98, 228
soul, 15, 18, 21, 86–89, 149–50
Southern Baptist Convention, 113
Spare the rod and spoil the child, 213
Spinoza, Baruch, 51–52
spirit, spiritual, 18–21, 22, 23, 35, 86

Spong, John Shelby, 38
Sprenger, Jacob, 171–2
stable, Jesus born in, 89–91
stealing, 160
Stephen of Bourbon, 234, 237
Stephen, Saint, 231
stereotypes, 5, 7, 9, 11, 135
storytelling, 6, 7
suicide, 1, 147–50, 205
Sultan, Wafa, 143
supernatural, 21–23, 41, 171
Sweden, 36, 42
Sword Verses, 139–42

Talbi, Mohamed, 161
Tanka, 193
Taoism, 12, 14, 15, 16, 19, 22–23, 27, 30
temples, fire, 165
terrorism, 1, 39, 43–44, 123, 125, 137–9,
    148, 153–7
Tertullian, 107, 231
Theodosius, Code of, 25
Theravada Buddhism, 16, 30–31, 192
Thirty Years' War, 39, 41, 42
This too shall pass, 214
Thomas of Monmouth, 68, 69
Thomas, Cal, 129
Thor, 209
Tillich, Paul, 16
To err is human, to forgive divine, 214–215
To thine own self be true, 213–214
torture, 68, 172, 224–6, 230
Trinity, 25, 111, 117, 133, 178
Tripoli, U.S. treaty with, 116–117
Turek, Frank, 207
Turkey, 125
Tutu, Desmond, 93
Twain, Mark, 187

Ultimate Reality, 10, 26, 182, 183, 184,
    189–90
Unitarian Universalism, 178–80
United Kingdom, 197, 209
United States of America, as Christian
    country, 115–21
untouchables, Dalits, outcastes, 186–7
Upanishads, 10, 183, 189
urban myths, urban legends, 7–8

Vaishyas, 185
varnas, 185, 186
Vedas, 182, 183, 186
violence, 6–7, 13, 36, 39–44, 103
    in Islam, 138–42, 143, 148, 156, 157
virgin birth, 133, 164, 165
Virginia Statute of Religious Freedom,
    32, 116
Vishnu, 26, 183, 190
Vodun, 167
Voodoo (Voudou, Vodu), 166–9

Warren, Rick, 202–204, 205, 206
Wars of Religion, 41, 42
Washington, George, 70, 72, 116, 119
Watts, Isaac, 215
Wellhausen, Julius, 52–53
Wesley, John, 211
White, Andrew Dickson, 106
Wiccans, 173–4
Winthrop, John, 115
witches, 22, 169–74
work ethic, Protestant, 215
World Religions, 12
worship, 11, 21, 94, 95, 118, 132
    in ancient Israel, 46–49
    Buddhists as worshipping the Buddha,
        190–3
    as essential to religion, 28–31
    hero worship, 7
    as purpose of life, 202–203
    witches as worshipping Satan, 169–74
    Zorastrians as worshipping fire, 163–6
wu-wei, 19, 22, 27, 30

xenophobia, 7, 45, 123, 129, 163

Yahweh, 28–29, 46, 47, 48, 49, 52
yoga, 170, 184
yoni, 188
Yousafzai, Malala, 143, 146

Zarathustra (Zoroaster), 164–5
Zealots, 95–96
Zen Buddhism, 192–3
Zeus, 16, 23
zombies, 168
Zoroastrianism, 10, 12, 149–50, 163–6, 220